LOOKING IN THE MIRROR

BARBARA TURNBULL

THE TORONTO STAR

ISBN 0-9690388-5-2

Published by
  The Toronto Star
  One Yonge Street
  Toronto, Ontario
  M5E 1E6

Co-ordinating Editors:
  Phil Bingley and Brad Henderson

Design:
  Ian Somerville

Printed and bound in Canada
by Quattro Marketing Inc.

This book is dedicated to:

Mom;

and Grandpa, for teaching me to love and respect books;

and Denise Baby, for special friendship and guidance in critical years.

LOOKING IN THE MIRROR

Look

into the mirror

of someone else's eyes

to see the beauty

in yourself.

Search

in that mirror

for the secret existential messages

which traverse the gap

that separates you.

Discover

in that reflection

the full

dimensions

of your own intricacies.

Gary D. Goldberg

CONTENTS

FOREWORD

I remember the moment it all began.

I was co-anchor of the six o'clock news at Citytv and was standing by the news desk late one afternoon, getting my script together, when reporter Mark Dailey approached. "The Turnbull family wonder if you would go and see Barb. They feel a visit from you might help."

I knew her story well. Barb had been the lead item on the news for the past week. She was working at a local Becker's store when three men entered at closing time and shot her, leaving her paralyzed from the shoulders down.

My stomach was in knots. What the hell would I say to an eighteen-year-old stranger whose life had just been shattered by a bullet? What could I possibly tell her? In the end I went, although I really can't tell you why.

Barb was in the intensive care unit hooked up to all kinds of machinery and monitors, with a tube attached to her throat to help her breathe. She couldn't talk, so I had to read her lips, our faces inches apart.

I don't really remember what I said, but I remember being really nervous. Within the first ten minutes I made her laugh, and I knew then that we could be friends.

More than a dozen years later, Barb and I are still friends, good friends, and we are still laughing. I love her sense of humour, her intelligence and her quick wit — and besides, she always laughs at my jokes!

I now host a national talk show and I've interviewed lots of incredible people — and among the top ten most amazing people I've ever known is Barbara Turnbull. Over the years, I have watched her grow from a victim of violence to a strong, passionate woman in charge of her life — like a butterfly she has left the cocoon, spread her wings and is learning to fly.

A few summers ago, we spent a week together in the country. We had a really good time. Let's just say there are some stories that Barb has left out of this book, and for that I'm grateful! But Barb also made an important decision that week. She decided that, in spite of her obvious physical restrictions, there were still many things she was capable of doing and so many things she wanted to do. She was going to live for the present and the future and stop feeling haunted by the past. "I have to stop watching people's hands as they flick on light switches and turn doorknobs so I can remember what it feels like," she said. "I've been in this chair long enough. I've been good, done everything that was expected of me — now someone please stop this merry-go-round, I want to get off." At moments like these, there is nothing I can think of to say.

Barb has always faced her disability with cheerful determination. Her tragedy scared the hell out of most of us, so we wanted her to play Pollyanna and smile for the cameras. We wanted her to be brave and sweet and let us believe that everything was really okay, because we didn't want to hear the truth. Barb played her role well.

I've been encouraging Barb for a long time to write this story, to examine the entrails of what happened, try to make some sense of it and then leave it behind. It was time to face it, and time to bury Pollyanna.

I believe in Barb, and in her dreams, and I've been doing a lot of applauding lately as they all start to come true. This book is one of them, and I take great pleasure in saying "I told you so!" I'm proud of her success as a journalist; I never doubted her talent. I believe that someday soon spinal cord research will give her back arm movement — she wants that more than anything else.

And I will be the flower girl at her wedding and throw rose petals by the thousands and I will dance with joy.

I have learned that there are two kinds of courage: the one to face your death, and the other to get out of bed each morning and face your own life. Barb and I made a deal one afternoon that we would get together and ask each other the questions we'd never asked before. I really only had one: "How do you do it?"

I don't think anyone can answer that question, and really, I don't need to know. I only care that she does.

Barbara Turnbull is my friend.

Dini Petty

ACKNOWLEDGMENTS

There are so many people to thank I'm almost afraid of naming anybody for fear of whom I might forget, but here it goes:

Several people deserve credit for this book being what it is and for making the writing process so easy and enjoyable from start to finish. They are: Lee Davis Creal, who not only acted flawlessly as a literary agent, but was even willing to help me sort through mountains of accumulated research; Catherine Marjoribanks, a wonderful editor. Behind every good writer is an even better editor, which is what I had in Catherine. She miraculously unblocked my blocks, gave valuable guidance, acted as a great sounding board and also helped with research (oh yeah, she edited the whole book, too). And Phil Bingley and Brad Henderson, who made every aspect of this project a pleasure.

Special mention goes to Dini Petty. People across Canada know Dini from her television show. What they don't know is that she is intensely loyal to her friends; I am happy and proud to be one of them. And to Gary Goldberg: my deep and heartfelt gratitude for years of support, friendship and enthusiasm, and for the steps he is taking to help me reach my dream (thanks also for the title and poem for this book!).

Love and thanks to my whole family, Mom, Dad, Chella, Lynn, Christine and Alison, who have been tremendously supportive and, in particular, were instrumental in getting me through my year in the hospital. I feel lucky that we are friends, too, and that there is so much laughter when we are together.

I am blessed with an amazing and very wide circle of friends, people who have helped smooth my path before, during and after the roughest spots, and continue to layer my life with depth and brightness. You know who you are.

Thanks also to: Judy Steed, my personal cheerleading team; Bill Whitlock, whom I first met in an ambulance racing for the hospital, and who, along our subsequent road, became a friend; David Greenberg, for thoughtful advice and refreshingly honest e-mail conversations; Dr. Charles Tator, for valuable input, for Bill, and for years of expertise and friendship; Lucy White, for pursuing the powers that be; Mary Deanne Shears, whose initial thought about my potential opened the door to a job and career I love; Shonagh Jabour, for patience and artistry; Christine Mortimei, for great transcribing skills; Sue and Shonagh for the "breakthrough" evening; Sandy and Michael Harding from the Self-Directed Learning Place; and the friends who got me through the anxiety attacks I had over this project.

Many other people were generous in helping me piece together and recreate the last thirteen years. They include (but are not limited to): Leo McGuigan, Brian Trafford, Brian Donnelly, Bill Gorewich, Bruce Day, Marg Bourke, Virginia Edmonds, Joan Dunn, Glen Woolvett, Hazel Self, Val Lusted, Rosie DiManno, and Karen Kelln of KCI Medical Canada, Inc.

INTRODUCTION

I focus so steadily on what's ahead of me — the challenges of each day and my hopes and goals for the future — that I rarely make an effort to look back. Looking back is much more difficult. There are many memories there that I have kept at arm's length, acknowledging them in a superficial way while simultaneously deflecting them with a protective coat of armour. At some point, however, we all have to look in the mirror.

When I was just eighteen years old I became a public figure. It was not because of anything notable that I'd done — I was just an average teenager — but because of something that was done to me. I was shot during a hold-up at the convenience store where I worked part-time and left paralyzed from my shoulders down. This act of violence, almost unheard of in Canada in 1983, sent shock waves across the country and beyond. My tragedy became a symbol of the increasingly violent nature of Canadian society.

The media spotlighted me as a "celebrity victim," though that wasn't how I saw myself. My life was divided into two — before and after. What became important was finding direction in my new life. I refused to let my tragedy and disability define me.

Then one day a mirror was held up to me. It revealed an image I could no longer ignore. I realized that I needed to look back at what had happened and try to make some sense of it all.

Would you like to know what I saw? It began with a dream.

I was on vacation in a town called Sedona, an artisan community north of Phoenix, Arizona, where I attended university. It is a magical, spiritual place that will always lay claim to a piece of my soul. Apart from its indescribable natural beauty, Sedona is also at the centre of four of the Earth's few vortexes, or energy centres. A vortex, simply defined, is a place where the natural electromagnetic field of the Earth is particularly strong, like a fountain of energy. The energy affects us both physically and spiritually. It expands our consciousness and has great healing properties. It is said one should pay close attention to dreams after spending time at a vortex.

In May 1995 I attended the wedding of a close friend, at a campground in Sedona, and my friends and I decided to spend four days there to really enjoy what the town has to offer. One friend in our party had a bad back. In looking for some therapy, she came across a pamphlet for a place called Therapy on the Rocks. They offered a procedure called Myofascial Release that she wanted to try, so we dropped her off for a treatment and went to lunch.

When we picked her up, she came out to the van to talk to me.

"Barb, you have to come here for a treatment. You just have to. There's a guy coming out to talk to you."

As if on cue, the door of the building opened and out into the bright sunshine walked one of the most beautiful men I'd ever laid eyes on. With long black hair and a dark, European complexion, Jonathan appeared to glow inside and out. Despite his youth (he was twenty-three), peace and tranquillity emanated from him. While he explained the principles of the therapy treatment, his eyes kept dropping to my neck.

"Has anyone ever released those scars?" he asked me.

"Released my scars?"

He explained that Myofascial Release treats the fasciae, a saran-like covering underneath our skin that binds our musculature. When impacted by trauma, either physical, mental or emotional, the fasciae become almost crumpled. MFR is one method of stretching it out. In addition, because of its strength, the fasciae are usually stitched up with the skin after surgery. Many believe that scars hold the memories of the events that create them, memories that can be released through a procedure like MFR. Jonathan saw me as a challenge and thought giving me a treatment would be a learning experience for him, too.

"What the hell," I thought. I agreed to come for treatment later that afternoon, though I still wasn't sure about his ideas. My expectations were low as I entered the small, squat building that overlooked Sedona's rich, red rocks.

Standing behind me, Jonathan placed his fingers on the scars on my neck and pressed in hard. It hurt, a lot.

"Relax, keep breathing and try to accept me into you," he said.

Most of what he did was painful. He moved my head around, doing something called "unwinding." The hour whipped by quickly. I can't remember much of the actual treatment, except that it wasn't anything like a relaxing massage. I said goodbye, figuring that was the end of that, and we left and went out to dinner.

But I was curiously depressed all evening. The last place I wanted to be was in the fancy restaurant we had chosen to splurge on. It was hard pretending to be interested in the conversation, and I had to keep forcing the occasional comment so it looked as though I was participating. I was completely lost in my thoughts and wanted to be sitting quietly in front of a roaring fire back at our cabin.

As I got ready for bed that night I joked with my friends about the great dreams I could look forward to. After all, I'd been to a vortex and had the beautiful Jonathan's hands on me for an hour.

What I actually did dream about took me totally by surprise.

I relived the shooting. For the first time in a dozen years, I actually dreamt about the shooting. My dreams have been widely varied over the years: sometimes I'm fully able-bodied, sometimes slightly disabled, sometimes a combination of both. But once the initial nightmares stopped, the actual crime never returned to my sleep.

This dream wasn't an exact reenactment of what had happened in 1983. This shooting took place in a stairwell of the building where I currently live. As well, Jonathan was the shooter, and I was not the victim but the only witness. Most upsetting was that, in my dream, the victim died.

There may have been changes, but it was unquestionably my shooting. The choreography was the same, the shooter and victim standing exactly as he and I had in the Becker's store. For the rest of my dream, I kept trying to get back to my home, through the stairwells and halls of my building. As I met up with people, including Jonathan, I pretended I hadn't seen anything and that I knew nothing of the shooting. I tried to pretend I hadn't been there and it hadn't happened, or at least that it had not affected me.

Although completely flabbergasted by the dream, as I thought about it, it made perfect sense. First of all, a part of me did die on the floor that night. Had I ever properly grieved for that girl who used to be me? Also, I had to admit to myself that I had been experiencing a form of denial all along. I had never dealt with "the big picture." I could never even bring myself to say "the shooting." I always referred to it as "when I was hurt." I never called it an accident, but I never called it what it actually was.

The truth was staring me in the face. This was a strong message telling me it was time to go back to the beginning and sort it all through. The thought was depressing and overwhelming. How does one go about digging up twelve years of deeply buried emotions? Something told me Jonathan's treatment had only started the ball rolling; MFR wouldn't keep the process happening.

Over the next few months I looked into every kind of therapy imaginable. I checked out hypnotherapy, classic psychiatry and psychology, spiritual yoga. I even briefly considered psychic over-the-phone counselling (very briefly). Nothing felt right, and I was trusting my instinct on this one. I knew what I didn't want, and I didn't want to sit and talk it over with someone.

One afternoon, six months later, I found myself sitting in front of my computer at home. Without any forethought, I started writing about what life was like in the hospital. The next day I wrote more. It felt right. That is how this book was born. The next time I hear an author say "This book started writing itself," I'll understand perfectly what that means.

Through this process I've come to the conclusion that there can be no closure for me. I had originally expected it from the justice and parole systems. When those processes failed to deliver it, I expected it from this book. But reading the trial transcripts and speaking with people for background has only brought the horror to the surface. I now have to decide whether to chase it or let it go again.

What I found I could do, though, was put the pieces in place. When we read about tragedies in the news, we get the facts — of a shooting, a fatal accident, a natural disaster — but not the whole story. With this book I offer the whole picture, at least from my point of view. It's my way of looking in the mirror and not turning away.

Chapter One:

FIFTEEN MINUTES

In real life, guns don't sound like they do in the movies.

At least what I heard September 23, 1983, at 11:15 p.m. was different. It was an innocent "pop," not a loud or menacing bang. That's why I thought it was a tranquillizer gun.

I don't remember falling backwards and hitting the floor, everything happened so fast. I was stacking cigarettes, with my arms raised high above my head as I straightened the top shelves. It was just before the store closed, in what had been an otherwise regular shift. The last hour had been very quiet, with only the occasional customer.

The Becker's convenience store was on the fringe of Mississauga, a residential area bordering the western side of Metropolitan Toronto, with homes on one side and a service road and highway on the other. It was a logical target for a robbery. In fact, the gas bar next door had been hit more than once, and during one robbery the gas attendant had been viciously beaten — a guy I knew fairly well.

But none of that was on my mind that Friday night when the door opened and two figures entered, their faces covered with ski masks. I saw the first figure raise his arm, point a gun at me and I heard that "pop." The next thing I knew I was lying on my back with my eyes closed. I didn't see the third masked person enter the store. I heard feet running around the counter and some beeps as someone pressed keys on the cash register.

Keep your eyes closed until they're gone.

I pictured the guys kicking me or stepping on me. Or shooting me again. A spasm of relief went through me when I heard the drawer open and feet go running back around the counter. "Let's get out of here!" were the only words I heard any of them say.

Wait a minute, then call for help. Make sure they aren't coming back. You'll be able to get up in ten or fifteen minutes. Don't freak out and you'll be okay.

In my mind I saw one of those tranquillizer darts you see in the movies sticking out of my neck — you know the kind, with feathers on the end. Why else wouldn't I be able to move? Fifteen minutes.

That's going to hurt when they pull that dart out.

I had a sick sense of foreboding in my stomach. It was the same feeling I had on my kindergarten field trip when I got separated from my class at the zoo. I found them within a few minutes, but the panic didn't leave my gut until I was safe on the bus, headed back to familiar territory.

Why are my arms and legs in the air?

It felt like all four limbs were in the air above me. I decided to open my eyes and look at my arms. I looked to my right and was shocked to see blood on the floor beside my neck. And my arm lay on the floor, it wasn't up in the air at all. I quickly looked away, realizing that it wasn't a tranquillizer dart I'd been hit with, but a real bullet.

Okay, then you should be able to crawl for help. Get up. GET UP!

I couldn't move. That didn't make sense either — in the movies the good guy can crawl for help. Too afraid to look at the growing pool of blood, I looked to my left, at the cooler that held the Becker's milk products and pop. I stared at the neatly stacked bags of 2 percent milk, my mind racing.

I always hated going into that cooler. It was a big walk-in room about fifteen feet long and eight feet wide. Every time I went in there I imagined someone locking me in it, and created wild scenarios of daring crimes and heroic rescues in my head. Funny that the cooler should become my focus now that I was really in trouble.

Don't blink.

Lying on the floor beside the cooler, one thing struck me with absolute certainty: if I closed my eyes again I would die. I knew it as surely as I'd known anything in my life. I also knew that I did not want to die. The will to live is incredibly powerful. It's the strongest urge I have ever encountered. It wasn't something I had to summon, it was just there when I needed it. So I lay there, my eyes fixed on those goddamn bags of milk, and I talked to myself.

Everything's going to be fine if you keep it together. You need to blink. Do it quickly. Okay, ready, get set, BLINK. Keep your eyes open. Good job.

I kept up a steady stream of chatter in my head, coaching myself through every blink and making sure I didn't look to the right at the blood. I had no sense of how much time was passing and I never considered the possibility that I might not be found until morning. I was breathing in short, shallow gasps.

I need water.

Suddenly I heard the door open and knew it was a customer. It's really a little miracle that Cheryl Corcoran came in at all. It was 11:30 — fifteen minutes after I was shot and right at closing time. She'd been visiting family in the neighbourhood and stopped in to get cigarettes on her way home. As she later testified at the trial, she waited a few moments and was about to leave, thinking no one was there, but something made her turn around and look over the counter.

Dear god, help me.

All I remember doing was motioning toward the phone with my eyes, but apparently I was also mouthing "Help me, please." The phone hung on the wall between the store and the back room. It was hidden by a plastic curtain and I knew she'd have trouble seeing it. She ran to the back room, then out of the store screaming.

Where the fuck is she going? Please don't leave me!

I heard her say something about her children. She was hysterical and I didn't think she was coming back. What I didn't know was that her children were sleeping in the car and she was afraid whoever hurt me was still around.

As she came running out of the store screaming for help, two people saw her. One, Alan Banks, was on his way home from a movie. The other was Andrew King, who lived next door and was arriving home on his motorcycle. I knew most of the King family: Andrea King, who had worked in the store when I was first hired, and the two youngest kids, Anthony and Adam. Andrew and Alan went to the store and called 911, then Andrew went back to his house and woke his parents to come help. Mrs. King, after seeing the blood, went home for some clean towels.

Water.

Police reached the store very quickly, three minutes after the 11:32 call. Constable Keith Brodie was the first officer on the scene, followed closely by Constable Mike McFadden. Despite all the blood on the floor, they didn't automatically assume I had been shot. They thought I might have been stabbed or hit with an instrument of some kind. At that time, a shooting of this sort was an incredibly rare occurrence.

Please, water.

My memory of the rest of the night is a series of brief flashes — Keith Brodie telling me to lie still while he tried to stem the bleeding, then switching places with Mike McFadden and going to a phone. I was bleeding badly, and though Mike McFadden used a cloth, he also had to stick a finger in the half-centimetre hole caused by the .38-calibre bullet on the right side of my neck. What was left of the bullet could be felt just under the skin on my left shoulder. They could tell by the coagulating blood that I had been there awhile. He kept talking to me, trying to comfort me and keep me conscious. I saw Mrs. King, with a fur coat thrown over her nightgown and Andrew beside her. I thought it was Anthony.

They shouldn't let him in here. He's too young to see this.

An ambulance stretcher was wheeled close to my head. The ambulance attendants, who had started giving me oxygen immediately, reported that I could move my legs and squeeze my hands on command at the store. By the time I reached the hospital, however, I could no longer move anything.

I remember a chipper nurse in Emergency brightly asking me if I'd ever been in the hospital before, as though I were in to have my tonsils removed. Three times my blood pressure dipped so low I had to be resuscitated with fluids.

The only way I could communicate was by blinking, once for yes, twice for no, and vice versa. One thing I was priding myself on was that the police had me blinking one way and the hospital staff the opposite way and I was able to keep it straight. Constable McFadden rode in the ambulance to Mississauga Hospital, then was replaced by Detective Bill Whitlock, who stayed on with me to Sunnybrook Health Science Centre, at that time the major trauma and spinal cord centre for the Toronto area. I remember the police asking me a few questions: How many robbers? What colour were they? What were they wearing?

And pain. Sudden, blinding pain.

*   *   *   *

Meanwhile, at my home, my mother and two of my four sisters were out for the evening. My twelve-year-old sister Alison was in bed asleep. My sister Lynn, who, at nineteen, was a year older than me, was doing homework downstairs. Up until three weeks before, Lynn had worked at Becker's too, but she'd quit when she started a full-time job. The Friday night closing shift had regularly been hers. Hearing a strange noise at the front door, she went upstairs to find a uniformed police officer standing in the hall. It was shortly after midnight, an hour after the shooting.

"You should never leave your door unlocked, I was able to walk right in," he told her sternly. "I'm here because there's been an accident at Becker's."

Though he gave her no more details, Lynn's entire body started to shake convulsively. The officer needed one of my parents. It was the one time my mother had not left the number where she could be reached. She was out playing bridge. My parents are divorced, and my father lived in an apartment close by, so Lynn went in the cruiser with the officer to pick him up. They were taken to Mississauga Hospital and left in the chapel. A doctor would come to see them, they were told.

"She must be dead," my sister thought. "We're sitting in a chapel. She has to be dead."

Shortly afterwards, although it seemed like an eternity, a doctor came in. He had my blood on his hands. He told them that I had been shot in the neck and that it was serious; they had stabilized me, then sent me on to Sunnybrook.

"I'm sorry to tell you this, but in cases like these there is usually paralysis, and it's usually permanent," the doctor said.

Constable McFadden then drove my father to Sunnybrook. The other officer was to drive Lynn back home to find my mother, but first she was told to follow the doctor to collect my things. She was still trembling from head to foot, and even walking was difficult.

She was handed a large, heavy paper bag with handles. Opening it, she saw my blood-soaked, once-white blouse sitting on top. Feeling as though she were watching a movie, she was halfway down the hall when somebody suddenly realized the police might be interested in keeping my clothes, and they took the bag back.

A short time later, back at our house, my mother arrived. She had been located and told I'd been shot. She doesn't remember driving home. By that time, close to 2:00 a.m., my sisters were all home. Chella and Lynn left with my mother for the forty-five-minute drive to Sunnybrook, leaving fifteen-year-old Christine home to answer the phone and be there for Alison when she woke up. It was to become a very familiar route for all of them.

At about 3:30 a.m., just before I was wheeled into surgery, my parents and sisters were brought in to say a brief hello. My oldest sister, Chella, recalls me looking at her and rolling my eyes, as if to say "Look what I got myself into *this* time."

None of us had any concept of what was to be.

*   *   *   *

I got the job at Becker's when I was fifteen. I had looked for some part-time jobs in some local malls, but with no experience I had no luck. A job wasn't a serious need, but I liked the idea of extra pocket money — it helped take a bit of pressure off my mother — and the manager let me have summers off so I could work as a camp counsellor. School, my job and an active social life filled my days and nights.

That night had been my first time closing the store. In most ways the shift had been like any other. My mother called at dinnertime to see if I was hungry. She would often drop off a plate of whatever they'd had at home for dinner. It was always wrapped in foil, with a tea towel over it to keep it warm. I asked her to bring the heavy sweater I had bought in Mexico in case it was cool when I walked home at 11:30. As she dropped off her homemade pizza she reminded me to call my sister Lynn and find out what she did on her Friday night shifts.

Lynn had been held up a few months before, and since then she had started locking the door sometime between 9:00 and 10:00 p.m. She would only let in customers she knew or who looked safe. I had been away at camp when Lynn was held up, so the robbery had very little effect on me. I called her around 9:00 to ask her about it.

"Lock the door whenever you feel like it, whenever you'll feel safer," she told me. That was the problem: I'd never had a reason not to feel safe in that store. I'd worked there for three years and nothing had ever happened to me. I also felt a bit silly locking the door.

I wish I'd spent a Friday night shift with Lynn and watched what she had done — I would not have felt stupid then. Even more, I wish I had just locked the goddamn door.

*   *   *   *

The Surgical Intensive Care Unit (SICU) at Sunnybrook is not a place for the weak of heart or stomach. Also known as the Respiratory Failure Unit, it houses only the most serious cases at the hospital. The fatality rate there is 25 percent. Every patient is hooked up to life support, and the constant hiss of respirators is punctuated every now and then by the screams of alarms going off as patients are momentarily taken off the machines to suction secretions from their chests. Alarms also go off when patients go into cardiac arrest, something that happened to the patient beside me in my first days there. That death frightened me enormously, though I tried to block it out of my mind.

Two rows of beds lined the unit. Mine was the last on the right, beside a window. To reach me, visitors had to pass all the other patients, each like me, with tubes, wires and machines surrounding their beds and invading their bodies, keeping them alive. I found out months later that it took each family member, and many of my friends, more than one attempt to reach my bed the first time. Weak in the knees, they would have to turn back and gather their strength before making it all the way across the unit to see me.

My first memory of intensive care after the surgery is of the bed I was put on. It was a new invention called the Roto-Rest, and I was the hospital's guinea pig. The bed is a motorized monstrosity, with panels sandwiching both sides of the patient's trunk and each limb. It moves constantly from side to side, turning its occupant like a carcass on a spit, sixty-two degrees in each direction. Terrified, I was sure I was going to fall out. I begged them to stop it; it made me dizzy. They told me it could only be stopped for one hour a day. I asked them to stop it right away for the allotted hour. They didn't. I still have a T-shirt that came with the bed: "I've Been Rotated," it reads.

The idea behind the bed is sound. The constant movement prevents pressure sores and keeps the organs moving, also lowering the risk of pneumonia. In eliminating the need to be turned from side to side, the bed provides maximum stability for a newly fused spine to heal.

The seven-hour surgery I had undergone in the early hours of September 24 removed the bullet, which had hit my spine then lodged in my left shoulder. There is still shrapnel in my neck, visible in every X-ray I get. Surgeons also removed the bone fragments that were pressing into the spinal cord, which is what caused the paralysis, and they fused three vertebrae of my spine with a piece from my hip. Curiously, losing the piece from my hip was one of the things that upset me most of all in those early days.

How will I be able to walk with a chunk of my hip gone? Couldn't they have used something else?

For months I wanted to ask about the long-term effects of that hip graft.

The first few days are hazy. I kept asking how I was going to the bathroom. My mother repeatedly told me I had a catheter in my bladder. Even though I had lost all sensation, as well as movement, below my shoulders, I kept insisting the catheter hurt, so they finally took it out. That meant having to be catheterized every few hours to drain my bladder; bowel and bladder function are also lost with spinal cord injuries. I wanted them to know I was expecting my period any day, but I was told it had started already, apparently triggered early by the trauma. After that my cycle stopped for over a year, another effect of the trauma and stress.

I had lost the ability to breathe on my own, so I had a tube that passed through my nose and into my lungs giving me oxygen. After ten days I was given a tracheostomy. A hole was cut in my windpipe, or trachea, and a tube went into the hole to provide air. I had no voice because the oxygen was going directly to my lungs without passing my vocal cords. Media reports that I couldn't talk weren't exactly accurate. I could mouth words, but no sound came out, so people had to read my lips. My family and many of my friends got pretty good at it. I kept asking for paper and a pen so I could write what I wanted to say.

My lips were terribly dry, but it was a few days before someone understood the word "chapstick." With any major trauma, fluid intake is strictly controlled for the first couple of days, so I was allowed only a few drops of water each hour, squirted through a syringe into my mouth. This wasn't nearly enough for my parched mouth, so my mother would keep a filled syringe behind her back, and as soon as the nurse looked away she'd quickly squirt it into my waiting mouth, like a mother bird feeding her chick. I wasn't allowed food for the first week.

Two days after the shooting the police came to take a statement. I answered everything, but couldn't provide a lot of information, except that the shooter was about my height, five feet, ten inches. Their final question put me over the edge and I started to cry.

"If we showed you some masks could you identify them?"

I couldn't look at them.

Psychologically, I was in rough shape. Every time I closed my eyes someone shot me. The nightmares were horrific and plagued me all night long, but I couldn't seem to tell anyone about them.

My family was hoping a visit from a celebrity might cheer me up. When I was younger, and I was asked what I wanted to be when I grew up, I'd say I wanted to be a famous television personality, "just like Dini Petty on Citytv." So my family contacted Dini Petty, who was then co-anchor of the six o'clock news. She came about a week after the shooting.

Dini and I hit it off right away. After running from side to side several times because of the moving bed, she suddenly said, "I feel like I'm at Swiss Chalet." Her face was inches from mine, since she had to read my lips. She picked up the skill immediately — in fact, she was better at it than some of the nurses. She asked me how I was sleeping, and I confessed about the nightmares.

"Tell me exactly what happened that night," Dini said. I told her.

"Tell me again," she said when I'd finished. I repeated the story.

"Tell me again," she said. She made me repeat it five or six times. The nightmares stopped.

My mother's presence was the most important thing to me at that point. She read to me a great deal. And my father could put me to sleep by stroking my forehead, which suited us both, because I don't think he knew what to say. No one did. Whenever my good friend Rob came in he would put one hand under the blanket and hold my hand. I couldn't feel it, but I could see it and it always made me feel better.

I think I'd watched too many "M*A*S*H" episodes, because I was terrified of getting hooked on morphine. I would wait as long as possible before finally giving in and asking for a shot. I couldn't get warm. I would have ten blankets heaped on me and still feel cold. I kept asking for my Mexican sweater. I also kept asking my mother to put my hands together and tuck them between my knees, wanting to curl up in the fetal position, the way I always used to sleep. Every once in a while my nurse would bring a flannel from a warmer and put it on me underneath the other blankets, pulling it up high around my chin where I could feel the heat. I loved those hot flannels.

I was distressed that they had cut off my camp bracelets. Moorelands Camp, where I'd been a counsellor for the three previous summers, was the most important place in the world to me then, and the bracelets were a symbolic tie to the place. Leather, beads and gimp — I must have had at least ten on each wrist.

Oh well, I'll get more next year when I'm at camp again.

I was in a type of traction called a "halo vest." It was a hard plastic shell with sheepskin on the inside. Four metal posts protruded up from the vest, two on each shoulder, front and back. The posts were attached to a ring around my head (hence the name "halo"), which was fixed to my head by four bolts that were screwed an eighth of an inch into my skull. There was one bolt over each eyebrow and one behind each ear. They had put it on me in Emergency, just before the surgery. That was what had caused the sudden pain.

The bolts were so tight against my skull that the upper half of my body could be lifted by the two front bars and I wouldn't feel a thing. Once, though, during the nearly four months I wore that vest, the bolts needed to be tightened. I don't know which was more painful, having loose bolts or the process of tightening them, but all told it led to one miserable afternoon.

A few days after the shooting, my mother, who kept a three-week vigil at my bedside before returning to work, washed my hair. To do it, the bed was stopped flat and the panel under my head was removed. A large bucket was put on the floor, to catch the pitchers of water that were poured over my head. The entire back of my head was bruised and sore from hitting the floor. I must get a large part of my strength from my mother, who silently emptied bucket after bucket of water, stained red with the blood caked in my hair.

Though my mother is strong, that doesn't mean she coasted through this time with ease. For the first three weeks, she would take a tranquillizer each morning after arriving at the hospital, and another each night before bed.

Squeamish even before the shooting, I have not been able to look at blood since. When I needed a transfusion they would cover the bag of blood somehow, once with a large paper plate with a happy face drawn on it. I still can't handle a cut, or anything else that bleeds, mine or anyone else's.

My friends were incredibly supportive — a little too supportive, in fact, for the hospital's liking. There were so many people virtually camped in the waiting room they were spilling out into the hallway. Before long the hospital approached us and said the multitudes were affecting the families of other patients, plus some staff had been complaining. So I had to choose two friends who could visit any time, and I could have unlimited visitors Saturdays and Sundays from 2:00 until 4:00 p.m.

The first time I went down the hall into the waiting room I understood the hospital's position. The room was tiny. It was where people received news of their loved ones, which was always serious and often tragic. My supporters had practically overtaken the room, and once I had stabilized there was no reason for it.

There is now a much larger waiting room, with a sign prominently displayed on the door: "Maximum three visitors per patient." Both the larger room and the sign, I'm told, are a direct result of my residence there. On a recent visit to the unit I looked at that sign with a bit of pride — I consider it a tribute to the family and friends who stayed by my side.

Though my friends were unwavering in their support, not all of them could handle the situation. Some could hardly look me in the eye when they visited. When that happened, I found myself doing the entertaining. It got so I could tell within thirty seconds how I had to behave to best suit my visitors. It came to me automatically. Sometimes, though, I wanted to scream in frustration when my expectations from a visitor weren't met. One night one of my favourite English teachers came to visit me and just stood there reading letters from students.

Put down those goddamn letters and talk to me, please. Anyone can read to me. I need some wisdom and guidance here. Why is this happening to me?

After a few weeks I got a crude type of call bell, unique to me and another patient in the unit with a halo and no voice. The bell had been designed and made by a friend of the other patient. It snapped onto the halo bar closest to my face and had a small plastic tab that stuck out in front of my mouth. When the need arose, I would stick my tongue out, pushing the piece of plastic, which would set off a distinctive buzz.

Without the device set up, the only sound I could make was a *cluck* or a *tch* with my tongue on the roof of my mouth, audible only to someone close to my bed. The need for a call bell became apparent when my respirator tube fell or was pulled off a couple of times. When it happened, it would take twenty long seconds before the alarm would sound to alert the nurses, and, because alarms were constantly sounding, another several seconds before someone would realize something was wrong.

One time I noticed my respirator tube was caught on something and, as the motorized bed moved away, it became obvious the tube was going to pop off. My nurse was not there right then, and my desperate *tch tch* sounds were not heard by anyone. Logically, there was no way I would die before someone noticed, but terror has no logic. Those were some of the longest seconds of my life, waiting for the alarm to sound, then waiting again for someone to respond. I was pretty hysterical by the time I was hooked back up. The call buzzer was a wonderful thing.

*   *   *   *

The doctors told us that I was paralyzed below my shoulders. They said that it was most probably permanent. Although I knew, technically, what paralysis meant, at a deeper level I couldn't accept it for myself. I knew I couldn't move, but my body was so traumatized that I wasn't really trying. We were dealing with life day by day. The future was never mentioned.

I did have one fantasy I played over and over in mind. Dave, one of my good friends from camp, whispered something in my ear when he first visited me: "I want to be the first to see you wiggle your toes." I cared a lot about Dave, and I desperately wanted to do that for him. I'd lie awake at night and concentrate on my toes, trying so damn hard to make them move. I had the happy scene all mapped out: me knowing I could move them, but not telling anyone, just sending for Dave. I'd get him to fling back the covers off my feet, astound them all, then we'd all have a joyous celebration.

Soon after Dini's visit she sent me a Walkman. It was brilliant. I put that headset on and didn't take it off for a second for three days. When I finally did my ears were numb and stained blue in parts from the headset sponges. I shut out everything by listening to music, mostly soothing instrumental tracks. To this day I can't bring myself to listen to most of those tapes I played in the first few weeks; they transport me back to that time. The music drowned out my thoughts for the most part, but when my thoughts did drift, it was to the past, not the future. I replayed happy memories in my mind, mostly centred around camp and my friends from there. I spent countless hours in my mother's little red Honda all over Ontario's roads mentally driving, driving, driving. When cold, I imagined I was being held in someone's arms.

When I was finally allowed food, it was liquids only the first day. I had been craving a Caramilk bar for a few days and I begged them to allow me to have some, reasoning that I would let it melt in my mouth — that way I would be swallowing liquid.

By this time I'd heard about the layout of the hospital and the Harvest Room, a large cafeteria-type lounge with vending machines and tables. It was clear on the other side of the massive hospital, a good ten- or fifteen-minute walk each way, and my friends and family were quickly getting intimately acquainted with it.

11

My friend Rob offered to go get the chocolate bar when I got permission from the doctor for the treat. As soon as the first piece was put in my mouth, I realized I'd made a mistake. After a week without food and with very little water, my mouth was not ready for chocolate. But I knew that Rob had gone all the way to the Harvest Room for it, so I figured I had to make it worth his while. I forced myself to eat half the bar. What a mistake that was! I felt so sick after that. It ended up curing me of a sweet tooth for years.

My first taste of solid food was wonderful, even though it was hospital fare. In fact, my appetite soon exploded and I started polishing off many of my meals. I looked forward to the menu coming each afternoon so I could choose the next day's meals. My five-foot-ten frame had plunged to ninety-five pounds in the first few weeks, and I needed to gain some of that back.

*   *   *   *

Now that I was becoming more aware of the world around me, limited as it was to the hospital staff, family and friends, I began to feel uncomfortable about certain things. I would be willing to bet that there are no finer medical personnel anywhere than at Sunnybrook's Surgical Intensive Care Unit, but I was afraid that some of the nurses didn't like me, because they'd asked *not* to be assigned to me ever. I never knew their reasons — it likely had something to do with all the media attention — so I could only imagine that they didn't like *me*. For as long as I can remember, I've had a hollow, sick feeling in my stomach whenever there was someone I knew who didn't like me. I thought maybe these nurses assumed my head had swelled with all the attention and that I was a spoiled brat.

I used every opportunity to show them I wasn't spoiled or conceited. Here I was, shot and paralyzed, on a respirator and unable to take a breath, but I would beam a smile if one of those nurses came near my bed, which they did fairly often because the unit's morphine was kept in a nearby cabinet. I would jump through hoops to try and change their minds. I once overheard one of them saying her face was dry and asking if anyone had moisturizer. So I quickly *tch tch tch*-ed with my tongue to get my nurse's attention and mouthed that I had some face cream and please give it to Joanne. Joanne thanked me and seemed friendly enough, but she still never got assigned to me. It drove me nuts.

I got along very well with most of the staff. Generally speaking, patients in SICU recovering from severe trauma or major surgery need to be on a respirator for only two or three days, and they aren't in the most alert state while they are there. I think it must have been a welcome change for the staff to have a long-term patient, especially one who was fully conscious and capable of conversation.

Occasionally I'd get a nurse who was hopeless at reading lips, though. That would make the shift frustrating and boring for me, since there would be little communication. Often I couldn't even convey what tapes I wanted to listen to. I was usually patient enough to repeat myself several times, but once in awhile my patience would run out. One day a nurse couldn't get the simplest word.

"Chapstick," I said over and over again. Finally, disgusted with the magnitude of her incompetence, I decided it just wasn't worth it.

"Fuck off," I mouthed. She didn't get that, either.

I quickly grew familiar with the ebb and flow of the unit. The staff had their ways of dealing with the pressures of such an intense job, usually involving humour. One afternoon I heard a few of them singing "Oh, we're the trauma team" as they were settling in a new, unconscious patient. Another day, soon after the shooting, a young man who had attempted suicide came in. He had put a gun in his mouth and pulled the trigger, but the gun was angled a bit, so all he'd managed to do was blow off the left side of his face. Some of the nurses joked about starting a school for suicide wannabes.

"If you're going to shoot yourself in the mouth, shoot straight, for crying out loud," one said.

"Yeah, and learn the proper depth and direction to slice your wrists *before* you try it," another nurse chimed in.

This kind of banter usually made me laugh, but not that time. I couldn't believe that someone would deliberately do that. I was furious at that guy for shooting himself. I wanted to yell and throw things at him. How dare he treat his body like that?

The jokes only flew around the unit at night, when visitors had gone home. I liked the unit in the late-evening hours before I fell asleep. The whole room was darkened, with faint lights glowing from each bedside. The atmosphere was more casual, and no one worried about censoring what came out of their mouths. Once in a while I even felt on par with the staff. One evening the nurses were all ordering takeout from a nearby restaurant I'd heard them talk about. Cheryl, my nurse, asked me if I wanted anything.

"They've got great Greek salad," she told me.

"No thanks, I'm not hungry," I lied. I would have loved to order something in along with the staff, for the novelty of it if not the Greek salad itself, but I had no cash, no wallet or purse. That was the first time I felt my disability separate me socially. It wasn't because they were staff and I was a patient that I didn't participate, it was because I was paralyzed and had no physical control over my sur-

13

roundings or belongings. The next day when my mother came in I had her put some money in the toe of a slipper. I hoped for an opportunity to join the nurses another night, but it never happened.

*   *   *   *

One morning, three weeks after the shooting, I was about to hungrily gobble my first bite of breakfast when a voice thundered from across the floor.

"Nurse, don't give her that food!"

It was Dr. Charles Tator, my neurosurgeon. Dr. Tator had been on call the night of my shooting, which is how he came to be in charge of my case. I'd been told he was among the very best in North America, most certainly in Canada, but I wasn't sure if I cared for his bedside manner. Every few days he'd do rounds with a different entourage of residents, medical students and sometimes visiting doctors. He'd talk about my case, give the history and then piss me off by pulling the respirator tube off my throat and commanding me to "BREATHE." I'd lie there helpless and angry. Then he'd take a pin and start poking me from my face on down, a critical early test to see if any sensation is returning or changing. I felt like an animal in a circus. My traumatized, eighteen-year-old logic resented his visits and I took to calling him "Chuck Spud" around my family.

On this particular morning he was there to deliver some bad news. An X-ray showed my bone graft had slipped off my repaired spine; they had to perform surgery immediately and reattach the bone with a metal plate, which would stay in my neck. The news was devastating. It meant the halo-vest traction would have to stay on three extra weeks. It meant starting all over again.

*   *   *   *

Although it took months and many gradual stages for me to understand what my disability meant, I can remember the day my mind first grasped the significance of my injury. It was a sunny morning, and beams of light danced across my bed from the window. I was upset because my physiotherapist was moving on to another unit. I looked forward to her daily visits. She would pound each side of my chest to loosen and then suction out secretions. This was done to prevent pneumonia. She also stretched my legs, arms and hands, trying to keep some manoeuvrability in my joints. My muscles were atrophying quickly from the sudden cessation of activity. I liked her a great deal and enjoyed our daily chats. I felt as though I was losing a friend.

Though I don't remember any of the exact words that passed between us, she had the misfortune to be the one I asked about my paralysis. For the first time since the shooting, it started to sink in that this might not completely go away.

Up until that point I had pictured myself back at high school the next semester on crutches. I thought glamorous thoughts about boys carrying my books and helping me up the stairs and holding doors. This was going to make me popular with everyone. Maybe I'd even score some hospital greens that I could wear — they were trendy back then.

I felt the walls come crashing in on me as the realization hit that I was never going to be the same. Never. I cried for hours, overcome by a mixture of despair and fear. It was so wrong, so unfair. I shouldn't have been there. I belonged in Mississauga, at high school, and with my friends.

But this still wasn't "acceptance." It was partial understanding only. I still pictured myself sitting up in bed, eating pizza with my friends, feeding myself. I had an image of my fingers curling, like those of other people I'd seen, but surely I would still be somewhat self-sufficient. Surely I could push myself in a wheelchair, feed myself, dress myself, drive a vehicle *by myself*. It took months for the full impact of my disability to sink in.

One afternoon, a couple of days later, I was alone, turning back and forth on that bed, when an image of something I *might* have been doing popped into my head. It was a memory, actually, of my friend Alise and me. The two of us would often sing together, while Alise played guitar or piano. We were in her basement, a cold, unfinished area with the half-stripped piano sitting among unpacked boxes on a sheet of plastic. As I remembered the words to a song we used to sing, my eyes started gushing like Niagara Falls. It was a Carole King song, called "Home Again": *"Sometimes I wonder if I'm ever going to make it home again / It's so far and out of sight / I really need someone to talk to, and nobody else / Knows how to comfort me tonight."*

I didn't particularly like the nurse assigned to me that day, so I wasn't in the best of spirits anyway, but that memory tore at my soul. I cried and cried and cried. My nurse was on lunch, but when another nurse on the unit caught sight of my face she came over to me and stood helplessly by my bed. What could she say? I sometimes get choked up when I think of it, me as a scared, confused, hurting teenager. I was the loneliest person in the world at that moment.

In the year I spent in the hospital I came across all types, but the most insensitive had to be the resident who took it upon himself to deliver a dose of reality. The "dose" was administered on a Saturday night, about a month after the shooting and not long after that last session with my physiotherapist. My mother was with me, reading to me.

The resident came over to my corner and started chatting. The unit was quiet that night. With one foot casually propped up on my bed, he said words to this effect:

"Face it, you're a quad and you'll always be a quad. You're never getting off the respirator. The sooner you learn to accept it, the sooner you can get on with your life."

He said this to me barely one month after I'd been shot. I'd never heard the shortened term "quad," for quadriplegic, used before. I thought he was making fun of me. He hadn't turned his back to walk away five seconds when my mother and I burst into tears. We just cried for the rest of the evening.

The next day was one of the worst days my family had. Everyone was upset and trying to grasp this news. I could not fathom what my life would be like being on a respirator forever. It was a nightmare, and I desperately wanted to wake from it.

That evening something strange and wonderful happened. A man named Howie arrived at the waiting room. He didn't give a last name, address or phone number; he said he'd driven in from upstate New York. That in itself wasn't unusual — the publicity surrounding the shooting had brought visitors from far and near. Some brought food, some brought gifts, a couple of folks wanted to dance and chant around my bed. Some of the people were absolute kooks who belonged in institutions. One afternoon when I was alone a stranger got in to see me by saying he was a clergyman and a relative of a family friend. He made me repeat a prayer, telling me I would go to Hell if I refused. Mine is a family of lapsed Catholics, and none of us is particularly religious, but that was the most vulnerable point of my life and I believed everything he said. And in those beginning weeks I was certainly praying a great deal to "God," or anyone else who might be listening. We all were. Terrified, I repeated the prayer, too frightened to be angry.

But Howie was different. He didn't ask to see me. Instead, he gave my mother a plain, white statue of the Sacred Heart of Jesus and three rose petals that had apparently been blessed by someone and laminated. He told her to put the statue where I could see it, and one petal under each hand, one under my head.

As I said, I'm not a religious person, but for some reason that statue filled me with a sense of peace I hadn't felt since the shooting. I could hardly take my eyes off it. It was the first night I didn't get upset when my mother left — in fact, I was anxious for solitude. I lay awake long into the night, my eyes steady on the statue. It was on the windowsill, and because of the motorized bed I kept turning away and back toward it. For hours my eyes strained to keep it in my sight as much as possible. When I finally slept, it was the most tranquil sleep I'd had since the shooting.

The next day Dr. Tator came with his usual entourage. Just as he had done during each round for the month I'd been there, he pulled the respirator tube off my throat.

"BREATHE."

I took my first breath.

Chapter Two:

GASPING FOR AIR

It is difficult to describe how excited we were that I had taken a breath. I don't know whose eyes popped wider, mine or Dr. Tator's. I was suddenly filled with the most thrilling kind of hope. Who knew what else I might recover? There was a flurry of phone calls that afternoon, letting everyone know the good news, followed by a couple of days of absolute euphoria. I was particularly elated because it had happened so soon after being told by that callous resident that it wasn't possible. "I'll show him," I thought. Then there came a solid month of incredibly hard work.

For the most part, it was up to me to get my diaphragm back in shape. It had been completely idle for four weeks and didn't exactly jump back into action by itself. I was still relying on the respirator, and I had to be constantly reminded to take breaths. At first, each time a visitor arrived at my bed, someone in my family would want to show off my new trick.

"Barb, show how you breathe," they'd say, chest puffed out with pride. I would obligingly screw up my face and, mustering every ounce of effort I possessed, suck in some air.

"Did you see that, isn't it *great*?" they would say. My visitor, usually not quite sure what they had seen, would nod in confusion.

Taking each breath was tiring, and even though I was taking only two or three an hour, I found it exhausting. Before long I grew resentful of the work. I was getting tired of always being tired. We are born breathing, it's automatic. It shouldn't have been so hard. I should have been able to take breathing for granted. It became a relief when my mother left each night and I could just let the respirator do its job. I rarely took a breath on my own initiative.

The process of weaning myself off the respirator was slow, accomplished by lowering the number of breaths per minute the machine was giving me as my diaphragm strengthened. It went fairly smoothly until I got down to six breaths a minute. Then we hit a snag. I had been told that I could easily survive on six breaths a minute without having to supplement it with my own, but once the machine was turned down to five breaths, I would *have* to consistently help out.

I was terrified of that responsibility, and stayed at six breaths for longer than I had at any other level. Each time someone suggested turning it down, I would start crying and tell them I wasn't ready. I wasn't acting like a prima donna, I was genuinely terrified. What would happen to me if I fell asleep and failed to do my part? I had no proof my breathing had become automatic. I knew I was hooked up to respirator and heart-rate monitors that had alarms, but that was not enough to ease my worries.

Finally, one afternoon SICU director Dr. Ross Reid came over to my bed and told me he had to lower the respirator. I burst into tears and begged him to wait a bit longer. He said he couldn't, but stood there calmly while I threw as hysterical a tantrum as a severely paralyzed, respirator-dependent person can throw. It lasted about ten minutes. Then, as my sobs started to subside, he matter-of-factly pointed out that he had put the respirator down on the sly, and I had been surviving just fine.

Feeling somewhat sheepish, I immediately jumped another hurdle when I fell into an exhausted sleep and woke to the news that I had taken some breaths on my own. After that, things moved quickly. A couple more weeks and I was at one breath a minute.

The next step, going right off the respirator, was as psychologically difficult as going from six to five breaths a minute had been. For the first time in two months, I would be breathing completely on my own. The day I came right off the respirator was very memorable. It was quiet with the machine turned off, but except for the odd anxious moment, I was doing pretty well. Then that afternoon Dr. Tator came to see me. He said he was pleased with my progress, and that I could also come off the bed "in a few days." Then, unbeknownst to me, he walked out of the room and ordered that I be taken off right away.

About an hour after he left, a regular bed was brought into my room.

"You get to get off the Roto-Rest today," my nurse said, as though she was delivering good news, as she set about making up the bed. "I'll get some help to move you over."

"What do you mean today?" I mouthed in panic. "Dr. Tator said I'd come off it in a few days, not today. I can't get off it today. You can't make me do that today, too." Psychologically I had become just as dependent on my motorized bed as I was on the respirator, spending those two months rocked in constant motion.

I was thunderstruck. I was also angry. I was as scared of a regular bed and the prospect of lying still as I had been of the motorized bed two months earlier. This would mean lying in one position for a couple of hours, then being turned to another side to avoid pressure sores. The timing could not have been worse. I was psychologically dependent on both machines and he was taking both away at the same time, without discussing it with me.

"I'm not moving until I talk to Dr. Bugaresti," I said, insisting they contact the resident in charge of the bed's research project, a woman I got along with very well. I was offended that she hadn't been a part of the decision. I stayed put for a few hours, until she reached the hospital.

Despite my "lie-down" protest, I was moved off the Roto-Rest later that afternoon. I talked with Joanne Bugaresti and she deferred to Dr. Tator's judgment. I was disappointed. I wanted to fight his order, but I needed her to fight with me. I couldn't see it as a positive step.

So, for the first time in two months, I was fully in charge of my own breathing *and* I was lying still. No amount of fiddling could get me in a comfortable position. My shoulder and neck kept cramping. It was almost motion sickness in reverse. I kept waiting for the bed to move. The stillness was unsettling; the quiet, with both machines silent, eerie.

That night was probably the worst I had. I certainly didn't sleep. Unfortunately my nurse was not one of the unit's regulars, but a relief nurse from an agency. She was unsympathetic from the start of her twelve-hour shift and was obviously annoyed that I buzzed her every few minutes.

"Can I have a drink of water?" I'd ask.

"Can you change the TV channel?" the next time.

"I need to be bagged," I said numerous times, having her attach a resuscitation bag to my trach tube and pump a few breaths of oxygen into me. Choked with fear all night, I felt as though I was drowning and couldn't get enough air.

After silently fulfilling each request, her mouth taut with disapproval and impatience, the nurse would turn and swiftly walk out of the room to sit in a chair just outside the door. What I needed was somebody sitting beside my bed and talking to me all night, as one of the unit's regular nurses would have done. I needed reassurance, understanding and a bit of sympathy. I got none of that, nor did I get a wink of sleep.

After a week of breathing well on my own, I was given a "talking trach." It was too premature to take the trach right out of my throat and let the hole close over, but this trach was sealed and allowed the air to pass over my vocal cords. I had a voice, my voice, back. I was warned to limit my talking for the first couple of days, since my vocal cords hadn't been used in nine weeks.

Limit my talking after nine weeks of forced silence? Yeah, right. There was no shutting me up. I talked all day, I made phone calls to friends, I talked excitedly to my mom and sister when they visited that day, I talked the nurses' ears off long into the night. And when I woke up the next day I had lost my voice!

The first time I saw Dr. Tator after getting a talking trach I duked it out with him. He had come on his usual rounds. I quietly let him give his spiel to the underlings, then, as he turned to walk away, I hit him with it.

"Dr. Tator, I'm never going to forgive you for what you did."

This was not the kind of greeting this most-respected surgeon and researcher was accustomed to, particularly from patients he had put back together to the best of his considerable ability.

"What did I do?" he asked, his eyes wide with surprise.

"I'm angry about the way you took me off my bed."

I'm quite sure no patient of his had ever spoken to him that way. We talked about it briefly and he agreed that I had a point. He said he had to continue rounds but would come back later, and he kept his word, returning that afternoon.

"What questions do you have?" he asked me. There were so many things I wanted to know.

"Why did my breathing come back?"

"Could I get movement back in my arms?"

"Is my spinal cord severed?"

"How do you know I won't get more movement back?"

"Am I ever going to walk again?"

The two of us had a lengthy and honest chat. He didn't know the answers to many of my questions and didn't pretend he did. "We don't know," he stated simply about why I'd started breathing. But he did explain a great deal about spinal cord injury. With the vast majority of these injuries it's the swelling of the cord cutting off the nerves that causes the paralysis. Within the first few months, it's possible for the swelling to go down enough to bring back some function. Cords themselves are rarely actually *severed*, he said. But he didn't hold out much hope for more movement for me in the near future. My injury was complete, he explained. The spinal cord is like a telephone cable, with thousands of wires, or nerves, carrying messages from the brain to the body. A complete injury cuts off all the messages, whereas an incomplete injury leaves some of the nerves intact, so a few messages can still get through.

Leaning on the bed rail beside me, he told me about the research he and many others were doing. He told me he thought it was possible to cure spinal cord injuries, but that he had no idea how far away that breakthrough was.

Since that discussion we've been friends, and he has gone "above and beyond" for me many times. The two of us have formed a mutual admiration society. I've become a staunch supporter of the research he does, and I even have an annual golf tournament, named in my honour and run by the Canadian Paraplegic Association, that raises funds for his research laboratory. He cares deeply and is passionately dedicated to finding the cure that so many of us are hoping for.

Two more weeks passed and the trach was taken out permanently. The hole was allowed to close, although an obvious scar remained until I had plastic surgery on it nine years later.

On another temporary high, I bet one of the head nurses five dollars I'd be moving my arms enough to feed myself before I left the unit. I lost that one.

*   *   *   *

In December I left the SICU. I had mixed feelings about leaving. I was excited and scared. The move was a step forward, but there were many truly special people working there and the unit had become my home. It was the only home I knew in my new life.

I spent two days in a less serious intensive care unit, then I finally moved to the neuro floor, the next step in transition toward rehabilitation. By that time my body was showing classic signs of spinal cord injury. I'd started sweating profusely above the injury level, so my face, head and neck were constantly soaked. It's one of the effects of paralytic trauma, and it usually lasts a few years. My muscles were starting to spasm, as well. This was particularly a problem when the nurses came to catheterize me. It was never an easy job for anyone because my urethra was quite small, but my legs started to spasm shut as they tried to insert the catheter into my bladder.

I am amazed how many times I was told to "relax." Muscle spasms almost always occur with spinal cord injury. They are completely involuntary and are set off by a number of things, like motion after sitting still for awhile. It's a paralyzed body's way of stretching muscles or changing position. They look a little freaky to people who don't know anything about them and have never seen one before. In fact, the worst part about spasms is how uncomfortable they make people who aren't used to seeing them. Big ones look almost violent and can pitch a person out of a chair.

Spasms are actually a good thing for two reasons: one, they keep some tone in atrophying muscles, and two, they can alert the person that something is wrong. I know my body so well now that I can read exactly what the spasm is telling me. I know if it's just a regular stretch, or if I'm getting a bladder infection, or, most important, if something is doing damage that would cause pain if I could feel it. Twice I've burned myself with boiling water, and the spasm was severe enough that I high-tailed it to an emergency department. But spasm is not caused in any way by tension or fear, and those nurses should have known that.

I was still being catheterized every few hours, including once during the night. It was usually timed for when I would need a turn. The interruption in the middle of the night was hard enough to take, but some of the nurses regularly made it a horrible experience, coming in and turning on the bright overhead light, not even making a pretense of trying to be quiet and let me stay a little sleepy. One night my legs spasmed every time the nurse tried to insert the catheter.

"Relax," she kept telling me.

"I can't control that," I replied each time, through clenched teeth.

Suddenly she lost her temper and walked out. "I'll be back in a few minutes when you've learned to relax," was her parting shot. She didn't even bother to cover me.

It was about 2:00 a.m., and there I was, most of my body paralyzed, lying completely exposed, the room flooded with light. And I was eighteen years old. Large tears started to roll out my eyes and down into my ears. She eventually returned, silently finished her work and left again. And I let her get away with it. I've asked myself many times why I didn't confront her or, more importantly, report her. I have no answer, except that I wasn't assertive at that point in my recovery. Boy, would I relish a round with her now.

I did lose it once with nurses on that floor. It was not long after that episode and I was starting to get fed up with their ignorance. One afternoon three nurses were trying to catheterize me. Each time I spasmed one turned to me and said, "Try to relax." It was too much and I burst into tears.

"I CAN'T CONTROL THAT," I screamed. "It's a muscle spasm, it's involuntary, and it doesn't matter how much I try to relax. GOT IT?" They got it.

As I got closer to discharge, someone decided I needed a psychiatric evaluation. A young psych resident was sent to my room. Posters covered my walls, and a Cabbage Patch doll — the hottest toy that year — hung upside down by her foot from the ceiling. The resident, stuffed into a shirt, tie, vest and corduroy jacket with patches on the elbows, was a very solemn sort. Since I'd known for a few days he was coming, I was prepared.

"Hey Doc, how many shrinks does it take to change a light bulb?" I asked him. Without waiting, I gave him the answer: "Only one, but the light bulb has to *really want* to change." He didn't think it was funny, and he launched right into his evaluation. He even asked me what my earliest childhood memory was, a question I managed to answer without rolling my eyes until he was gone. I passed his test and was pronounced ready for rehabilitation.

*   *   *   *

In January I moved to Lyndhurst Rehabilitation Hospital, which is very close to Sunnybrook. Lyndhurst is a spacious, two-storey, red-brick building set on the edge of a ravine and surrounded by trees and flowering bushes. Paved paths weave their way around the centre. Inside, large picture windows ensure natural light all year round. The walls are covered with art, painted and donated by local artists and former patients. Open spaces dominate, and hallways are wide enough for passing lanes. There are some private rooms, but most, like mine, house four patients in each. In the rooms, each section has a bed, desk, closet and floor-to-ceiling window. A privacy curtain can be pulled around the section.

I clearly remember my first afternoon at Lyndhurst, because I thought my admitting nurse was a miracle worker. At Sunnybrook I had been plagued by the constant sweating, and I was sick of feeling soaking wet all the time. When I was turned from one side to the other it would stop for about ten blessed minutes, then start again. Lying on my side the sweat would start dripping in my ear. When I couldn't hear anymore, I'd call a nurse to come and mop me up.

I was admitted to Lyndhurst by Glenna, an impossibly cheery person. With her blond, always-coiffed hair and a quick, easy laugh, she was a favourite on the ward. Clucking disapprovingly about how much general hospitals *didn't* know about spinal cord injury, she got me a tiny, pink, bitter tablet. Within twenty minutes, my sweating stopped. The relief was so incredible I just lay there in bed all afternoon enjoying *not sweating*. She told me my doctor would write an order for me to take the medication four times a day.

Lyndhurst observed a "no fuss" policy, which I learned right away when I tried to tell Glenna that I kept a towel roll under the pillow on either side to prop my head. Glenna explained that they discouraged "little extras like that."

My first day was a little strange. I didn't see any of the hospital because I was transported by ambulance and just put right into bed. But I soon met my three roommates. One was a married mother of two, named, if you can believe it, Lynn Hurst. With a name like that, we used to joke, she was destined to end up breaking her neck. Then there was Tammy. Tammy was two years younger than me. Her injury was low and incomplete, so she had a lot of movement. She and her stepfather greeted me with a baseball cap that had "Quad Squad" stencilled on it. Our fourth roommate was a woman we privately called "Wendy Whiner." She complained about everything and insisted on using an electric wheelchair, despite having an incomplete injury. She ultimately walked out of Lyndhurst.

I was awakened my first morning by a nurse whose face was inches from mine. She introduced herself as "Caroline, the bowel lady." She had so much make-up on she scared me. Caroline was a woman who took great pride in her work. She took me to a sterile, tiled room appropriately named the "Bowel Room," where I was given the lovely greeting of an enema. She explained that my bowels would be cleaned out, then trained to work on schedule, three times a week. My schedule would be Monday, Wednesday and Friday mornings, so the nights before I would take laxatives. In the morning a suppository would be inserted and *voilà*. It's actually amazing how quickly my system caught on to that.

It certainly made a lot more sense from a lifestyle point of view. That's also why I started keeping an indwelling catheter in my bladder, with a bag that I wear on the side of my leg. Although it's much healthier to be catheterized several times a day, avoiding many bladder infections and keeping my bladder filling and emptying, it makes day-to-day life much more complicated than necessary. Without an indwelling catheter I would have to transfer out of my chair several times a day, get undressed and be catheterized. Try working full time if you have to do that.

The staff of Lyndhurst are primarily good at their jobs. There is no pity to be found on the premises. The philosophy in rehab is to learn to live as best you can in the real world with what you have left. I felt a certain lack of sympathy, but I needed to learn how to live as independently as I could, keeping reality firmly in mind. Anyone who finds rehab too tough won't make it very well in the real world.

There are three wards in the hospital, each with its own physiatrist, a doctor specializing in rehabilitation. I feel fortunate that I landed on Ward 1A. I think I had the best doctor on staff, Dr. Nimmi Bharatwal, known by all simply and affectionately as "Dr. B." There were three ward aides as well. Ours was Rowena, part den mother, part friend. We used to think Rowena didn't get the respect she deserved, and we'd sometimes find ways to keep her busy with us to give her a break from some of the more menial clean-up jobs she might otherwise have been given.

Therapy did not start off well for me at all because I was quite sick. I couldn't even get out of bed for several days. For the first week, when I did start trying to sit up, I passed out. That's common for quads — it's a combination of general weakness from the injury and the change in elevation after lying down for weeks or, as in my case, months. Nursing notes state that I "begged" to be put back in bed during this time. I was eating next to nothing, vomiting several times a week and had a near-constant low-grade fever. A couple of times each week my temperature would rise quite high, and I'd need medication for it. There was something brewing in my body.

When I did manage to get up and go to occupational therapy, I'd spend most of the time leaning forward on a pillow on the table because I was so faint. Part of the problem was that I was sitting upright for the first time. At Sunnybrook, the wheel-chair backs reclined and could be set at different angles. Not here — the theory was that patients needed to get used to sitting properly right away. After months of lying flat or sitting reclined, being completely upright jolted my equilibrium. It's not that staff just sit the patients up and leave them to pass out, though. There are devices designed to help push blood back up to the brain. One was an abdominal binder that would be stretched tight around the person's waist and velcroed shut. They also used thigh-high stockings which were very tight and went on each leg with a fight. And there was a pill that was *supposed* to help, though it never felt like it did. Despite all these inventions, I kept passing right out. When this happened they would tip the whole chair back until I was ready to try again.

One afternoon, while my father was visiting, I passed out while getting up. I came to in time to hear the nurse ask my father, tragedy dripping from her voice, "How tall *was* she?"

"I still am five foot ten," I used all my strength to retort.

I was eventually sent back to Sunnybrook to investigate the problem with my temperature and nausea. For three weeks a battery of tests was run.

One test stands out clearly in my memory. The name of it escapes me, but it involved an injection of some sort of substance and a trip down to Sunnybrook's Nuclear Medicine department. The day before the scheduled test, someone from the department came to my room and injected the substance into my big toe. During the injection, which took a solid couple of minutes, a chemical stench filled the air, which lingered for a couple of hours afterward. I couldn't bring myself to look at the needle or what was in it, but my mind pictured a giant syringe full of a thick, sil-ver, mercury-like substance travelling slowly through my body. The smell alone was extremely upsetting, and it wouldn't have surprised me if I'd glowed when the light was turned out.

The next stage was to get my bowels emptied. I had to drink a horrid concoction that evening that was supposed to do the trick. The following morning, I was taken down to the department by an orderly. Patients were always transported the same way, feet first on a stretcher, pushed by an orderly. One of the most difficult aspects of hospitalization is the loss of control and personal dignity. With paralysis, the loss is even greater. You never know who is going to walk into your room, for example. But nowhere is the lack of privacy more evident than when moving through the hospital — for an X-ray, a test, or even just to another room. It's impossible to escape the fact that hospital hallways are public places. Everyone looks — hospital visitors and staff alike. That total lack of privacy was a normal, everyday part of my life.

Nuclear Medicine was in the basement of the hospital, and the closer we got to it, the fewer people I saw. The actual test involved lying on a table while a giant piece of equipment, positioned a few inches above me, moved slowly from my head to my feet and back again. Since it was an X-ray, naturally no one was in the room with me, making the long test even more disconcerting.

When they got the test results, they discovered my bowels had not been sufficiently emptied, and the test had to be repeated. This time I couldn't stop the tears from flowing when they gave me the injection in my toe. Amazingly enough, the second test was skewed for the same problem — my bowels weren't completely cleaned out. This time they asked for my permission to repeat the test a third time. I refused.

They finally discovered that I had a huge abscess in my neck, basically a large pocket of infection. By the time they found it I needed immediate surgery. They opened my neck again, drained the abscess and took the metal plate off my spinal fusion.

The period following that surgery was the toughest I faced. By the time they discovered the problem I was extremely ill. Another problem was the surgery itself; because I had been on a respirator for so long, it was very risky to give me a general anaesthetic. As I was being wheeled into surgery, the anaesthetist, the same one who had performed my other operations, told me he couldn't put me to sleep the same way as before. I had to be awake while they put the intubation tube down my throat.

For the longest time after that operation I kept reliving those moments before I lost consciousness: lying there filled with fear, not knowing what I was going to be put through, shivering uncontrollably in the sterile, freezing room, the doctors and nurses all wearing masks and caps covering their hair, the anaesthetist telling me to open my mouth so he could squirt a freezing spray down my throat, and the tube going into my mouth and down my throat. I would wake suddenly in the middle of the night, gasping for air. I became afraid to go to sleep.

The reality of the paralysis also started to sink in around this time, plunging me into a deep, deep depression. My low spirits were not bolstered by the hospital unit I was in — in fact, the opposite was true. The negative atmosphere at Sunnybrook's Neurological Intensive Care Unit (NICU) was almost palpable. This unit had one nurse for every two patients, but the difference between the NICU and SICU unit nurses was like night and day. Maybe they were unable to rise above the mood of the unit, but whatever the reason, they were far less cheerful and friendly. My depression undoubtedly contributed to it, but it was definitely not the whole problem. Dini Petty describes that period as the only time she was ever scared for me.

"I came to visit you one day, looked into your eyes, and I could see you had given up," she told me years later. In a way I had. I lay in bed all day not caring about anything, not the future or the present. I didn't care what I ate, or if I ate. I couldn't entertain visitors the way I had before. I don't remember what my thoughts were. I was totally listless.

One day my nurse gave me a warning.

"Be careful. People won't want to be around you if you aren't happy."

That comment had a profound effect on me. From that moment on I felt incredible pressure to mask my depression, particularly when that nurse was working. That comment has actually never left me. I cannot rid myself of the fear of being alone if I am not consistently pleasant to be with.

Things were especially bad at night. I discovered that the nurses must have been taking double breaks and covering for each other. It seemed that every time I asked for something, I was told my nurse was on break. And it's not as if the other nurse would get me what I needed; I kept being told to wait until my nurse returned. I started having anxiety attacks every night when my mother left for home, sometimes almost hyperventilating myself unconscious.

Finally I raised the issue with the unit's head nurse one morning. She said she would look into it. I never heard any more about it, but things immediately changed on the night shift. I also became despised by the staff. So the nurses were around more at night, but they resented me. My depression got worse.

One morning I got a surprise visit from one of the SICU nurses. Annette had become a favourite the first time she was assigned to me, soon after the shooting. We'd connected right away, and after that first shift she'd said, "I think you and I are going to be friends." It used to be the biggest treat when she was assigned to me. She would give me facials, or do my nails. We would talk endlessly: I'd tell her all about my camp experiences, and she'd tell me about her New Brunswick background. We are still friends.

Annette had just finished working a twelve-hour overnight shift. I knew she would be exhausted, but I needed a friendly face too badly to insist she go home. She started to give me a manicure as we sat together.

"Word has travelled upstairs that you're depressed," she said.

Hearing that, I started sobbing. Until that point I hadn't acknowledged my depression even to myself. I had just been existing. The fact that the news was travelling through the hospital made me realize how obvious and serious my state was.

"I can't live like this," I told her.

Annette listened to me for a while, then took me up to visit the SICU. No miracle solutions were reached that morning, but I realized that I had to do something to save myself. It was sink or swim time again. I chose to swim, but I knew I needed help.

I started by telling my family that I couldn't be alone during the day anymore. It was hard to do that, because my family had already sacrificed a great deal. After the first three weeks when my mother had to go back to work, my oldest sister, Chella, decided to drop out of university and come to the hospital every day. For the rest of that semester she took public transit every day from Mississauga to the hospital, stopping first to pick up my lunch (I was starting to get tired of the hospital fare). The trip took her well over an hour. My mother came in almost every evening after work, except for the nights my father visited. Most nights my mother also brought me takeout food for dinners, except on the weekends, when she'd try to make one of my favourite dishes to bring with her so I could eat homemade food. My whole family spent Saturdays and Sundays there. Anyone who has been hospitalized will understand how much I looked forward to visits.

This depression hit close to six months after the shooting. Chella was now back at school, and it wasn't easy asking them all to give up more time again. I felt I had no choice, though; I simply needed them to be with me. So my mother and father took turns taking days off work and my closest friends came in and spent days with me. Dr. Tator even arranged for me to have my own nurse for a few nights.

Something else happened that had a huge impact on my psychological state at that time. A Mississauga milk store clerk, a young boy named Nizam Ali, was brutally murdered on the job. A video camera recorded part of the attack, which reportedly took over forty minutes. His store was only about a mile from mine. So much kept going through my mind: how the attacks might have been reversed, how much his parents must have wished he could have lived, even as a quadriplegic. I was really shaken by that crime and couldn't stop thinking about how it related to me. Was I supposed to consider myself lucky because all my attackers did was point a gun and fire it? Of course it was good that there had been no long, drawn-out drama first. I had no time to feel terror or wonder what they were going to do to me, and I hadn't been sexually assaulted. But did that make me lucky? Was I really fortunate to be alive? Did I want to live a paralyzed life? Should I have closed my eyes forever that night? No matter what the crime, there is always the question "Why?" For me it was, "Why shoot without giving me a chance to cooperate? Why did he fire the gun without saying a word?"

There was also the "if only" aspect that plagued me. If only the bullet had hit a few millimetres to the left or right, it probably would have missed my spinal cord and I would not have been paralyzed. But then it might have hit a major artery and I would have bled to death in minutes. If it had been a few millimetres lower I'd have had arm movement and could feed myself, drive a vehicle and be a whole lot more independent. If it had been a bit higher, again I probably would not have survived and wouldn't have had to live through the agony of it all. Why couldn't it have hit my shoulder?

So I did whatever it took to get out of the black hole, whether it was watching a movie with a friend or being read to. When I needed to cry, I cried, no matter who was there. One night three close friends stood by my bed in awkward helplessness while I poured out my sadness and frustrations.

"I can't believe they just shot me without saying a word," I sobbed.

*   *   *   *

Once I'd recovered from the surgery, I left the NICU and transferred to the neuro floor, and then went back to Lyndhurst. Again I was there only a short time when I started spiking a temperature every evening. After what had recently happened, they wasted no time and shipped me back to Sunnybrook. Another three weeks passed, and another battery of tests. The source turned out to be a kidney stone, which took so long to discover because I could not feel the pain.

I was shipped back and forth a few more times, and it was April before I really started rehab. I was set up in a daily routine of physio and occupational therapy (OT). By then I wasn't passing out every time I sat up. My physiotherapist was excellent, but I really bonded with my occupational therapist, Janet Campbell. Seeing Janet every day was like getting a dose of sunshine. She's one of those people that anyone and everyone immediately warms to. I have always been able to cope better when I have the right kind of people around me, and Janet definitely belonged in that category. I don't just cope better, I find it easier to focus on the positive aspects of life and push the negative things aside.

In OT I learned to use a mouthstick to turn pages and work an electric typewriter. I set up books on stands on my desk and could read by myself for the first time. I was grateful for the two typing classes I had taken in high school — I could only hit one key at a time, but at least I could type faster knowing where everything was on the keyboard.

I spent a whole lot of OT time with Janet learning how to work an electric chair. There weren't many options for someone with my level of paralysis. I could have chairs that were chin or breath operated, or one with the controls behind my head. Since I didn't want anything in front of my face, I chose the latter. To make the chair move, I pressed my head against a sponge-covered switch and held it. There were two "leaf" switches above each shoulder, which I reached by shrugging my shoulder. One shifted the chair from forward to reverse, the other turned it on and off.

I quickly learned why Lyndhurst's wide halls were important. For the first several days I was dangerous in that chair. The very first thing I did when I sat in it was crash into a tall trolley piled with trays. I remember one friend coming to visit me, and as he left he bent down to kiss me. I hit the switch and plowed him down. It took countless hours of practice and trial and error to figure out the intricacies of it.

Janet pushed me to try other devices designed for "high quads." One was a contraption that assisted people with limited arm movement. I had none, but Janet thought it was worth a try. She thought I might be able to feed myself and play cards this way. I didn't like the look of it — I wanted to feed myself close to normally or not at all — but I humoured Janet. She put a splint on my wrist with a fork sticking out and lifted my arm onto a fitted platform that swung back and forth. The idea was to lift my shoulder high enough to bob my hand down to a plate of food on another platform, try to shove my shoulder to scoop up some food, then push down hard and shove again to swing my hand to my mouth. It didn't work, though I had such a negative attitude toward it I barely tried.

I was more interested in an environmental control unit called TOSC, Touch-Operated Sensory Control. Using my tongue to press on two silver rings fixed on a microphone-shaped device, I could select and control certain appliances plugged into it. One was a radio, one a tape deck, one a hands-free telephone, which I could dial by holding my tongue and counting beeps. It was set up by my bed. I had no privacy, since I had to speak into a microphone and the person on the line was on a speaker, but it was an independent link to the outside. The day it was set up I spent hours trying to make a call. I kept making mistakes, and then I'd give up for a while. By the time I successfully dialled a number, it was close to dinner time. I'd decided to call Dini. My three roommates were back from therapy, my mother was sitting with me, and there were a couple of nurses there as well. In other words, there was a full house when Dini came on the line. Our conversation taught me to warn people whenever they can be heard:

"Dini, I dialled this myself," I said triumphantly.

"How did you do that?" she asked.

"With my tongue," I proudly replied.

"Oh, are you practising oral sex?" she asked. The room erupted with laughter.

"Dini, say hello to about ten people who all heard you."

There wasn't much I could do in physiotherapy, besides trying to keep my muscles as limber as possible. Most people have muscles to strengthen, and they work with weights and exercise machines. Physio also teaches people with enough movement to transfer themselves from their wheelchairs to various other places. There was a car permanently parked inside for patients to practise on. There were also parallel bars for those lucky enough to be able to walk. Once a day my therapist transferred me to a low table and stretched my arms, shoulders, hands, legs and heels. There was also a tilt table, where patients got strapped in tight, then tilted up as high as they could take it — as far as standing up straight. I only tried that once. I couldn't get far at all before passing out. It made me nauseous. I couldn't see the point of it anyway, since it wasn't something I could continue at home and I didn't see walking in my near future. At that point no one was talking about a cure happening in my lifetime.

I had been finishing my last high school credit when I was shot. One of my goals was to get my diploma before leaving, so I could start university. Lyndhurst has a school teacher, who arranged with my physio a credit in Phys Ed. My "curriculum" wasn't exactly challenging: it included increasing my sitting tolerance and learning to drive my wheelchair over grass and up curves. It was ridiculous, actually, but I wasn't going to say anything. Paralysis turned out to be one hell of a way to get out of Canadian History. Not one I'd recommend, though.

*   *   *   *

Throughout my whole life I've never belonged to the "in" group anywhere. I've never been able to figure out how these groups are defined and who decides who is "in" and who isn't — I've just always been acutely aware they didn't include me. The worst repercussion of that was being the brunt of jokes. It still bothers me how quickly I can get that sick feeling in the pit of my stomach if I've done or said something stupid that might come back to haunt me. That feeling of *not* belonging is an all-too-familiar one for me and remains a sensitive issue.

In high school I was rarely invited to parties, though that didn't bother me too much. One incident that did bother me was not getting an invitation to join a sorority that had been formed by some members of the cheerleading team. Members had to be approved and personally asked. The only reason I was upset was because

Alise, my best friend in those years, had been invited and I was afraid she would join and leave me behind. Being principled, she made it clear she wouldn't belong to any group that practised such exclusivity, and we went on hanging out together.

In starting rehab I had to discover where I fit in socially. At first I found it quite scary. I was intimidated each time I left my room. I have always been prone to shyness and discomfort in new situations. Even before I was hurt, I hated standing by myself at a party or bar. The "correct" small talk doesn't come easily to me.

There was one group at Lyndhurst I had nothing at all in common with. I'm sure some would have considered them cool. Their friends would visit and they'd spend evenings in the parking lot drinking beer and come in smashed. Drugs were pretty common, too. One quad named Joe used to get his paraplegic friends, who had finger movement, to separate his lines of cocaine for him. He was able to snort the stuff without assistance.

The publicity I was still receiving only made me more uncomfortable. I went in as the "celebrity quad." This wasn't how I viewed myself, but I was acutely aware that the media attention that came my way might make other patients ostracize me. I have never seen myself as different from other spinal-cord-injured people. I don't think it matters whether a person dives into shallow water, gets in a car accident or gets thrown from a horse. Some people might be acting more recklessly than others when they are injured, but no one asks for such consequences. So though I saw us all as equals, all of us in the same boat, my fear was that they would think I considered myself somehow superior, or at least different.

Although I was getting up and going to therapy every day, I would go back to bed for meals for the first while. I used the excuse that after so many months of eating in bed, it was difficult for me to swallow in a sitting position. The truth was that I hated going into the cafeteria.

Cafeteria tables were set up in rows, each table seating four people. Chairs were clearly not a necessity, since all the patients had their own, but several regular chairs lined one wall for aides and volunteers to use while helping patients who couldn't feed themselves. Mealtime had a social atmosphere, and I didn't have any friends to sit with, the way so many of the other patients did. My stomach would twist into knots when I tried to find a table. I was usually helped with my meals by a volunteer, most often a senior citizen from the area. Often they would want to use a spoon instead of a fork, which instantly got my back up. I was overly sensitive to any treatment I considered childish — adults eat with forks, children with spoons. One day I sat watching one elderly volunteer cut up a hot dog and feed it to me in small pieces. It was depressing. I wanted to scream "THAT'S NOT HOW YOU EAT A GODDAMN HOT DOG!" but I kept my mouth shut.

One day my roommate Lynn stopped by my bed and said that she always ate her meals with two buddies. She asked me if I wanted to join them in the fourth spot at the table. So Lynn, Bill, Donny and I became a foursome.

As a tight group, you'd be hard pressed to find four people with as little in common as us. Lynn was in her late twenties, married with two kids. Bill was in his thirties, a former police officer who had broken his neck tubing down a ski hill while drunk. He had two divorces under his belt and was a bit of a playboy. Then there was Donny, who was my age. I don't think Donny had ever read anything other than a *Hot Rod* magazine. He had wanted to be a mechanic before his injury. Lynn and Donny had suffered diving injuries.

Spinal cord injury and a wicked sense of humour were all we had in common at first. It was all we needed.

Just knowing that I had a place to go to every meal made me feel as though I belonged. I started looking forward to my cafeteria trips. My old spunkiness returned. We had a lot of fun, but, more importantly, we were incredible support for each other. If one was having a bad day then the others would boost him up. We shared everything that we were going through and became very tight. They largely made rehab a good experience for me. Lunches often lasted well into the afternoon, dinner always stretched to bedtime. Televisions were not allowed on before 6:00 each night. Our regular table was right in front of the TV at the front of the cafeteria. Majority ruled on which channel we watched, but there were two other TV lounges in the hospital.

We sometimes talked about the "walkies" — people who had broken their necks the right way, without damaging their spinal cords. They moved around the hospital fully decked out with the halo-vests on, but actually walking behind their wheelchairs, leaning on them for support. We looked at them with envy, humour and, well, more envy.

It didn't take long to get into a comfortable routine. Soon, I told my mother to stop coming in after work for the evening. I started going home on weekends. My father still came twice a week, since I didn't see him on weekends, but it was more important to have the support of the other injured patients at that point than family.

Sometimes a sympathetic voice would be heard where it was least expected. One day I was sitting alone at our regular table in what I thought was an empty cafeteria. There was a small piece of paper on the opposite end of the table. For some stupid reason, it bugged me sitting there. It was taunting me to knock it to the floor. I took deep breaths and tried with all my might to blow it off. Being a high quad, with no stomach or chest muscles to back me up, my might wasn't very great. The damn piece of paper wouldn't budge, but I kept trying. After several tries I heard someone stir. Looking up, I saw a patient sitting in the doorway watching me. He was known as "Baby Quad." Quite short to begin with, his usual sitting position was hunched down in his wheelchair, resting his chin in his hands.

"I know just how you feel," he said, shaking his head. We burst out laughing.

Lyndhurst is at the end of a quiet street. A few blocks from the hospital is a restaurant known as "the Laird." An easy roll for anyone drunk or sober, the Laird made a fair business from the rehab patients. One night — for the first time since the shooting — I went out independently with a gang for drinks. I was ridiculously excited — it was my first time out drinking since reaching legal age. The evening wasn't particularly memorable, but the trip back to Lyndhurst was. I was going back with a friend, Tim, a cop who had been hit by a truck while standing on the side of a highway one night at work. It was a warm summer night, around ten o'clock, and neither of us was feeling much pain. As we made our way up the middle of the road I started slipping out of my chair, butt first. Every few feet Tim had to lower my chair control behind my head for me to reach it. I was enjoying myself too much to worry, but Tim was starting to panic. He wasn't sure if he should zoom ahead and get help or stay with me. By the time we reached Lyndhurst I was practically out of my chair.

One of my clearest memories of rehab was a video that was shown to us patients. This was some time after the movie *The Other Side of the Mountain* had been released. That movie and its sequel were based on the life of American skier Jill Kinmont, who broke her neck in a 1955 skiing accident and went on to become a teacher. I'd watched those movies as a youngster when they were first released. I loved the scene where Kinmont's boyfriend, fellow skier Dick Buick (played by oh-so-handsome Beau Bridges), shows up at her hospital bed. He picks her up and puts her in a wheelchair, then pushes her into the middle of a busy intersection and tells her he is going to stick around, so she might as well get used to it. It's a wonderfully romantic scene, perfect fodder for fantasies. I can say now that those movies did little to show the public what life with a spinal cord injury is really like.

What we were shown was a film of the *real* Kinmont, made twenty years after her injury. It was about ten years old, so we were watching a woman who had been a quadriplegic for thirty years. *Thirty years*. The movie was titled *Jill Kinmont: From Tragedy to Triumph*, and it was narrated by Beau Bridges. It shows Kinmont in her real life, at her job and with her family, along with a few clips from the movie. It ends with her and her new husband sitting by a lake as the sun sets, her Prince Charming not on a white horse but driving a van equipped with ramps.

"Do you miss walking?" one of her students asks her.

"It's been so long that I don't think about it anymore," she replies.

"Do people stare at you?"

Yes, but it's okay to look, is her answer. "Instead of staring at someone, go up and say hello," she tells them.

It was no doubt meant to inspire us, show us what we could achieve. To say the movie's effect was depressing, though, is an understatement. A friend of mine aptly chalked it up to "well-intentioned professionals who don't have a clue."

Kinmont made it clear that she had totally divorced herself from her "before" life, but there wasn't a soul watching that film who was even remotely prepared to do that. We were all just trying to get by each day, still in a bit of shock over it all. When the film ended, a patient sitting beside me, a man in his thirties who had broken his back, was quietly sobbing, his face buried in his hands. He was a teacher.

I went back to my room, feeling as though I had been hoofed in the stomach. I felt almost winded. I could not fathom giving up the notion of walking, nor did I want to try to fathom it.

Thirty years. There's no way I can live like this for five or ten years, never mind thirty.

I felt such panic, and so trapped — the proverbial deer caught in the headlights. Absolute panic.

It's a feeling I still get once in a while, more often when things in my life aren't going very well. It might hit me in a quiet, reflective moment, or I might be doing something that I never would have been doing had I not been injured, or perhaps when an attendant is doing something for me. I'll get hit with a wave of panic. I'll have to pause and take a deep breath to clear my head, letting the panic subside before continuing. Sometimes it's still so hard to believe this is happening to me.

Toward the end of my rehab, Janet, my favourite therapist, got another job. I was upset at the thought of her leaving and grew quieter and more depressed as her final day approached. On her last day, a Friday, I was miserable. When I went into the OT department I was barely holding myself together. We started to work on one thing or another, but she could see I was in rough shape and suggested taking a walk outside. I wasn't even through the door before the tears started streaming down my cheeks.

We went to a bench where Janet could sit down and I started pouring out my heart to her. All the thoughts and feelings I had been holding in came rushing out.

"I miss walking and dancing and making love," I sobbed. "I miss my life."

She listened and simply said, "I know." We both knew there was nothing she could say, and there was certainly nothing she could do besides listen. It's too bad it happened on her last day, but it was good for me to voice some of that.

That night, having gone home for the weekend, I was lying in the hospital bed in our living room with my sister sitting beside me, again trying to hold back the tears. My mother was heading out the door to run an errand, and it was all I could do to wait until she left before crying. My mother had been through enough and I didn't want to saddle her with my depression. My sister didn't know what to say either.

"Barb, if you ever have an itch you call me, no matter what I'm doing," she said. It was not the response I was looking for. There was probably nothing that would have helped, but I was unfairly disappointed in her response.

I passed the first anniversary of the shooting quietly with my roommate Lynn. I could never stay up very late, because I required so much assistance from the nurses to get to bed, so I was lying down. Since she had more movement and independence, needing little from the scaled-down night staff, Lynn had more control of her schedule. She sat by my bed as the minutes ticked toward 11:15 p.m.

"Have you accepted this?" I asked her. I'd wanted to ask someone that for months.

"I don't accept not walking," she said. "I'll adapt as best I can, but I won't *accept* this."

That made perfect sense to me, and, more than thirteen years later, it still does.

Five days later I was discharged. It was time to face reality.

Chapter Three:

CELEBRITY CRIP

No matter how depressed I was on the inside, or how difficult the adjustment to my new life was for me, I always smiled brightly for the camera. In a strange way, I had a reputation to uphold. It was a reputation partially created by the media, which turned its eye on me that September night in 1983 and didn't turn away for a long, long time.

It was a radio, left on near my bed in intensive care, that gave me the first indication that I had become a news story. Every hour, as the news came on, I would hear bits of what the announcer was saying. "Barbara Turnbull ... shooting ... life support ... paralyzed." These were scary words that I was in no way prepared to hear. Because of the respirator, I had no voice, so it took me awhile before I was able to convey the message that I wanted the radio turned off. It was a great relief when they finally took it away. My family tells me they showed me the newspapers, but I don't remember that.

My shooting likely meant different things to different people, but it seemed to mean something to everyone. It had an enormous impact on, most significantly, the greater Toronto area, but also on the whole province. The story rippled across Canada and even to little pockets outside our borders (we heard from people as far away as Australia and Europe). As recently as the autumn of 1996, I received a passionate marriage proposal from a young man in Libya who had read a 1992 story about me in *Reader's Digest*.

There were several reasons the media and the public embraced my story. Perhaps the biggest aspect was the shock of it for the whole community. As I said before, back in 1983 this sort of thing just didn't happen. I was a young student, from a nice, large family headed by a single, hard-working mother. I was just trying to make a little pocket money to help support myself. I was an average teenage high school student working late hours for pretty low pay. I was everyone's daughter, sister, niece, friend. Everyone could relate to me, because what happened to me clearly could have happened to pretty much anyone. The picture released to the media didn't hurt either — people saw an attractive youth with a huge, toothy smile.

Three suspects were arrested the day after the shooting. They had been identified by a girl named Farah Ali, the sister of one of the accused's girlfriends. On the afternoon of the shooting, the guys had picked her up under the pretence of giving her a ride home and taken her to a secluded area. There they tried to scare her into prostituting for them. In a show of bravado, one of them, Sutcliffe Logan, fired a gun into the ground and presented her with the casing as "a little memento." Then they dropped her off at a subway station, with a final warning to hit the streets and start making money for them. Instead, she went to the police and told them what she'd overheard of the guys' plans to hold up an unspecified store that night. So even before the 911 call came in, police were already on the case. There was little doubt that these were the people responsible.

On Saturday, September 24, police arrested Hugh Logan, Sutcliffe Logan and Clive Brown. A warrant for Warren Johnson was also issued. Clive was sleeping in the basement of the Logans' house when police went in with a tactical unit at 6:00 a.m. One pointed a 9-millimetre pistol at him, another pointed a shotgun, and they asked him if his name was Clive Brown.

"What's going on? Who the hell are you? Did you get Hugh and Warren? Did they tell you?" he was quoted by detectives as saying. "Give me a break," was his response, when told he was being arrested for the forcible confinement of Farah Ali. "Did that no-good bitch come running to you?" he said. He then refused to elaborate on what he had meant by his comments.

Hugh Logan was arrested at his aunt's place. He confessed, in police custody, to having pulled the trigger. His brother Sutcliffe was first taken in for questioning, then charged. Warren Johnson turned himself in the next day.

What shocked everybody was the fact that one of the four, Clive Brown, was from my high school. As you might imagine, the media played up that angle — somehow it seemed to bring it closer to home. No one could comprehend it. How could they? It didn't make any sense to anybody, least of all me and my family. Suddenly, violence leapt into everyone's living room. People correctly guessed that things would never be the same again. We'd all lost our innocence, and the city had changed forever. I once saw a television program on how crime has changed society over time, and a police officer cited my shooting as a major turning point. He actually referred to it as "The Barbara Turnbull Era." The shooting caused a shift in our society that, in different ways, affected everybody.

I believe I became a symbol of that lost innocence for people. And my fight to recover became, in a way, everyone's fight. Everyone was pulling for me to triumph over evil. People wanted updates, they turned to stories in newspapers and listened up when they heard my name on TV and radio. Parents wanted their teenage children to follow the case. Every step of my survival and my attempts at recovery were followed intensely by the media and the public. Even now, nearly fourteen years after the shooting, it's not unusual for people to recognize my name.

All media requests were going through the hospital's public relations department, whose job was mostly to keep the press at arm's length. Early on, however, one reporter from a local tabloid showed up in the waiting room to talk to my family. The woman seemed so sincere and so comforting, talking soothingly and carefully noting everything they said. Then she pulled out a camera and asked if she could come in and take a picture of me. My mother just about pushed her face in. That's what they *all* wanted to do.

People were calling around the clock, trying to find out more details. But hospitals release only a one-word condition to the media and public, such as "critical" or "serious," and everyone at Sunnybrook was conscientious about not giving away any information. Sometimes the intensive care unit would get a phone call at 4:00 a.m. from someone pretending to be a family member.

"I'm her father checking up on her. Is she sleeping okay?"

Certainly nobody could have had access to me where I was in that unit. I wasn't in a room that somebody could sneak into, so I was pretty well protected. Nevertheless, for the first few weeks I was a bit paranoid, imagining that many people wanted to hurt me. I made my mother throw out some baked goods that a nice woman had dropped off, just in case they were laced with poison.

As for the accused and the case against them, interest was just as sharp. Clive Brown was let out on bail for about two weeks, and the public outcry was instant and very clear. Petitions were started and members of the public were canvassed for their thoughts. His bail had a particular impact on my high school, Clarkson Secondary School, because one of the conditions was that he attend classes. The situation must have been particularly rough for his younger siblings, who were students there as well, some in my sisters' classes. For my family, one of the worst aspects of his bail hearing was that a gym teacher — the coach of my sister Christine's volleyball team — testified as a character witness. My poor sister was beside herself and my family was astounded. My sister wanted to quit the team, but sports meant everything to her and provided an important physical outlet, particularly at that time.

At any rate, Clive was probably safer in jail than out. One friend told me that her brother almost ran him over one day when he saw him walking down the street. Given the circumstances, the school promptly suspended him. Within two weeks, the Crown successfully appealed the bail decision. Clive went back to jail.

Then, in a preliminary hearing about a year after the shooting, charges of attempted murder against Clive Brown and Warren Johnson were "discharged," or dropped. Ontario attorney general Roy McMurtry promptly intervened and reinstated the charges.

McMurtry's involvement was, and still is, extremely unusual. "When someone is discharged of an alleged offense at a preliminary hearing, we do not lightly interfere with that process. But, clearly, the public interest was involved," he said at the time. I've been fortunate enough to have met the Honorable Roy McMurtry (now Chief Justice of Ontario) many times since, and I've always found him to be a man of great warmth and grace.

*   *   *   *

As many words as we have in the English language, I have yet to find one that adequately describes the public's swift response to my shooting.

Incredible.

Unbelievable.

Fantastic.

Heart-warming.

It was all that and more.

Mail immediately started pouring in from all over. One postcard, mailed from Turkey and addressed only to "Barbara Turnbull, Toronto (Mississauga or Bramalea), Canada" actually made it to me. The Barbara Turnbull Fund was started for me by a woman who used to come in to the store for milk and would usually end up staying half an hour chatting. Joan Dunn, a young, recently married woman who lived a few doors away from the store, started the fund unintentionally when she went door-to-door to raise money to send flowers. When she got home she discovered she had more than $250. This was reported by the media, which inspired the public to send more mail and boost the growing fund.

Because I was injured on the job, the Workers' Compensation Board would cover the cost of attendants, medication, equipment, environmental control equipment and home and vehicle modifications, as well as a monthly pension. But there were suddenly so many new expenses, and I was once again dependent on my mother.

The money from the fund was to be used to help relieve the financial burden, and to buy a new house and a van to accommodate me and my wheelchair. Anything left would be invested for my future.

My family told me about all the attention, the people calling and the public outcry about the shooting. From where I was lying, I couldn't relate to any of it.

There were people showing up in the waiting room of the intensive care unit. Some were very strange — like the man who showed up with a huge stick to "save" me and had to be removed by security — but most were sincere and just wanted to express their sorrow or anger. The phone calls to the house were incredible too. Eventually, though, to protect ourselves from some of the creepier callers, we had to get a new, non-published number.

Helpful people wanted to do whatever they could. The owner of a video store near the hospital let me have free movies whenever I wanted, for as long as I wanted — even the popular new releases. Two paramedics with St. John Ambulance transported me from the hospital to my home every time I went, until I was able to be transferred to a car. They did this without payment, on their own time, even on Christmas Eve that first year.

Many, many fundraisers were held the first few months after the shooting. There was a live, televised auction and telethon, there were walk-athons, kiss-athons, dance-athons and haircut-athons. Metro Police Chief Jack Marks and several Ontario mayors got pledges to "Shed Pounds for Barbara." There were more dances than I could count, and even a comedy night and a concert for the fund. Obviously I couldn't attend these events, but I loved to hear all about them. Craftspeople and shop owners donated items in every price range to be auctioned off. If my name was attached to it, the answer was "Yes." Many stores called, asking if they could put out cash donation boxes. There was a "Barbara Turnbull Day" in Toronto and surrounding areas, with canvassers and huge posters with my smiling face on them at every major shopping mall. That day Burton Cummings, one of Canada's best known rock singers, appeared at Toronto's Eaton Centre to sign autographs and boost the turnout. I can still see him on the news, waving to the camera and saying, "Hi Barbara." Inmates at a Guelph, Ontario, medium/maximum security prison passed a hat around and came up with over $520 — a little over $1 for each inmate there. That was a huge sum, considering that many of them didn't work, and those who did probably only earned that much a day.

As one might expect, a few fraud artists also emerged. One printed some sort of coupon books, selling them door-to-door. There was at least one dubious dance that I heard about; the couple involved were charged with fraud but later acquitted.

It was as incredible to me then as it is now that so many strangers organized and participated in these events. I think the degree of community involvement is what separates the public reaction to my story from any other I have ever heard of. When a news story touches the public, donations might pour in, but the multitude of events that took place in the months following my shooting was almost unprecedented. Perhaps it was because I was there, still smiling, a living, breathing person that they could extend their sympathies to by helping in a very practical way.

Of all the fundraisers held for me, two stand out most in my heart.

One was put on by some of my most special friends, people from my summers at Moorelands Camp. Moorelands, a camp for inner-city children, is run by the Downtown Churchworkers' Association; parents contribute what they can, the rest is covered by donations. Campers get to spend two glorious weeks on an island on a large lake in Ontario's Haliburton Highlands. I went first as a camper, and then later as a counsellor. My summers there were carefree and full of friends, fun and adventure. Even now, nearly fourteen years after my last summer there, I occasionally dream that I'm on the island, walking along the paths, or with the sun baking my skin, the shouts of children playing in the background.

My Moorelands friends were keen to show their support for me in any way they could, and they organized a Portage-A-Thon. Symbolizing all the portages and canoe trips we had done at camp, they carried canoes from the camp office at Jarvis and Adelaide Streets all the way to Sunnybrook Hospital, about eight miles and a hell of a distance to carry ten heavy canoes. It was very well organized. They had police escorts and the streets along the route were blocked off. And they had an incredible turnout, with current and former staff coming in from all over Ontario and Quebec. They got pledges and collected money along the way.

I had recently come off the respirator and it was just my second day with my new talking trach. My family brought me down to a room near the parking lot, where everyone had gathered. The plan was to bring in all my friends from camp in small groups, a few people at a time. Before they started, I remember someone pulling back the curtain to show me all my friends out there. It was a cold, overcast day in late November, and there were over a hundred people standing there. Those people I loved so much. Standing out there for *me*. When they moved the curtain everyone saw me and started to cheer, sending the first of many tears to my eyes. One cameraman actually started to scale the wall, using a trellis so that he could get the first media photo of me through the window. I remember hearing that my friends ran over to pull him down and threw a hat over the lens of the camera (he didn't get a picture). It was a very emotional day. Successful, too. They raised more than $10,000.

Back at my high school, the students also galvanized themselves. Fundraising wasn't new at Clarkson Secondary. Every spring we used to have a cancer drive. It lasted two weeks, during which we staged all sorts of money-raising events — bake sales, car washes, auctions. In my four years there, I had always looked at that drive as Clarkson at its best; there was a positive energy that was totally contagious. In the last drive we had before the shooting we raised $10,000, the most ever. I knew very well what went into those drives so I was completely blown away by their efforts, which raised $25,000 for the fund. I was, and will always be, deeply touched and proud of what they did for me. I only wish I could have been there for it all, part of that beautiful, spirited collective, raising money for somebody, or something, else.

My family and friends were trying to do things to keep my spirits up, including trying to get celebrities to contact me. A couple of weeks before the shooting I had gone to see a David Bowie concert with a group from my high school. We'd had an amazing time, and that must have been fresh in their minds, so they contacted Bowie's agents in New York and tried to get him to telephone me. Thinking back now, it's pretty funny, considering I had no voice. It sure would have been a one-sided conversation! Some celebrities took it upon themselves to send their best wishes. Veteran Canadian actor Gordon Pinsent sent a signed picture of himself. Sir Edmund Hillary, the first man to conquer Mount Everest (with Tenzing Norgay), sent me a signed poster. I also heard from many politicians, including Ontario's premier, Bill Davis, and federal Opposition Leader (soon to be prime minister) Brian Mulroney.

Through Yuk Yuk's Comedy Club, a favourite hangout of mine, my friends succeeded in contacting Kelly McDonald, a comedian I had seen the week before I was hurt. A friend recalled me raving about how funny he was and they sent word to him in Los Angeles. It was thrilling to get a signed picture and letter from him.

When Kelly came back to headline Yuk Yuk's again in January, I made my first public outing to see him. The club was packed with my friends, and the air was electric. The MC for the show asked the standard "Anyone here from out of town?" question. One of my friends yelled out "Mississauga!" and the entire place erupted in loud cheers. Dini Petty was there with a cameraman to make a report for Citytv's ten o'clock news, but she was the only reporter. Someone at *The Toronto Sun* must have been watching the broadcast, though, because they rushed a photographer over. The front page of the next day's paper had a photo of me being introduced to Kelly.

When Kelly came to see me in the hospital the next day, he was carrying a bouquet of flowers and the newspaper. "Can you believe this?" he said. "You should be my publicist!" I'm happy to say that Kelly and I are still friends.

The first media interview I did was with Dini. It was in November. By then I was off the respirator and had my speaking voice back, but I still had the halo vest on.

I was taken into a room in the hospital that had been specially set up with cameras and lights. What I wanted most of all was to thank the public for their outpouring of support. I said something to the effect of "You've been great and I appreciate it," but it rang hollow in my ears. It didn't begin to express what was in my heart. How could I adequately thank people for thousands of cards, dollars, presents, prayers and good wishes?

By that time I had moved to one of SICU's isolation rooms so that I could have a bit more privacy. Fairly soon after that I got a small television. Dini visited me the day the TV arrived and reminded me to watch the newscast. At the end of the hour Dini said to her co-anchor, Gord Martineau, "We can welcome a new viewer tonight. Barbara Turnbull got a television today and she's watching us." The two then spoke directly to me — it was such a thrill!

I remember the morning DJs from popular Toronto radio station Q107 came to see me with a present. Scruff Connors and Gene Valaitis came with a gigantic boom box and taped a show from my room. They started the taping saying, "We're standing here in Barbara Turnbull's hospital room, and you should see the cases of beer lined up along the wall!"

Sometimes all the attention was overwhelming and hard to bear. For example, I had agreed to be a special guest at Sunnybrook Hospital's Valentine's fundraiser. The problem was that I was extremely ill by the time the event rolled around. The doctors were running all kinds of tests, but they had not determined what the problem was. I was spiking a temperature every night and sweating profusely from the top of my head to my chest all day, every day.

The fundraiser was a black-tie affair, and Alan Cherry, a prominent local fashion retailer and designer, had offered a gown for me to wear. It was to be my first real official outing in public, and the hospital was expecting a ton of media. So I got into this dress and a pair of slippers from the rehab hospital, which I was hoping the long dress would hide, and off I went with my friend Annette, the nurse from the SICU. Soon after we got there I was wheeled through the rooms and then parked in a corner so I could be gawked at by the people who had bought tickets. Sweat was just pouring down my face, so I asked Annette to see if she could find a couple of tissues or a paper towel. But as soon as she left the press converged, and I was completely surrounded. I may have exaggerated the number of media in my mind, but I remember looking out and seeing nothing but hot, bright lights and vague outlines of faces. I was still really weak and I couldn't talk very much and it seemed like Annette was taking forever with the tissue.

"What's your temperature tonight?" one of the reporters asked me.

"I don't know, I haven't taken it," I replied, starting to panic. I was so scared.

Suddenly, at the back of the crowd I recognized a familiar face. It was Gord Martineau from Citytv. Though I'd never met him, I had been watching him with Dini every night, so I felt as though I knew him. I managed to get the attention of a man beside me and asked him to bring Gord Martineau over. As it turned out, even though he was the last one in the door, he was the only member of the media who got to speak directly to me that night.

What really bothered me about that night was reading in *The Toronto Star* the next day that I'd been wearing a gown and "fluffy" hospital slippers. I guess the dress wasn't as long and concealing as I'd hoped!

*　　　*　　　*　　　*

After awhile it seemed as though everybody — reporters, the public, doctors, nurses, even orderlies — knew all about what had happened to me.

One weekend, though, when I was in rehab, I was sick enough for the nurse to bring in the doctor on call. Unfortunately it wasn't my doctor but the one in charge of another hospital ward. This doctor was considered by all to be Lyndhurst's absent-minded professor. Most patients had a story about something he'd said or done that made no sense whatsoever.

Above each patient's bed was a card with their last name and the date of their injury. The first thing he asked was my first name.

"Barbara," I answered.

"How were you injured?" he asked.

This question surprised me. No one had ever asked me that before. This was January, four months after the shooting, and it was still in the news fairly regularly. Had this man been living under a rock? It wasn't that I thought everyone in Toronto *should* know my name, it's just that everyone did. Considering that mine was a spinal cord injury, his area of expertise, I was taken aback. Even the nurse looked surprised.

"I was shot," I said.

He continued with his examination as if I had cited a car accident or diving injury as the cause. Minutes after they left the nurse came back, almost doubled over with laughter. She filled me in on what was said after they'd left my room.

"How was that young girl shot?" he'd asked her.

"It was a convenience store hold-up."

"What the hell was she doing holding up a convenience store?"

*   *   *   *

The media interest continued, even a year later as I was preparing to leave rehab. We were starting to get media inquiries about my pending discharge to home. I knew for sure that I wanted to leave Lyndhurst Hospital quietly, like every other patient, so we decided that the best way to handle it was for me to have a press conference about a week before I left. We could do all the interviews in one fell swoop.

As I think back now, it was an odd and almost surreal experience: I was wheeled into a room and behind a table, where I was confronted with cameras, reporters and lots of personal questions. I couldn't understand why there was so much interest in *me*, a year after the shooting. Even now, when I look at press conferences from a reporter's point of view, I sometimes shake my head to think that they all turned out to hear what I had to say that day. We did the press conference and then I did individual interviews with a lot of reporters.

After the press conference it was uncomfortable to go back to Lyndhurst. I always felt a little bit awkward around many of the patients anyway, and I was extremely sensitive to the ways in which the media and the public were perceiving me as different from the others. Here I was getting phone calls from Q107 and visits from Dini Petty — I was the "celebrity crip."

Though the fundraising activities had slowed and then stopped a few months after the shooting, the Barbara Turnbull Fund wasn't formally closed until soon after I moved home from rehab. I was at a restaurant one night with my mother and some friends when a tall woman in a long fur coat swept up to our table.

"Is that Barbara?" she asked my mother, who was sitting right beside me. After my identity was confirmed, she continued: "I wanted to donate to the fund months ago, but you never *really* know if the money goes where it's intended."

With that, she leaned down and kissed me, put something on the table and walked out of the restaurant. On the table was $100. I sat there feeling greatly embarrassed and like, well, like a charity case.

From the beginning the fundraising had taken on a life of its own, instigated by a public that felt a need to express their outrage and support and responded the only way they could. We *were* concerned about money and my future at that point and welcomed the efforts, though we didn't initiate them. Obviously my life had been turned upside down and I was mainly just trying to survive and adjust, so all of the implications of being the recipient of such generosity didn't hit me until that incident. I called my lawyer the next day and instructed him to officially shut down the fund. In total, the public donated $250,000.

For another four or five years I continued to be treated as a celebrity. I was invited to many ritzy events, one as a "Celebrity Gourmet" at a fundraising gala, where I was paired up with actress Rita Tushingham. Because I'd been unable to attend all the early fundraisers, I'd never had a real, concrete sense of how the public felt about me. Even the thousands of cards and letters I received didn't bring it home to me. Then one night, very soon after my discharge, I was asked to be a special guest at a hockey game. It was a fundraiser for a local children's centre. One of the teams was made up of officers from the Peel police force, which had handled my case; I was to be presented with a plaque and some flowers by the chief. As my name was announced and I was wheeled out onto the rink, a deafening roar went up. Everyone was on their feet, clapping and cheering, and the players were all banging their sticks on the ice. It seemed to go on forever. I'm sure it lasted a full two or three minutes, while I sat with a lump in my throat. I was totally overwhelmed. Fortunately there was no microphone, because I don't know what I ever would have said to that greeting.

One of the most memorable of the public events took place in London, England, when my mother and I were there in 1985, in the middle of the trial. British Airways had given me a return trip on the Concorde. For the first time I was meeting Roy McMurtry, who by then had been appointed Canada's High Commissioner. After tea and a tour of Canada House, McMurtry invited us to stay and meet representatives of the National Hockey League — players, coaches and executives — who were having their annual meeting in London and were expected for an afternoon reception. It was only a couple of months after the Stanley Cup finals, so the invitation was a thrill.

As the NHL members started trickling in and introducing themselves to the High Commissioner, McMurtry would introduce himself, then say simply, "And this is Barbara Turnbull and her mother Iris, from Mississauga, Ontario." Just about every guy stuck his hand out to shake mine, something that happens frequently. When people do that and I don't lift my hand up, they usually feel like an idiot, which they shouldn't at all — my hands don't look paralyzed. If I had some arm movement, the muscles would have curled my fingers in permanently, but since I can only shrug my shoulders, my hands rest comfortably on my lap, looking totally normal. But it's awkward when someone tries to shake my hand, and I have never found a way of putting people who do it at ease. I've tried humour — like saying "Nice watch!" — but that hasn't worked either. I finally had my mother put my purse on top of my hands, hoping that would discourage the guys, but to no avail.

Not far into the arrivals Alan Eagleson appeared. The man who started the Canada Cup is a controversial figure, but, like him or not, his is undeniably a colourful, dynamic presence. He recognized my name immediately, then took over the introductions. As each player stepped up to our little welcoming committee, Eagleson introduced McMurtry, then said, "And this is Barbara Turnbull. Some punks shot her in cold blood a couple of years ago. We're lucky to still have her with us." It was absolutely hysterical to watch these poor hockey jocks, who didn't know anything about me or my background, try to react the "correct" way — "Do I look angry, shocked, sorry, or what?" their faces seemed to say. Though Wayne Gretzky and the Stanley Cup champion Edmonton Oilers weren't there, it was a particular pleasure spending time with Lanny McDonald and Darryl Sittler. I had such vivid memories of the Maple Leafs in the glory days of the 1970s. That those two heroes turned out to be such genuinely nice guys made the afternoon all the more enjoyable.

Being a public figure sure has had its bizarre moments, too. One evening in the early days, a black man, knowing that my assailants were black, showed up at the door to "apologize for my race." My mother assured him that was not necessary, but he was not easily dissuaded.

And sometimes I've felt as though my life has become public property. Ridiculous rumours have surfaced from time to time. I remember hearing stories soon after the shooting that I'd supposedly recognized Clive Brown at the store, leaving the guys with no other choice but to shoot me.

Recently, however, another rumour came to light that was not easy to laugh at. A friend was taking a week-long series of workshops, and during one of them someone brought up my name. The subject was motive and the group was discussing what goes on in people's minds when they do certain things. A man stood up to address the group. "I heard that Barbara Turnbull was in on planning the robbery with those guys," he said.

Though immediately incensed, my friend preferred not to say she knew me and just sat and listened a while longer. Most of the group dismissed his claim, but he continued with such an air of authority that my friend soon leapt to her feet in my defence. Amazingly enough, he didn't back down right away but challenged her on how well she actually knew me. Eventually he admitted defeat, saying somewhat petulantly, "I was just repeating what I'd heard."

It was bad enough that he spoke as if this crazy notion were factual, but what upset me the most was picturing groups of people at dinner parties or other informal get-togethers over the years, theorizing that my shooting resulted from my own criminal involvement with my attackers. I could imagine the conversations where there was no one to defend me.

Ironically enough, it was in Arizona, when I was studying journalism at Arizona State University, that I really learned the value of privacy and security. In my third year, when I was living off campus and renting a house in a nearby suburb, my attendant's eleven-year-old daughter and I were the only people home one afternoon when an unknown man rang the doorbell. I was working at my computer on a table in my bedroom, which was easily visible from the front door of our open-concept house. Amy opened the door as I was backing up from the table to go into the living room, but the man spied me and walked right into my bedroom, leaned on the arms of my wheelchair and kissed my cheek. I was so shocked and scared I could not think of a single thing to say. My immediate implulse was to end the situation as quickly and safely as possible.

"I'm from Mississauga," he finally said, after what seemed like an eternity. He looked around my bedroom, clearly taking note of the shelves, my work table, my bed. I was driving my chair forward, trying to push him out of my bedroom as he talked. He said he did business in Arizona a few times a year and had heard in the news that I was studying there. "So I went to the university and looked up your address," he explained, proud of his sleuthing ability.

By now we were in the living room, where he continued to nose around. I was being as pleasant as possible, since I had no way of knowing if he was a total nutbar and might go off the deep end if I told him he was carrying out a home invasion. The man had absolutely no concept that what he was doing was wrong and might be upsetting. He didn't have anything of any consequence to say, either; he was just on a celebrity hunt. It had never occurred to me that I shouldn't be listed at school — two thousand miles from Toronto.

And sometimes the media were no less intrusive than that unwelcome visitor. At one point, soon after my discharge from Lyndhurst, I was contacted by freelancers doing a piece for a cable channel on people with disabilities and relationships. When they approached me I made it clear that I might not be appropriate for the subject, since I wasn't having a relationship at that particular time — but they really wanted me. I guess they wanted a known name. They insisted that the show was not specifically about romantic or sexual relationships, just about relationships in general, particularly friendships. I reluctantly agreed.

They set up the cameras outside, and a woman and a man were both going to ask me questions. First the woman: "Can disabled people have romantic or sexual kinds of relationships? What are some of the differences/difficulties around them?" I hadn't worked out these issues for myself yet, and I was a little uncomfortable, but I was able to handle her questions in a general way. Then the man took over. The first question he asked was "What do you think of your body?" He then proceeded to ask questions like "What do men think when they look at you?" "What do you dream about at night?" "When you look in the mirror and you see yourself like this, what goes through your mind?" Unbelievable questions. They were so invasive that my attendant, who was sitting watching, went into the house. She told me later that she just couldn't sit there anymore and listen. I was in shock. I certainly didn't have the kind of assertiveness or media savvy then to simply refuse to answer. I just tried to be as evasive as possible. There was not one single question that I answered truthfully. It was the most awful experience.

Later they called back to ask for a photograph they needed to show during the voice-over introduction. By then I'd discussed the experience with my sisters and my attendant, and I was really angry. I told them they couldn't have anything else, that I was upset and felt invaded. I was most angry that they had misled me about what the interview was going to be about. They offered me the chance to sit in on the editing and take out anything I didn't like. But there was no way I was going to sit through their footage, and I told them I wanted them to edit out *everything*. I heard later that they did air the interview, though I don't know what material was used.

That incident led to one of my big regrets regarding the media. CBC TV's "Man Alive," hosted by the venerable Roy Bonisteel, was doing a segment on victims of violence. Two producers spent an afternoon with me discussing it. They were extremely pleasant, and we had a really good talk about my experiences and feelings. I know they left excited about my participation.

Unfortunately, between our meeting and the shoot came that interview with the freelancers. The experience was so awful that for a long time I closed off the media. I had my guard up constantly. My fists were raised to ward off everything. For the "Man Alive" shoot I remember giving only short, clipped answers. I was determined to protect my thoughts and feelings — they were all I had left. Several times the director stopped filming and tried to get me to open up, but I wasn't cooperating. I even refused to drive my chair so they could shoot it for a voice-over shot. I finally just asked them to leave.

For years afterwards I felt terrible about it — I even toyed with the idea of sending the producers a letter of explanation, but I never did. Years later I heard someone say that the "Man Alive" budget was so small that they had to carefully monitor every **foot** of film shot. That explained why the director kept stopping the filming, and it made me feel even worse.

In truth, I never did get used to the idea that people were interested in me. Over and over I would hear the same questions: "What do you see yourself doing in the future?" "How do you feel about your attackers?" and "Were you surprised by the public's response to your story?" But there was one question that would always stop me cold: "Why do you think this happened to you?" I would usually tell the interviewer something about the randomness of fate, or babble something about having to play the cards you're dealt. But I could never quite drown out the tiny voice in my head that said: "You know why this happened. This was no accident." Then I would feel sick with guilt, and I would quickly shift the conversation to another topic rather than have to deal with the feelings that lay waiting for me inside.

On the whole, it was difficult for me to be a news story. It wasn't glamorous or exciting, it was just strange. My own loss was so profound, and there were so many incredible changes to my life, that I was hardly aware of what was happening to me. I consider this my second life. Everything is divided between before the shooting and after. And this new life was just so much to get used to that the attention and the opportunities that would probably have meant a great deal more to me before I was hurt ceased to mean anything at all.

$$*\qquad*\qquad*\qquad*$$

Ironically, in the midst of this media maelstrom, while my thoughts and feelings were being probed and reported on incessantly, I felt completely numb emotionally. I seemed incapable of feeling grief or compassion for anyone else. It wasn't even something I was actually aware of until my Aunt Marina died.

Marina was not only my aunt, she was my godmother. Several years before the shooting she'd developed ALS, Lou Gehrig's disease, and as her illness progressed she moved from Montreal to Mississauga, to be closer to my mother. I can remember getting birthday presents from her when I was very young, and I wrote her notes on stationery with "Brainwaves from Barbara" emblazoned on the top. Later, she was the one who organized our family reunions. For the first few months after the shooting, Marina and our close family friend Denise took on the important job of handling the mountains of mail that poured in to me.

There were these reasons and more to have felt particularly upset when she finally succumbed to the ravages of the disease. I felt nothing. Without saying anything about my feelings, or lack of them, I sat through her funeral wondering what was wrong with me. I didn't feel grief and I felt no relief for her that her suffering was over.

A couple of months after that my grandmother died of colon cancer. As it had been for my aunt, the end was slow in coming and very painful. She had also fought a long battle. Years earlier she had undergone an operation that left her with a colostomy.

The last time I saw my grandmother alive is a visit etched on my brain. She was in a tiny hospital in a small town close to my grandparents' summer mobile home.

The shooting had put me on a different level than my sisters in my grandparents' eyes. The disability was a big part of it but the publicity provided an extra edge — my grandmother was very proud of her "brave, celebrity" granddaughter. I knew I was special to my grandparents, and I did small things that showed I cared as well. Once I wrote a full-page letter to them with a pen in my mouth, a letter that my grandmother carried in her purse until she died, showing it proudly to anyone who would look.

The afternoon we visited her for the last time, my sisters and I made the two-hour drive together. When we went into her room, she was lying in bed, obviously under a great deal of medication. Her speech was slurry and she was too weak to say much. What she did say made me wish I'd stayed home.

"Do you know who this is?" she asked a nurse, gesturing toward me.

"These must be your lovely granddaughters," the nurse said, tactfully.

"Yes, but do you know who *this one* is?" she repeated, pointing at me. "That's *Barbara Turnbull.*"

"Yes, I know," the nurse said, and quietly left the room.

That's all I remember of her last words to us. And far from being glad to see her one last time, all I could think of was how much I hated being singled out.

When she died a few days later, I said all the usual things: "It's good her suffering's over" and "She fought a long time." But, as with my aunt, *I felt nothing.* I didn't feel sad she was gone and I wasn't happy her pain was over.

This time I really was worried that something was wrong with me. I was dead emotionally — I didn't feel the slightest urge to cry, I wasn't even a little bit upset. Nothing excited me. I owned a house and a van, I had money in the bank, I'd just been to England and back on the Concorde — but I didn't get any kind of a kick from that or anything else. I wondered if I'd become some kind of sociopath. This was now almost two years after the shooting.

Then one tragedy happened that seemed to kick-start my ability to feel grief for others again.

My eight-year-old friend Nicholas had leukemia. I'd heard about him from a family friend while I was in the hospital. After I came home, she started bringing him over for occasional visits, and he never failed to charm us. Nicholas had the innocence and wonder that all children have, and the fragility characteristic of many terminally ill children, but he had something special above that. There was an air of compassion and humanity around him.

With logic only a child possesses, Nicholas had questions for me, like, "Why didn't you just tell those guys to shoot you in the legs, anyway?"

One day, when I was sitting on a sofa chair in the basement, my sister told him she'd take him for a ride in my elevator. Unbeknownst to them, the "Stop" button had been pushed, so it wouldn't budge. Nicholas approached me in a most solemn manner, putting one hand on my arm.

"I think we broke your elevator," he said. Then he paused and spoke slowly and gently, as though he were breaking terrible news to me. "You *may* have to walk."

Every time he visited he brought a gift of some sort, either candy (which he had to first test for me), a figurine or a picture.

As he got sicker, his family took him to Walt Disney World. One day they were in a McDonald's, and he passed a big poster of Ronald McDonald with a sign that read "Help Ronald help kids with cancer." Nicholas knew he was sick but he didn't know what he had. He started emptying his pockets, putting every penny he had into the box, saying, "Those poor kids with cancer ..."

It was that kind of precious soul we lost one August day. Unlike the previous two funerals, this one I wanted to attend. And as I sat there looking at the tiny casket, I started quietly sobbing. I could *feel* how wrong it was. I hurt for his loss, for his family's loss, for my loss. And though the pain I was feeling was sharp, it came tinged with relief as well. It was the first time in a long time that I'd been able to feel pain for someone other than myself.

Some years later, I was in my van and I heard a song that was played at my Aunt Marina's funeral. As soon as it started I got completely choked up as I thought of her and of my grandmother. I felt relief then, too, realizing that I hadn't been an uncaring monster, that my emotions had just been tied up with my own overwhelming loss. I wish I could have understood that sooner, because I beat myself up a lot over that time.

Nicholas's death was like CPR for my emotions, a trauma so strong it could not be ignored. In a way it brought me back to life. A short while after his funeral his mother Karin came to see me. It was the first time we'd met. She recounted a conversation she'd had with him one day when he'd just gotten home from visiting me, carrying a stuffed toy I'd given him.

During the first few months after the shooting, dozens of people gave me stuffed animals. I must have had more than a hundred. I sorted through them after coming home, keeping only twenty or thirty and donating the rest to the Hospital for Sick

Children. The ones I kept were sitting on a large shelf in our basement. That day I had told Nicholas he could choose one to take home with him. He stood in front of the shelf for several minutes, then chose one of the smallest toys, right at the front.

"You sure that's the one you want?" I asked, surprised he'd chosen such a small one.

About ten minutes later, he asked if he could change his mind. "Absolutely," I told him. After another long, quiet few moments standing on a chair in front of the shelf, he chose another small animal. Then ten minutes later he asked again if he could choose another.

"You can change your mind as many times as you like," I assured him.

This time he chose one of the big bears at the back of the shelf. Ironically, it was my favourite. It was not a cutesy teddy bear, see, but more like a real bear on all fours. It seemed appropriate he should like my favourite and I didn't hesitate to let him have it. Actually, I would have happily given him all of them.

Karin recalled that when he got home that day he told her about his three choices. When she asked why he kept changing his mind, he said, "I didn't want to choose her favourite."

I told Karin that it had been my favourite and she offered to give it back to me. What she dropped off, however, was much better than what Nicholas had taken with him that day: this bear had been loved by a very special little boy. The fur was all squashed on the sides where he had lain on it.

I'll always have a corner of my heart reserved for Nicholas. And thanks to his mother, I have a beautiful, tangible reminder that sits on my bed every day.

Chapter Four:

BEFORE AND AFTER

If I thought getting through the first year of my "new life" in hospital and rehabilitation was tough, I was totally unprepared for how difficult living in the real world would be. Instead of heading off to university with my friends and enjoying a new level of independence, I was living at home with my mother and two younger sisters, dependent on someone for every little thing. I needed someone to assist me in every aspect of getting up in the morning and going to bed at night — dressing, washing, brushing my teeth, getting me in and out of bed — but my requirements didn't stop there. I needed someone to pour drinks, prepare food and feed me, help me in and out of my van and drive whenever I went out. Instead of taking the next step into adulthood, I found myself thrown into two opposing states: I had to deal with far too much for someone my age, but at the same time, I felt I had regressed to the state of a helpless infant.

This kind of dependence was completely at odds with my personality.

Ask either of my parents to describe me as a child in one word and they would say "stubborn." I figured out what I wanted and I did whatever I had to do to get it. Even as young as two I would get what I wanted for myself, as demonstrated by one of my mother's favourite stories about me. We were not allowed to chew gum, which made it a huge treat. One day I came into the house with the forbidden fruit in my mouth.

"Where did you get the gum?" my mother asked.

"Off the woad," I matter-of-factly replied.

When I was thirteen it occurred to me that all of my friends had been on a plane and/or been to Florida except me. So I babysat and saved enough money to take myself to Florida to visit my grandparents over the March Break. I learned early on to work for what I wanted.

I was also a bit of a rebel, in my own way.

In grade seven a first-time teacher, Mr. Gallante, had the misfortune of being assigned to my class. I wasn't the only delinquent in the class by any means — there were several of us who would have made a good case for bringing back corporal punishment. I didn't do anything illegal, but I was insolent, rude and never showed a trace of respect. I can remember tilting my chair back, putting my feet on the desk and munching an apple one afternoon while Mr. Gallante was trying to teach a science class.

"Barbara, you shouldn't be eating in class, please put that away," he said to me, resignation and failure already clear to my twelve-year-old ears.

"No, I'm hungry," I replied with feigned innocence, and kept right on eating. He should have taken me by the ear and hauled me down to the office, but he just carried on, trying to teach around my defiance.

In our elementary school, detention punishment was staying late and writing out the school rules. They were typed in a small font that filled two overhead transparencies. I'm surprised I didn't have them committed to memory, considering how often I was in there after school. I felt triumph and resentment each time my attitude landed me in hot water.

Maybe I was reacting to my parents' divorce or trying to get the attention I wasn't getting at home, because I was also getting into trouble in other classes. Recently my mother was going through some old photographs and found a note written by one of my other grade seven teachers. Sent home with me on a Friday, the note said I was not to bother returning to school on the following Monday unless my behaviour was radically improved.

As summer approached, I sometimes got into trouble when we had an outdoor class. I once snuck away from art class and joined some high school friends who had already finished school for the year and were having fun skateboarding. Before long my absence was noticed and my teacher, Mr. Reidel, came looking for me.

"Get back and join the class, Barb," he said, with more patience than I deserved.

"Not until I finish with my friends, Thomas," I coolly shot back. This flagrant act of disrespect was particularly terrible because I had overheard him telling another teacher that he hated his full name and always went by the short form Tom. How he stopped himself from strangling me I don't know.

Growing up in a family of five daughters, I was no pushover. We all knew how to stand up for ourselves, though we each did it in our own way. Chella, the oldest, probably had the toughest job. Naturally, parents cut their teeth with the first child, and Chella bore the brunt of that. As in most large families, she was always expected to set an example for us, leaving her with an exaggerated sense of responsibility. She was exceptionally bright, from her early years on, and she was skipped from the first to the third grade. Her teachers probably meant well but shouldn't have done it; it made it difficult for her to fit in with her schoolmates. She always felt pressure to live up to the expectations put on her academically, but she thrilled her parents and grandparents by becoming the first professional in the family when she finished law school (even though she soon became disillusioned with the profession and left it after five years).

Lynn, next in line, had a particularly hard time with the financial problems our family had. She wanted the "in" clothes that my mother could not afford. She started working full time right after high school, bought a car and always had nice clothes — she worked hard and was proud of what she owned. She later went to law school, taking Chella's place as the lawyer in the family. She has always been the hardest worker of us all.

Christine, three years younger than me, has had a tendency to be a bit overly sensitive. I think she had some miserable years in high school, made worse by the attention showered on me after the shooting. She did blossom in university, though, meeting and marrying a great guy and settling down in northern Ontario, where she teaches high school. Christine has a sunny nature and outgoing personality and is probably the most balanced of the bunch of us.

Alison, six years younger than me, is the family charmer. Always witty and instantly likeable, she made it impossible to stay mad at her for long. The youngest child is sometimes coddled in large families, and in her younger years Alison got away with more than the rest of us liked. "Because she's the smallest" were words we frequently heard our mother say (and Alison impishly echo).

Even though we stuck up for each other as a rule, my sisters and I also had a pretty rough-and-tumble relationship. We fought like most siblings, and most of our battles were played out around the dining-room table. The chaser and the chased would square off with the table between them, then the offender would get into the best position to race down the stairs into the bathroom. Once there, you would usually be safe until the other party calmed down.

But you had to be careful, because the bathroom lock could be turned with a knife. I can remember standing there, my whole body trembling, chest heaving and adrenaline pumping, holding on to the lock with both my shaking hands. The bathroom was at street level and there was a window that opened to the driveway. Sometimes the angry party would engage another sister to help break into the bathroom. It depended on the offence and if the recruit was holding any grudges against the captive; if a good enough case was made, she could gain an accomplice. When that happened your goose was cooked. One sister would pick the lock while the other opened the window from the driveway — it was impossible to defend yourself on both fronts. No matter what side you were on, you usually ended up losing some of your skin underneath someone's fingernails and gaining some of her skin under yours. Our immediate neighbours must have wondered sometimes if they should send in the cavalry.

Our house was not large and there wasn't much in the way of privacy. There were two bathrooms, but only one had a shower, so morning routines were scheduled and cooperative — in theory, anyway. Sleeping in could throw everybody off.

The two youngest in the family always shared a bedroom. For many years we three older ones shared two bedrooms, taking six-month turns with a room to ourselves. The hardest part of those moves was taking down our posters. We were always competing for wall space to display the objects of our latest celebrity crushes — from TV stars to rock stars to hockey players. When I was fourteen a friend of my mother's built a small bedroom in the basement for me. It was freezing down there in the winter, even with an electric blanket and a space heater, but it was worth it to have my own room.

I am the middle child, although I don't think that's significant. I don't believe I got any less attention than my sisters. With five children being raised by a single parent, none of us got much individual attention. That my mother kept a roof over our heads and kept us fed is, I think, a great testimonial to her. After all, none of us is strung out on drugs or has ever been in trouble with the law.

Four of us went through university and have professional careers. Alison chose not to go to university and lives and works in Vancouver. It wasn't easy having so many people in our small house, but now, as adults, it's great having such a large family.

One thing that has always bound us together is a good sense of humour. Our family get-togethers are always filled with laughter, jokes and good-natured teasing. We even managed to find humour in the horrible circumstances caused by the shooting. My first Christmas home I found a card that was so well suited I bought every single one I could find. On the front was nothing but a green blob. The inside read: "I did this with my ear and thought you might like to have it. Merry Christmas."

I don't know what life was like at home for my sisters that year I spent in the hospital, but I do know that my younger sisters were kind of orphaned for several months. It had to have been difficult for them, considering how much time my mother spent at the hospital. For the first three weeks she was with me from morning until late evening. Then after she went back to work she'd still come directly to the hospital from the office, staying again until late evening and checking in with the others by phone. Talk about latchkey kids! My sister Lynn managed much of the grocery shopping and cleaning. For the first few weeks prepared meals and frozen casseroles kept appearing as if by magic, and that really helped. We had wonderful neighbours and friends. Alison, who had just turned thirteen when I was hurt, spent a lot of time hanging out with one friend or another, often being invited to their homes for meals. It was close to eight months before I was in a stable enough situation that I didn't need my mom to come during the week.

From my sisters' perspective, everything revolved around "Barb" for the entire year I was hospitalized, and, in fact, for much longer. It was the same way with their friends. Every member of my family was always greeted with "How's Barb?" before "How are *you*?" It was a rare occurrence when someone asked them, *really* asked them, how they were doing.

It's understandable that couples sometimes break up after a tragedy like losing a child. When a sudden death or an injury of such magnitude happens, everyone in the family is traumatized. I think every member of my family had to heal themselves. In some ways it brought us all closer together, but in other ways, from the time of the shooting we were all looking out for ourselves.

Meanwhile, time and life march on, so each person had to try to keep up with her life while dealing with all the emotions and changes and *stresses* that go hand-in-hand with tragedy. Christine remembers wanting to go to a party one Friday night a couple of weeks after the shooting but feeling guilty about it.

"How can you think about a party at a time like this?" Lynn said to her.

Why wouldn't she think about a party? She was a high school student who had been spending a lot of time at the hospital, all her friends were going to be at this party and, damn it all, she just wanted to go. There wasn't anything wrong with that, and Lynn's comment only made the guilt worse.

Guilt. Everyone felt it. My mother felt she should have stopped me from working at Becker's (though I never would have listened to her). She felt helpless and responsible. She didn't have a bath for almost a year, remembering that I had loved taking long soaks and reading a good book. She figured if I couldn't, she shouldn't. My sister Lynn felt enormously guilty because Friday closing had been her shift until she'd quit — only three weeks before. My other sisters felt guilty because they were whole and life was continuing. The manager of the store was taking his first night off the evening of the shooting, and there are no words to describe the guilt he felt. Not only did he leave the Becker's company, he had something close to a nervous breakdown to boot.

How long should my family have waited before rejoining their lives? They weren't paralyzed, I was. Did the fact that my sister wanted to go to a party mean she didn't care about what happened to me? Of course not. Each person's grief is her own. If a friend or acquaintance loses a loved one we can express our sympathy, we can feel absolutely horrible, but our lives don't suffer the same interruption. It might make us ponder our own mortality for a while, but for the most part we still carry on with our daily activities.

Life goes on for people, it's as simple as that. After Christopher Reeve broke his neck and appeared on "20/20" with Barbara Walters, she told television viewers that she would "never complain again." I wanted to throw something at her head for making such a stupid comment. I don't believe for a moment that her life changed quite that dramatically because she spent a few hours with a man who was thrown from his horse and wound up in a wheelchair; I don't care how stoic he is. And that is not to detract in any way from the accomplishments of Christopher Reeve, or myself or anyone else who carries on with life. The suffering of others can't totally and permanently eliminate a person's own frustrations. No matter how badly off someone is, guaranteed there is someone else in the world worse off — and that fact won't make our own difficulties disappear.

Everyone's struggle is personal, and each of my family and friends had to deal with my injury and how it affected their lives in their own way. For my two younger sisters, things were particularly difficult because they suddenly weren't getting the attention and support they needed. No one was home when they finished school, and they were frequently alone all evening. There might have been food in the fridge, but there was no responsible adult; an older sister just doesn't cut it. By the time my mother got home from the hospital each night, it was late and she was exhausted.

Once, not long after the shooting, Christine appeared in the local newspaper with her volleyball team. This was, understandably, a big deal to her. That weekend at the hospital she was riding up in an elevator with our father.

"Hey, I was in the paper, Dad," she said excitedly.

"Yes, eh," he said.

He was distracted, obviously immersed in other matters, and by then he was accustomed to seeing our family name in the news every day. But his response was devastating for my sister.

*   *   *   *

My family lived in the same house I'd grown up in until a couple of months before my discharge from rehab. There was no question about moving back to it. It was one of those split-level, semi-detached houses with four small floors and lots of stairs. This was where I went on weekends. We rented a hospital bed, which was kept in the living room, because at that point I still needed breaks from my wheelchair during the day. Each night a family friend carried me upstairs to my mother's waterbed, and then I'd be carried back downstairs the next morning. We started looking for a house better suited for me to go home to.

We wanted to stay in roughly the same neighbourhood, so my mother hunted there for a house that could easily be made accessible. When she found it, I went to look to give the final approval. For half of the cost we used money from the Barbara Turnbull Fund. My mother and I became co-owners. Despite it being a bungalow with a finished basement, it still needed a fair amount of renovation to make it work for me. The garage door had to be raised to fit my van, which had been modified with a raised roof and hydraulic lift. An elevator was built right behind the garage, which took me up to the main floor and down to the basement. With funding from the Workers' Compensation Board, we turned one bedroom into a large bathroom with a wheel-in shower and had it open into another room, making that my bedroom.

I wanted to take a last look at my old bedroom before we moved. It was down two flights of stairs, so getting there was no small feat. I hadn't been in it since the shooting. My mother had made sure it was untouched, everything just as I'd left it. Being in that room was gut-wrenching. The last time I'd been in there I had walked in and walked out, or maybe run out, on my way to Becker's. I badly wanted to relive that last time, to savour it, play it over and over in my mind, but I couldn't recall it. Why would I have? September 23 had been like any other day, right up until 11:15 p.m.

Sitting surrounded by all the reminders of my "before" life, I got very depressed. There in my face was the brass bed I had always meant to polish. And so much more. One corner was full of my stuffed animals — the Woody Woodpecker I'd won at a summer fair when I was eleven, a Mickey Mouse from my trip to Florida when I was in grade eight. A Muppet poster was still tacked to my wall. My jewellery was carelessly tossed down on the table beside my mirror. My school essays and projects were all there in my closet, dating back to elementary years. I had all the letters I'd received from my camp friends alphabetized and crammed into two wooden fruit baskets. Near them was a pile of some of the early mail that had come in from friends and acquaintances after the shooting.

I didn't notice it at the time but there were a few things missing. The night of the shooting, while Lynn was waiting for my mother to get home, she'd gone through my bedroom, found every single item that had "Becker's" on it — bags, pay stubs, cash receipts — and ripped them into tiny pieces.

61

Now, with a friend's help, I started throwing everything out. It all reminded me of what I had lost, what I would never be or have again. I even threw out pictures (I learned much later that my mother snuck into the garbage bag and took out some of the photos — I wish she had kept the whole damn bag).

One of the cards I threw out, from a high school classmate, was one of the most special pieces of mail I received after the shooting. I had a vague recollection of who she was, but we had never had much to do with each other. She wrote about two incidents in particular in which I had played a part. One was a day in class when we were told to break into groups. She said that she had been very shy and always dreaded having to team up. On this day, I turned to her and invited her to join my group. Another day, she was walking down the hall with a friend, and I came running up behind them, threw my arms around their shoulders, said something of little consequence and ran off. She wrote how the two incidents made her feel included and how surprised she had been that I, as popular as I was, would have counted her in.

Me, popular? I didn't see it that way at all. When I'd started high school I'd changed immediately and dramatically from a grade eight brat to someone who really enjoyed school. I was no star academically — in fact I was a very lazy student in those years and my marks reflected that — but I had great respect for my teachers. I sat up front and I was quick with one-liners, never hesitant to talk out. Class participation was definitely my strong point, even if most of it was unsolicited. Mouthy, many would have called me. But that confidence and cockiness always vanished in a social setting, like a party.

In grades nine and ten there was a part of me that needed to leave the brat in me behind, and the other students my age were too much of a reminder. So I skipped ahead a year using the semester system, to be with older students. As a result, I didn't really fit in socially with either year. That suited me fine — my camp friends were my life anyway. I got along well enough with other students, but I never belonged to any of "in" groups. My closest friends in the high school were in the drama club. I was a pretty marginal member and rarely socialized with them outside of school.

I would never have considered myself popular. It would be just like me to invite a person sitting alone to join my group, but I'd do that because there had been so many times in my life when I was praying someone would do the same for me. I know very well what it feels like to be left out, feeling like a misfit. Anyhow, her card made me feel good about myself, and I'm sorry it ended up in the garbage.

At home in my new life, it wasn't easy getting back into the swing of things. My two younger sisters and I were often at odds. I started seeing a social worker once a week. It was a good outlet for whatever was on my mind, and I used the sessions to talk about day-to-day issues. I still had not dealt with the "big picture," although I didn't know it at the time. I had my hands full just living every day. I was very afraid of long days with nothing to do. I tried to get at least one thing accomplished each day, no matter how small.

I had one attendant, who worked Monday to Friday, and nurses who came in three mornings a week to help me with my bowel routine and shower. Nurses weren't necessary, but it was a way to get extra coverage from the Workers' Compensation Board. They gave me a monthly allowance for attendants, but it was nowhere near adequate to cover the cost. They would pay for nursing separately, so my doctor wrote an order saying that's what I needed. I had attendants from an agency at night, who helped me get ready for bed and then stayed until 4:00 a.m. They were there in case I needed something, then came into my room to flip me over onto my other side before they left. On weekends my mother and sisters took turns helping me get up and go to bed.

One great surprise was that I could have Janet, my occupational therapist, back. I was eligible for temporary at-home OT through an outreach program, which is where she had been working since quitting Lyndhurst. She came once a week and helped me set up work areas around the house and install environmental control equipment. I had two TOSC units, like the one I'd had at my bedside in rehab, to control a tape-recorder, lights and telephone. Janet was helping me figure out what I was going to do with the rest of my life, or at least the next couple of years. I was starting to think about university. It was wonderful to be able to talk to her on a regular basis again.

Time seemed to pass quickly enough. I attended a local computer training centre for disabled people each week or two. My spine had started to curve and it was getting harder to sit comfortably in a chair, so every couple of weeks I was going to a seating clinic, where they would modify my chair to make it more comfortable and to improve my posture. Friends visited often and I started going to a lot of concerts.

I spent a lot of time reading through the thousands of letters that had been sitting waiting for me. I was astounded by the sheer volume of it, but also by the contents. There was a tremendous amount of love and support in those cards and letters. There were several people who had each sent many cards over my year in the hospital. Some of the names would come up over and over again. I wrote thank-you letters on my computer. I didn't respond to every letter — not by a long shot — but I did what I could.

I was having trouble letting go of my former life. I held on to it in my memory, what it had felt like to be physically able. I'd watch people and follow their actions simultaneously in my head. Let's say someone was filling the kettle — I'd recall how the weight of it increased as the water poured in the spout. I wanted to remember the simple activities, like opening doors, washing dishes or bending down and picking something up. I tried to hang on to the memory of textures and the temperature of household objects.

*   *   *   *

It was during this time that I went back to visit the Becker's store. I think many people go back to the scene of their injury — a few people in rehab had talked about it. For me, both nostalgia and reflection were enticing me back.

I could remember the first time I went into that Becker's store on Benedet Drive. It was during a holiday, when few stores were open. I was just running in for milk but it occurred to me that this would be an ideal spot for a job, since it was within walking distance from home in one direction and school in the other. I asked for an application, although I wasn't dressed for making a good impression and there wasn't a "Help Wanted" sign anywhere. I got a call from Martin, the store manager, almost right away saying I'd got the job.

I was so excited. My two older sisters had started working when they were fourteen and fifteen at the local McDonald's, but all I had to my resumé was paper routes, a whole lot of babysitting and helping a family friend who was disabled with her housework on Saturdays. This was my first *real* job, and I was thrilled at the prospect of learning to use a cash register.

It didn't take me too long to learn the job, though I can remember slamming my thumb in the cash register drawer a couple of times when cute guys came in. Martin was a pleasant guy and an easy boss, but quite soon after I started, he informed me that he was leaving Becker's. There were two other student employees, both from my high school — one was a good friend of my sister's and the other lived next door to the store — and we were assured that our jobs were pretty safe. Until another manager was chosen, the store was to be managed by an area supervisor named Dominick.

Under Dominick, the store took on a free-spirited, almost party-like atmosphere. He seemed to enjoy the company of us young women a little more than he should have. He started scheduling us so that often there would be two of us on at a time — a totally unnecessary move. It became so much fun to be there that it wasn't unusual for whoever wasn't working to come just to hang out. It was certainly less than professional! I can even remember cutting Dominick's hair in the back room one night. One Friday night, close to Christmas, he scheduled all three of us and brought in a bottle of rum. We drank rum and egg nog, though not one of us clerks was legally old enough to drink.

The worst change to occur with Dominick in charge was that we started helping ourselves to store merchandise. When Dominick needed a pack of cigarettes, he took it off the shelf without paying for it. He made it clear it was no big deal and we could do the same. Hungry? Grab a bag of chips. Thirsty? There was plenty of pop in the fridge. "Help yourself" turned out to be a habit too hard to break, and one that would come back to haunt me for many years.

Life for those few weeks was fun, but I always felt uneasy at the same time. It felt wrong, and I was secretly relieved when a regular manager was assigned to the store. New order was going to be a welcome change. The new manager, Bernard LeBars, was no stranger to the business of convenience stores. Managing milk stores was what Bernard had done for many years. He was a very able and responsible manager, and a kind and good man. Immediately a sense of order was restored.

In the last couple of years before the shooting, my regular shifts at Becker's were two or three weekdays from 4:00 p.m. until 9:00 p.m. and Sunday mornings from opening at 7:00 or 8:00 a.m. until 1:00 or 2:00 p.m. To open the store for 7:00 a.m., I used to get up at 5:30, shower and get ready, then take the twenty-minute walk to reach the store about ten minutes early. I don't know why I always got there early, since we rarely had customers before 8:00 (one of the changes Bernard made was to change the Sunday shift to start at 8:00 a.m.). I liked bringing the newspapers in and locking the door behind me while I got everything ready. I always felt a slight shiver of apprehension going into the store and locking the door behind me so early, but at the same time I enjoyed the solitude.

First I would make coffee. I've never been able to drink the stuff, but I've always really loved the smell. Then, with the smell of fresh-brewing coffee filling the store, I'd put the *Toronto Sun* inserts into the papers and try to grab a cigarette before finally turning on the lights and unlocking the door. It's funny now in this anti-cigarette era to think of smoking in the store back then, something I and other employees with the habit did regularly.

I believe I was the best cashier any Becker's store could have hoped for. I was efficient and very good at my job (except for smoking and eating some of the profits). I loved my job and I loved being good at my job. I even loved the *smell* of the store, a distinct smell to convenience stores that can still make me nostalgic when I go into one. I could read, write letters or knit between customers, though there was often someone to chat with.

I loved my regular customers and I'm pretty sure they loved me. When any of the regulars walked in, they never had to tell me their brand of cigarettes or type of milk. It was always "Two today, please," or "Just milk, I got cigarettes already." One customer would pull up, and unless I was serving others I would have his bag of 2 percent milk, loaf of bread and two bottles of Pepsi bagged and waiting for him by the time he reached the counter. If he was in a rush he'd sometimes slap down exact change and be gone without us exchanging so much as a "Hi, there ya go." One woman, an avid reader of trash romance like myself, would come in to buy books, then give them to me after she'd finished them. (I *think* she gave them to me — otherwise I owe her a ton of trashy paperbacks!) Another customer, one who lived about five houses away, used to stay chatting so long that picking up milk would take an hour.

To this day I think I could name the brands my regulars smoked if they were lined up in front of me. I remember seeing one guy who'd been a regular about ten years after the shooting. We crossed paths at a strip mall in Mississauga and it was as though no time had passed at all.

"Aren't you Barbara?" he asked me.

"Yeah," I replied, "and aren't you large Player's regular?" I was right. Damn I was good!

There were a lot of kids in the area and I was definitely their favourite cashier. I have always enjoyed children and been pretty good with them. I loved it when one would come in with a quarter or a couple of dimes clutched in his grimy little hand and, looking up at me with big eyes, ask if I could show him what he could buy. I would take each one to the candy shelf and point out all the different combinations he could get. Some of them would take ten or fifteen minutes making up their minds. Sometimes they'd ask to be shown again. It was a big decision for them and I understood that.

When changes to the provincial sales tax came in, suddenly twenty-five-cent purchases were taxable. Try explaining to a five-year-old that, because of the government, what she could buy yesterday for a quarter cost twenty-seven cents today — even though the prices of the candy were the same. It was far easier to ring in the kids' purchases twice as if they were two different sales, one for a dime and one for fifteen cents. I didn't know who swallowed the loss and I didn't particularly care.

My sister did not have the patience or affection for the children back then that I had, and they sure knew it. One of the local kids wrote me a letter after the shooting that said: "When I first heard what happened I thought it was your sister who got hurt, but when I found out it was you I cried."

The store was generally very safe and free from robberies. There was one period of time when a gang of youths tried repeatedly, and unsuccessfully, to hold up the store. One time one of them came in with an axe, stood in front of the counter and tapped the blade of the axe on one hand.

"What do you want?" my boss asked.

"I want money," the punk replied.

Bernard, a balding and not exactly muscular forty-something man, said, "Oh yeah?" and started around the counter, as if to chase the guy. The kid took off as fast as his legs could carry him. Another time one of them came in and asked Rita, Bernard's wife, for cash.

"Oh go home, get out of here," she said. And he did.

These attempts were more amusing than threatening. We all had a good laugh each time they happened, though I was always secretly relieved I had not been working that shift. I wondered what I would do if they came in when I was working, because we had always been told to hand over the cash, no questions asked. Considering how harmless these guys seemed, I would have hated to let punks like that get away with anything, but at the same time, I didn't want to take any chances.

Part of the irony about the shooting is that the guys who held up the store that night would have made substantially more money had they simply asked for it. After the shooter fired, he came around the counter and took the money from the cash register, plus a box of rolled coins from a shelf underneath — less than $200 altogether. A little further to the left was another box full of bills. Since we weren't supposed to keep much cash in the till, I'd continually empty it throughout each shift, putting the money in another box. That night, I would have willingly and immediately given them everything. All they had to do was ask.

On the afternoon I went back to Becker's, all I wanted to do was sit and look behind the counter for a few minutes. It would have been ideal to sit there alone, but I didn't want anyone to know what exactly it was I wanted to do. Why I thought I could casually and quietly drop in I don't know, but I tried one afternoon. First there was a step in, and my attendant, Sue, couldn't bump my chair over it and hold the door at the same time, so we needed help. I was in my manual chair, so I had no control over where I went or how fast. The manager, of course, recognized me immediately and started a running monologue that didn't end until we left. Sue pushed me up and down each aisle, while the manager chattered incessantly about nothing. I was frustrated; had I been in my electric chair I would have positioned myself with a view of the area behind the counter, then sat there pretending to listen to whatever she was saying. I know Sue would have done that had I asked her, but it was something very private I didn't want to share with anyone.

After touring around a bit, the manager asked me if I wanted to see the back room. I quickly said yes, realizing it would be my only chance to look behind the counter. I only got a quick glimpse as I went past into the back room and out again. I left feeling totally dissatisfied.

Oddly enough, the store was robbed a few days later. A reporter at the local community newspaper realized it was "my" store and interviewed the manager. Can you see the headline? "Scene of shooting robbed days after visit from victim." It seemed as though I could never do anything quietly or on my own.

*   *   *   *

During the year I spent in the hospital, my mother did her best to support me, but back at home, I guess she wanted to protect me, too — as she wished she could have that September night. And she tried to protect me from *everything*. If I got into a spat with a sister, she'd immediately take my side and tell her to leave me alone. She even started answering for me in certain situations.

"Barb can I wear your ...?"

"No, leave Barb's clothes alone. Wear your own clothes."

This was as infuriating for me as it was for my sisters. I was feeling smothered. Her unnecessary intervention often worked to my sisters' advantage, because I'd get so angry with her that I'd let them have whatever they wanted in a futile attempt to to take control. I'd point out what she had done, sometimes screaming in frustration, and she would sheepishly laugh, apologize and do the exact same thing the next time. She seemed incapable of backing off and letting me have a normal sibling relationship.

Things were different with my friends, too. And for me, the most difficult change was with my friends from camp. You see, at the time of the shooting, they were more important to me than anything else. I'd worked at Moorelands Camp for three summers before the shooting and it was paradise for me. I was happier at Moorelands than I've ever been anywhere at any time in my life.

Though my camp friends rallied around me after the shooting, things just weren't the same after I got home. When I did see them socially, I was always depressed for a few days after. Yet I was in no way prepared to give up on them. They were great. Often they'd pick me up in my van for a party or get-together, but for me it was just too different from what it had been. It was fine when I saw them one on one, but I couldn't handle large groups. Perhaps they reminded me of what I'd lost. Whatever it was, it was years before I could really enjoy their company again.

There was a definite limit to what I could do for myself and how much time I could spend on my own. I had some basic environmental controls, but that went no further than a telephone and a couple of lights in my bedroom. I could read a book propped in a stand with a mouthstick to turn the pages, and I could use a computer, but that was about it.

Many quads feel the cold very easily, it's partly a circulation problem and partly a temperature regulation problem. It's like an internal cold and an inability to feel really warm unless we're sitting right in front of a roaring fire or have the heat cranked high in winter. I felt cold almost constantly and drank gallons of tea all day long. Since I couldn't pour drinks for myself and I couldn't empty the bladder bag I wore on the side of my leg, I was dependent on someone being around most of the time.

This became an ongoing problem for weekend evenings. Friday and Saturday nights are synonymous with going out, being social and, well, *partying* — especially for people in their late teens, twenties and often into the thirties. If you don't have plans *at least* one of the nights you feel like a loner or a loser. I have always had a lot of friends, but by the time I got out of the hospital many were away at university. For once it was more common for me *not* to have plans than the other way around.

God, how I hated those two nights of the week. By that time my two older sisters were living in downtown Toronto. Chella came home weekend nights fairly frequently, but still, every single one of those nights I'd be painfully aware that I would have been doing something else had I not been hurt. It was slightly better if my mother had no plans. Those nights I'd usually rent a video. Sometimes my mother would watch it with me, but more often she'd be doing laundry or puttering around the house. My mother has always had a problem relaxing — she'll sit and stew about what she *could* be accomplishing. Those nights were solitary and extremely depressing. I kept asking myself how many nineteen-year-olds spend so many weekend nights sitting at home with their mother. What was far worse, though, was any night she had plans. It would start, sometimes mid-week.

"I'm going out Saturday night. Who's going to stay home with Barb?"

"It's not my turn."

"I've already got plans."

"My plans were made *ages* ago and I stayed home last time."

My mother usually tried to have these conversations in hushed tones or when I wasn't around, but I was always aware they were going on or had gone on, and I witnessed my share. I'd sometimes retreat to my bedroom, not able to bear being in the same room while the debate raged, but even then I'd sit and listen carefully to it, cringing, wilting inside.

I had become one of the household chores I used to argue about with my sisters, like vacuuming the house or washing the dishes. I felt as though I had to be babysat. No one was to blame for this. My sisters were at the age when the most important thing was to be with their friends. It's a selfish age. They would have been abnormal if they'd cheerfully said, "Oh, I'll skip my plans, who cares about that house party all my friends will be at." To their credit, they would be perfectly agreeable by the time the evening rolled around, but that didn't make it much easier for me.

I felt so helpless. I *was* helpless. The solution of hiring someone for those evenings was unacceptable to me; there was no way I could bring myself to pay someone to be home with me. That would truly be like babysitting, I thought. At that point I couldn't understand why staying home the odd weekend evening was such a big deal.

It's not as if they're affected like I am. I live with this every second of every minute of every hour of every godforsaken day.

I burned with resentment toward them and the whole situation — much as I'm sure they burned with resentment right back. Even if I'd found someone to run in, make tea, give me a hand in the washroom and then leave, I still would have been depressed about my solitary weekend evenings. It was a no-win situation.

Compounding the problem was the fact that on weekends I'd rely on my sisters and mother to do my attendant care in the mornings and evenings. I've learned that having siblings, parents, spouses, partners, "significant others" as attendants with any kind of regularity does not work. It throws off the balance of the relationship. When I was still in rehab and coming home weekends, I always left my electric chair back at the hospital. For some reason, I assumed my family was there for every one of my needs. The independence the chair would give me in every environment — including the house — didn't register for a long time. Maybe I was used to everything revolving around me and figured weekends at home would be the same. It was many months before I wised up and had attendants on weekends.

My sisters were trying to get on with their lives. They were normal teenagers; I wasn't. Naturally, the more independent I've become in my life, the better I've felt about myself and the easier it's been for the rest of my family. But it took a dozen years and an awful lot of money to reach that state.

In addition, I hated being an added burden to my mother. With her daughters all well on the way to being grown up and out of the house, she deserved to enjoy this phase of her life. Up until then, it had certainly been no cakewalk.

*   *   *   *

My mother was born Iris Gertrude Tapp in Barachois, Quebec, one of eight kids on a farm. Her father, Anthony Tapp, was an alcoholic, and the kids never knew what he might do next. She calls him a "very nice man" when he was sober. He fished in the summer and cut wood in the winter. Her mother, born Alice Paradis, was a devout Catholic. If she ever had a spare moment she would be found in her rocking chair saying a rosary. The whole family attended church on Sunday no matter what — her dad even sobered up for it. Both parents were extremely hard workers.

Her dad was usually gone during the week and home for boozy binges on weekends. Screech was his drink of choice. Once he came in drunk while they were having dinner and turned the table over. Another time my young, brave mother called him a "son of a bitch" after he hit her mother, and he chased her around the house. She ended up hiding in the potato cellar until she could sneak out, then she spent the next three days at a friend's house while he sobered up. By the time she returned home he had no memory of what had transpired.

They had plenty of food and a decent-sized house, so the kids never realized they had no money. They slaughtered their own beef and chicken, collected the eggs, milked the cows and made butter.

As were her other siblings, my mother was educated by nuns in a schoolhouse for both elementary and high school. As soon as they could, her older brother and sisters moved to "the Big City," Montreal, and started working. But Iris's mother had plans for her — she was to be the child to attend college. Mom started at teacher's college but got only one year under her belt before her mother became ill. Dependable Iris stayed at home to help out.

She was only nineteen, but her one college year allowed her to teach elementary school. So that's what she did, with her youngest sister in her first grade five class, until the day her mother had a heart attack. My mom had gone home to prepare lunch that day, sneaking in dressed as a nun to give her mother a chuckle. Shortly after she went back to school to teach that afternoon, her mother got up to get some mending out of a heavy chest. They concluded that the strain of opening the chest caused the fatal attack. Alice Tapp was fifty-five.

Some days earlier her mother had asked my mom to promise she would look after her younger brother and sisters if anything should happen to her. That's how Iris Tapp ended up virtually a parent at nineteen.

Her dad fell apart, but my mother, ever stoic and responsible for too much, didn't allow herself to cry for three months. The following summer she decided to go to Montreal with her young siblings, taking her father with her as he didn't want to be left behind. He died not long afterwards, at fifty-two, also of a heart attack.

Enter John Robert (Bob) Turnbull, introduced to her by a mutual friend. He was looking for an escape from his unhappy, unaffectionate household. My mother was on the rebound after having to leave her one true love, a man named Harold. He was Anglican, and her devout Catholic parents had *freaked* at the mention of her converting to marry him.

My parents were married seven months after they first met. Dad was nineteen, mom twenty-one. Things were rough from the start. My dad, practically a child himself, often fought with my mom's two younger sisters. Complicating matters further, my parents proved to be very proper Catholics, getting pregnant right away. Soon my mother's sisters went to boarding school at a local convent, then moved out on their own.

During their fourteen-year marriage things were never great. They were far too young in the first place, and neither had come from homes with solid, functional families that might have provided good examples. Looking back, my father realizes they never worked together; they were always at odds.

I was ten when my father moved out. I think ours was the first known family in our school to have a "broken home" (an expression I absolutely detest). It was a single-parent family, but certainly less dysfunctional without both my parents living there. It must have caused quite a stir in the school, because my teacher decided to use me as an example to teach the class about one-parent families.

"Who here doesn't have a father?" she asked the class. No one raised a hand. "Barbara, you don't have a father in your house, do you?"

"I still have a father," I hotly replied, my face burning with shame.

That my parents had split was not much of a secret. My mother, after joining a single parents' group, had been named "Single Parent of the Year" by the club. A story and picture of us ran in the *Mississauga News*.

Except for being seen as different for that reason, I don't think the split had much impact on me at the time, though it might be an explanation for my later rebellious stage. A short time ago, my sister Lynn talked about the day our mother told us our father was moving out. My mom was washing dishes and the three older kids were in the kitchen with her. Lynn said she had to grip the counter to keep from passing out when she heard the news. Then, about ten minutes later, she came into the bedroom I shared with Chella. We were both on our beds reading.

"What are we going to do about this?" she asked us. We both looked up.

"Do about what?" we replied.

We were pretty poor. My mother always worked, and did get some support from my father after he left, but we were definitely on the lowest end of middle class. We always had food, but by month's end my mother had to get creative with dinners. She called them her "dollar dinners" or "cheap, cheap nights." We'd have baked beans and homemade bread, or my mother would make several meals out of a utility turkey: pot pies, turkey à la king, sandwiches and, finally, with near-bare bones, turkey soup.

On her once-a-month payday we were treated to a meal at McDonald's. Lynn recalls that our mother's wallet would be fat with money on that day. "It was the only day I felt safe," she once told me.

When I think back, I'm amazed that we lived in a house we owned, or at least partially owned — it was certainly not mortgage-free. Family friends recall that my mother felt unrelenting financial pressures. There was just never enough money for what we needed or wanted, or for what she wanted us to have.

Life with five daughters wasn't easy for my mom. One thing I'm ashamed of now is that we didn't help out much around the house. You'd think with five girls my mom would have had most of the housework and cooking taken care of, but that was not the case. Anything she asked us to do would start an argument. "What has so-and-so done?" we would ask accusingly, each sure we were the *only* one who ever did anything around the house. I think my mom found it easier just to do it all herself.

Countless nights I would come home from my job at Becker's, at around 9:30, and walk by a sink full of dishes on my way down to my room, which was directly below the kitchen. My mother was often out in the evenings, at her single parents' group or earning extra cash by participating in one of those consumer test groups that would pay her thirty or forty dollars to sit and listen to a sales pitch all evening. She usually got home around 10:00 p.m. or so. I could hear her familiar step as she crossed the kitchen floor. While I lounged in bed reading, I would hear her fill the sink with water, do everyone's dishes, then go up to bed. It never occurred to me that it wasn't right, until years later, when it was too late.

*   *   *   *

I remember a conversation I had with my mother once, about a month or two before the shooting. Two people I knew, or knew of, had suffered spinal cord injuries that summer.

"I couldn't cope with that, if one of you were paralyzed."

"Don't be silly," I told her. "Of course you would cope. You deal with what comes your way and that's that."

Was it some kind of premonition?

One day, about a week before the shooting, I was driving with my friend Alise and out of my mouth popped the strangest statement.

"I've been memorizing my mother's face," I said. "I've been studying the lines in her face like something bad is going to happen."

I don't know if my thoughts were that something was going to happen to me or to her, because quite frankly I don't remember the incident. Alise reminded me of it years later. She said she remembered it so clearly because I just came out with it, in the middle of our otherwise typical high school conversation. She said it made the hair on the back of her neck stand up.

My mother has always loved her five children equally, but it would be dishonest to deny that I was a bit of a favourite. I think in some ways I had a maturity or responsibility my sisters didn't, and on top of that I liked to spend time with her. After my parents split, I usually hung out with my mom while she got ready for her dates. I can remember setting up her hair rollers, then sitting on the bathroom counter, handing them to her as she asked for them. The green ones were the largest, blue were medium and red the smallest. As she rolled each one I would hand her the clip, with the tip painted the corresponding colour. After they cooled and she'd combed and teased her hair, she would glue it together with her heavy-duty hairspray that came, in those environment-unfriendly days, in an aerosol can. The smell would linger in the upstairs hallway for hours after she left. She was often still finishing her hair or make-up when her date arrived, and I would entertain him while he waited. I'd get him a drink, then sit and make polite, grown-up (I thought) chit-chat. How this ritual started with my mother I don't know. Perhaps I was just at the right age.

I often went grocery shopping with her, too. We'd each take a cart, then I'd start at one end of the store and she'd start at the other. We'd meet in the middle and she'd check my choices. I always felt like such an adult doing that.

As I got older, I loved to surprise my mother with presents. When I was a teenager I came up with a plan to send her to Las Vegas. We got three of her friends to secretly plan to go with her. For the next year, all my babysitting and odd job money went into a bank account. My sisters all kicked in what they could, and we paid for her plane ticket, hotel for the three-night stay, ticket to see Frank Sinatra (her favourite) and provided $350 in traveller's cheques. We had it all set for her birthday.

As her birthday approached I could hardly sleep, I was so excited. I can still remember her face as she spread the tickets, pamphlets and traveller's cheques in a circle in front of her on the table, repeating "But I don't understand," with a look one would expect on the face of a winning lottery ticket holder checking the numbers a second time. I couldn't have enjoyed it more, even if I'd been going myself.

Another time, when I was sixteen and spending my first summer as a camp counsellor, I spotted a waterbed on sale. The owner of the store said he'd deliver it for free. Knowing my mother had a bad back, I bought it for her upcoming birthday, figuring I'd get my sisters to help pay for it later. It wasn't that my sisters weren't gung-ho for these endeavours — they absolutely were — but they tended to be my ideas and I usually paid more than one fifth. Of course, my younger sisters had little money of their own then.

My mother has had an unbelievably difficult life and she deserved everything any of us did for her and much, much more. In any case, all these things combined to put me in, perhaps, a slightly different place in my mother's affections.

That fact was not an issue before the shooting, but it became a huge one after I came home from the hospital and our family had to put itself together again. Through all that turmoil I felt smothered by my mother's overprotectiveness. The closer she tried to get, the more I held her at arm's length. The more she cared for me, the less I shared with her. Many times, when I'd be sitting at my regular spot at the kitchen table wallowing in self-pity, hating my life, she'd ask me if I was depressed.

"No, I'm just tired," I'd say, then pretend to be more animated so she wouldn't ask me again or suspect the truth. I'm sure I never fooled her.

Another thing that changed after I came home was that I became the family mediator. If there was an argument, I either settled it or repaired the damage afterward. I could make each person see the other's point of view. I was the voice of reason everyone listened to. I even became the go-between for my sisters and my mother. This was something new.

In my family there have been some rather long periods of time — some lasting years — during which two siblings did not speak to each other. In the longest, Chella and Lynn didn't speak for seven years; even they don't remember why. Except for the occasional loud argument, they completely ignored each other. After I was hurt, major conflicts among my sisters occurred, but for the most part, everyone got along with *me*. I'm sure this was directly related to the shooting and my disability — who's going to stay mad at her crippled sister? Perhaps I'm being overly cynical, but I know that was a factor.

I also became a crutch for my mother socially. While it was true I needed her help, I think she used that as an excuse not to socialize much herself. In some ways we became partners, or co-parents, co-dependants. We were co-owners of the house, so we made several decisions together that my other sisters had no part in.

In addition, I felt like a parent or figurehead in another way. When my mother's friends or older relatives came to visit, I felt obliged to sit with them. At times it was because I had nothing else to do, but more often it was because there was so little I could do without assistance of some kind. To go downstairs where the TV was would require help with the elevator, with a drink and the TV. Had I been able-bodied, I'd have been content flopping on my bed with a book sometimes. But then again, had I been able-bodied I probably wouldn't have been home.

Truth is, I didn't know what to do with myself at home. I was aimless and nothing made it better — except when I was out with friends. Nothing was the same. I wasn't interested in flicking through TV channels by myself. I'll happily sit beside someone else while they do it, but it's not an activity I enjoy alone. The fact is, I was used to being unbelievably active. The busier I was, the happier I was. In high school, I could barely fit my homework into my busy social schedule. The occasional free evening was precious and I would usually spend it on the phone catching up with friends from camp. I was probably the biggest social organizer among the camp alumni — the official reunions and many unofficial dinners and get-togethers were my specialty. About twice a year I'd find an evening to devote to myself, have a long bath, do a facial mask and read a good book. I was certainly never a TV junkie.

Suddenly that life was ripped away from me, and I was not adjusting well to it at all. I was used to doing *everything* for myself and suddenly I couldn't do *anything* for myself. I missed the girl who used to be me.

So when company came over, I had nothing better to do than visit. Plus, I felt an obligation because everyone was so interested in me and how I was doing. But I would sit there feeling resentful. There were times when I'd hear my sisters moving around in their rooms and I'd desperately want to be like them. Though I bitterly resented the situation, I didn't know what I could do about it.

And never far from the back of my mind were the words of the nurse: "People won't want to be around you if you aren't happy." I couldn't be angry, I couldn't show resentment.

But even worse than all that was one thought that was creeping into my head with increasing regularity:

You know why this happened. You're being punished. You had this coming.

Chapter Five:

THE TRIAL

About eighteen months after the shooting, the trial began. It was March 1985. There were 180 witnesses subpoenaed for what would ultimately be a four-month process.

Things took a dramatic turn just before the trial started when Sutcliffe Logan was charged with attempted murder. Sutcliffe Logan had been the only one of the four not facing this charge. He was not at the store during the shooting — that had been clear all along. He was at Heartbreaker's, a nightclub in Mississauga, where Hugh Logan and Warren Johnson met him later that night.

The Becker's crime was by no means this group's first foray into illegal activity. Far from it. It began when the group's karate instructor, Mike Shaw, moved into the Logan residence earlier that summer. He wanted to get guns, and brought the Logan brothers, Clive Brown, Warren Johnson and others into his plan. Shaw convinced them that local bikers had guns and were out to kill black men. One night, with Johnson creating a diversion by setting fire to a Bank of Montreal building, the guys broke into Shuriken Distributors Inc., a police-equipment supplier in Mississauga. Brown broke the door down, then the Logans broke the display cases with a sledge-hammer and stole thirteen handguns. One of them, a Colt .357 magnum, was used six weeks later to shoot me.

Once armed, the eight-member group began to argue among themselves. Shaw later claimed he wanted to make money through legal means, while Sutcliffe insisted on committing violent acts to get money. The group split up. Shaw and some of the others returned their guns to Sutcliffe, who then became the leader.

On September 16, a week before the shooting, Sutcliffe Logan and Warren Johnson tried unsuccessfully to rob a McDonald's restaurant manager. A few days later, the Logans and Johnson, wearing masks, robbed a Mac's Milk store. They ordered two employees to empty the till at gunpoint. The group, including Clive

Brown, also had grandiose business schemes. Sutcliffe Logan even saw a lawyer about incorporating an escort service, to be a front for a prostitution operation.

On the afternoon of September 23, the four men forcibly confined Farah Ali. Their next crime was the robbery and shooting at Becker's.

That their criminal activities are reprehensible is obvious, but their behaviour after the shooting was also astounding. While emergency personnel were working to save my life, Hugh Logan and Warren Johnson met up with Sutcliffe at Heartbreaker's. My oldest sister, Chella, was there with some friends, and one of them even pointed out the Logan brothers to her. Sutcliffe ordered champagne, telling the bartender they had something to celebrate. They each had $42 in bills from the robbery to spend. And they danced. At a second club, shortly after leaving Heartbreaker's, Hugh Logan went out onto the dance floor. Warren Johnson had requested Michael Jackson's "Billie Jean," and Hugh performed an impersonation of the pop star. Clive Brown, who had recognized me from school when he looked over the counter, complained of a headache and stayed at the Logan house. He went to bed with his headache and his conscience. He did not call 911.

Though Sutcliffe Logan was not at the Becker's store that night, police suspected that his involvement with the robbery and shooting ran deeper, so they sent undercover officers to the Metro West Detention Centre, where he was being held. He boasted to them about his role in the robbery. His exact words, in fact, were: "I set it up, I set the whole thing up." The Logans talked a lot about how much better things would have been for them had I died that night. The story would have faded, they said, taking the heat off them. The attempted murder charge against Sutcliffe Logan was largely based on the evidence of the undercover officers.

*   *   *   *

I first learned that a trial date had been set from a newspaper clipping, passed on to me from a friend's grandmother. Ironically enough, it was the first of several significant pieces of information about the trial that I would learn through the media. It was a little digest item, with the headline "March 4 trial for shooting clerk." Just a small blurb. I remember being quite surprised that I hadn't heard from anybody from the police or Crown Attorney's office about it first. I kept that clipping tacked to a corkboard by my computer for almost ten years — I don't know why. I still have the small, yellowed piece of paper.

Right after the shooting, Toronto lawyer Bruce Day had stepped forward and offered his services to me and my mother. He was extremely helpful as we waded through the paperwork and decoded the technicalities of Workers' Compensation and Criminal Injuries Compensation. And though victims aren't allowed their own legal representatives as part of a criminal case — victims are represented by the Crown — there were times when he acted as a liaison between me and the Crown's office. He billed us for only about half of the hours he worked.

I was a little bit nervous about the whole trial process, so Bruce arranged for me to see another trial first. I met him at a downtown courthouse and we sat in on a murder trial one day. We were the only spectators there. It was a little bit strange, but interesting, to see justice in progress. At a break, Bruce introduced me to the prosecutor. I remember him being a really pleasant person, funny and very friendly. A stereotypical "good guy." We chatted for a while, and as we were leaving he said, "Whatever you do, don't let the defence attorneys scare you."

That was my mindset as the trial approached: that the defence attorneys were going to try to discredit me, or scare me, or try to prove that I didn't know what I was talking about or that I couldn't possibly remember what I knew I remembered. My expectation was that the people I had to fear the most were the defence attorneys.

My first meeting with the prosecutors is unforgettable. My attendant was waiting outside, so it was just me and Bill Whitlock, the police detective in charge of the case, meeting with Leo McGuigan, the senior Crown, and Brian Trafford, second in command. At the time they were two of the best prosecutors in Ontario. Brian Trafford is now a judge, with a very solid reputation among both defence and prosecuting attorneys. Leo McGuigan, soon to retire, was content to remain a Crown and has turned down the opportunity to become a judge "two or three times" (that he admits to).

To start off our first meeting, one of them said, "We need to know exactly where you were standing behind the counter, so we're going to show you a picture of the store."

They opened up a huge photo album that was filled with pictures. One of them turned to a page and consulted with the others.

When they turned the book to me, I was shocked at what was in front of me. It was a full page of pictures taken behind the counter, all from slightly different angles but showing the same thing. They had moved me but not cleaned anything up, so there was a pool of my blood on the floor. There was a bloody smudge where my body had been lying, and then the large pool of blood beside it. The image was multiplied by six.

I was absolutely dumfounded. I couldn't believe they hadn't warned me. I still don't know how I should have reacted, or *if* I should have reacted, because I immediately clamped down on my emotions. By that point, eighteen months after the shooting, I had developed incredible control over myself. I calmly indicated where I had been standing, and the photo album was put away. In the seconds it took for the picture to register, the image burned into my brain to such an extent that the next time I saw it, a dozen years later doing research for this book, every detail was exactly as I remembered it.

The rest of the meeting was a blur. I held it together, but my mind and heart were racing and I felt sick. I couldn't understand why they would show me those pictures without a word of warning. Was it a test to see how I would hold up on the stand? I had no way of knowing what was in their minds. How anyone could be so insensitive as to show a victim pictures like that without a word of preparation was beyond me. Weren't they supposed to be on my side?

I left without saying anything about it to them, to my attendant or, later, to my family. There didn't seem much point in upsetting anyone else. I made it through the rest of the day and dinner, but I was just barely holding myself together. After dinner I went into my bedroom, where I had a phone I could use independently. I had my sister close the door behind me and I called my good friend Cathy. Fortunately she answered the phone right away and recognized my voice, because all I managed to squeak out was "Hi Cath," before collapsing in sobs. It was several moments before I could calm down and stop crying enough to tell her what had happened.

I was suddenly scared of the trial. I didn't know what to expect at all anymore. In the instant it took for the contents of those pictures to register, it suddenly looked as though it was all going to be much more difficult than I had anticipated. I wondered what tricks the defence attorneys would have up their sleeves if the Crown was pulling stunts like that. The thought of being cross-examined by the defence attorneys terrified me.

The next time I met with the prosecutors, my friend Cathy came with me. Nothing as upsetting happened, but it was nice having her there. She was someone I had been able to talk to about all that, so I didn't have to hold anything in.

I must stop here to say a word about the Crown attorneys. I hesitated to include the previous anecdote because I don't wish to paint them in a bad light. Though the episode with the pictures was extremely regrettable, to say the least, I chalk that up to being desensitized by a job that deals with crime every day. They treated me with tremendous respect and gave me much more attention than most victims get. They spent countless hours preparing for trial. I believe they cared deeply about the case and I don't think I'm wrong in saying they cared about me as a person as well.

The charge of attempted murder laid against Sutcliffe Logan was the second little gem I learned from the media, and it really shocked me. I turned on the six o'clock news one night and heard that he was charged with trying to kill me. Too bad no one had bothered to tell *me* that. Now, I don't know whose responsibility it would have been to call and tell me, and I do understand that everybody involved had an awful lot going on at that point, but I have always wondered why *somebody* didn't think to call. It was, after all, my life he was charged with trying to snuff out.

*   *   *   *

The trial started with two days of jury selection, marking the first time in Ontario history that a jury consultant was used. Such consultants, far more common in the United States, advise lawyers on how prospective jurors are likely to respond, based on background, occupation and the way they answer questions posed to them.

From jury selection and right through the Crown's case I got each day's highlights from the media. Because I was a witness, I was not permitted to attend court until I testified, and I was the second-last witness scheduled for the Crown. I certainly never expected my own daily briefings ahead of time, but I think a victim does have the right to hear major details firsthand, if they want to hear them. For example, I wish I'd been forewarned about some of the contents of the Crown's opening statement.

"The Crown said they will prove that Sutcliffe Logan set the robbery up, saying `Hugh should have killed the blood clot bitch,'" I heard a reporter say on the six o'clock news. Now, obviously, that "blood clot bitch" was me. Listening to it I felt the blood drain from my face. I couldn't believe anyone would say that about me, especially after what I had been living through. What had I ever done to them?

"Are you okay?" my attendant asked. She was leaving for the day but had stopped to catch the news.

"Oh sure," I said, swallowing hard.

I sat on my own after she left, waves of disbelief washing over me. There were two things I could not understand. First, why Logan would make such a comment. What on Earth did I ever do to deserve that? And second, why no one had warned me it was coming.

*   *   *   *

There were several voir dires held during the trial, some of them lasting several days. I was allowed to attend those. A voir dire is essentially a trial within a trial, without the jury present. The two sides argue points, such as whether certain evidence is admissible for the jury to hear. So there was one day when I was able to sit in the courtroom. There were no reporters, since voir dires cannot be reported on.

The courtroom was just about empty as the four accused walked in. I watched them closely, wanting them to look at me, afraid that they might.

81

None of them looked my way. They had been told that I was going to be there. They looked straight ahead and never turned around the whole time I was in there. I remember sitting staring at the backs of their heads.

What should I be feeling? I don't know, but feel SOMETHING, for Christ's sake. What's wrong with you? Where is your anger?

I felt completely dispassionate about the whole thing, about them. I didn't feel anger, I didn't feel fear. I didn't feel *anything*.

I've wondered more times than I can count why I have no great rage within me. When people close to me are mistreated or injured in some way, my anger is swift to rise and very intense, but for some reason, looking at the four young men who did this to me, I felt nothing.

The voir dire did provide an opportunity for me to meet the defence attorneys. Each of the four accused had his own counsel. Three of the lawyers were very nice men, and two of them are among the nicest men I have ever met. I spoke with both Brian Donnelly and Bill Gorewich a fair amount during the trial and met with them while researching this book. During the trial, I enjoyed kibitzing with them when there was a lull in the proceedings. Ken Danson, another defence lawyer, was also a very pleasant person, though I didn't interact with him as much.

I was happy to meet them because often defence attorneys are stereotyped as being somewhat sleazy. The three men I've named were anything but. They were doing their job, and I recognized that each accused was entitled to legal representation. It was refreshing for me to meet men of such integrity.

* * * *

Soon enough the day came for me to take the stand. I was hoping that the media wouldn't know ahead of time when I was going to testify, because I was afraid of the crush. I was hoping to sneak in unnoticed. Well, there was no chance of that happening. I testified on a Monday, and on the Friday before, I heard one of the reporters covering the trial say, "It is expected that Barbara will testify on Monday of next week."

So much for slipping quietly into the courthouse.

I had met again with the Crown attorneys and I had a copy of the questions I was going to be asked. We went over the questions and my answers. I was fully prepared.

In fact, my family had come up with an amusing plan for my day in court. Remember the prime-time TV soap "Dallas" and the huge "Who Shot J.R?" hype? My father's name is John Robert, and though he answers to Bob, he has always signed his name J.R. Turnbull. We joked about printing T-shirts to wear that day that would read "Who Shot J.R.'s Daughter?"

The day was bright and sunny. My mother and sisters were coming with me. My mother was a bundle of nerves that morning. She kept trying to get me to take a tranquillizer and I kept saying that I didn't need it. I'd never taken those things before and I wasn't about to start then. I wasn't worried about testifying, I wasn't even slightly nervous. By that time my initial terror had passed and I knew I was just there to tell the truth about what happened. It was also extremely important to me to testify without getting upset. So I convinced the others to take the tranquillizers and leave me alone.

We arrived at the courthouse in good time. The media were all in one huddle at the bottom of the building's ramp waiting for me, so we stopped a distance away so I could get out of the van without being filmed for the news.

As soon as the horde saw the van's hydraulic lift come down they all started racing toward me. I was just able to get off the ramp as they arrived. I guess Chella, who was pushing my chair, was a little stressed out about it, because she ended up pushing me so quickly that all the reporters and cameramen were forced to run backwards. I remember one falling into some bushes. They were all pushing each other, running backwards, trying to "capture the moment." This was the first time that the media really had a crack at "the famous victim." Looking back I feel a little silly about it, particularly since I'm now a member of that horde.

The courthouse building was wheelchair accessible, but the courtroom being used was not. It was the only room large enough to hold the trial, and unfortunately it had a flight of stairs. I had to sit in my manual wheelchair and be bumped down the stairs each time I went in.

I was in a small room that had been set aside for me, waiting to be called . A friend who was in the courtroom that day told me about the dramatic moment when it was announced, "The Crown calls Barbara Turnbull." There was a pause because they had to come and get me, and then we had to make our way across the entire building and down the stairs. So there was probably a good five minutes before I appeared. Apparently the "deafening silence" and anticipation was quite something.

I was pushed to the area immediately in front of the witness box. Obviously I could not stand or sit in the box. It was then that Brian Trafford motioned to my mother to stand in the box behind me. I remember feeling a flash of irritation because I didn't want it to be perceived that I needed my mother standing with me. I was an adult, not a scared child who needed her mommy. I love my mother, but I wanted to prove I could do it by myself. I guess they wanted her there for effect.

Leo McGuigan began asking me the prepared questions and I went through each answer with ease. He stuck pretty much to the script, beginning with a bit of my background, then quickly moving on to my duties at Becker's. He asked me about my sister Lynn's habit of keeping the door locked throughout late-evening hours.

"I called her and asked her what time she would lock the door, and she said whatever time I felt comfortable in doing that, around nine or ten or whatever. I didn't think to do it, I just forgot," I said.

He had me look at some police photos and identify several items behind the counter. We covered where I was standing and what I was doing, then what I saw when the door opened. After I described the events of the shooting, he demonstrated three ways a person with a gun might move his arm and shoot, and asked me which one best fit the motion I observed.

Then he threw in one question that hadn't been on the list: "From your observation, how would you describe that motion?"

I thought about it for a second. I needed one word that would describe what I saw Hugh Logan do on September 23. One word to describe the action that forever changed my life in the most devastating way imaginable. The word came to me fairly quickly: "Deliberate."

After we discussed the shooter's height and then what happened over the rest of the night, it was the defence's turn.

Hugh Logan's lawyer cross-examined me first. As he stood up, I thought to myself that I had to be on my guard. I wanted to be very careful with anything he had to ask me, because I knew if anyone was really going to try to challenge my testimony, it was going to be him. As prepared as I thought I was, his first question, a rhetorical one, caught me off guard.

"As I understand it, you were wearing moccasins that night?"

So that's where they went!

It made sense, since I hadn't seen my moccasins since the shooting, but I'd forgotten about them. I quickly agreed, as though I'd known for sure that's what I'd had on my feet.

He didn't catch me with anything else, although he tried. Under questioning about the clothes the robbers were wearing, I said that I hadn't noticed the clothes, I was taking in what was happening.

"And when you say that you were focusing more on what was happening, I take it you were obviously focusing, and if I can use the expression, perhaps almost being mesmerized by the movement of the arm and the gun?" he asked.

I could see him telling the jury that I, myself, admitted that I was *mesmerized* and therefore couldn't say for sure what happened.

"I wouldn't say mesmerized," I quickly replied. "He raised his arm and did what looked to me like deliberately shoot me."

I felt relieved and triumphant when he finished his questions.

Next to cross-examine me was Ken Danson, Sutcliffe Logan's lawyer. He basically asked me in several different ways about the height of the person who shot me. I kept reiterating that the person who shot me was approximately my height, five foot, ten. The reason for his emphasis on this point became evident later when his client, Sutcliffe Logan, would be accused by his brother Hugh of pulling the trigger.

Hugh Logan pulled the trigger. There was really no doubt about that. He'd admitted it in more than one statement to the police, and the rest of the guys told the same story. But Hugh would later recant on the stand, in an attempt to confuse the jury and cast enough doubt in their minds to find him not guilty.

All told, I was an excellent witness. I don't often boast — in fact, I am usually my own harshest critic — but I know I could not have improved my testimony at all.

I do have one regret about my day in court. I never looked at the four people who did this to me. I never even glanced in the direction of the prisoners' box. I don't know if any of them would have met my gaze, but I wish I'd tried.

*   *   *   *

It was interesting to watch the various newscasts that night and look at the newspapers' accounts the next day. One of the television reporters actually stated, factually, that I had testified without showing emotion. But the next day *The Toronto Sun* ran the headline "Barbara testifies in tears." It still astounds me when I think of it. It was so unfair. There had not been a hint of emotion in my voice, nor was there a hint of a tear in my eye at any time. I was outraged at *The Sun* for what they had done. When I saw people in the days that followed, it was pretty obvious which paper they had read, because some people looked at me with such *pity* in their eyes, no doubt picturing me reduced to tears on the stand. Considering that just the opposite was true, I would have liked to see the reporter, Zen Ruryk, flogged.

I was told that the guy was given quite a hard time by his colleagues for his blatant misreporting. He approached me the next time I was in court and apologized. He asked if I wanted a retraction printed, which struck me as pretty stupid:

Barbara did not actually blubber on the stand the other day. The Sun *regrets the error*.

I told him not to bother, but I couldn't look at him, I was so angry.

Soon after I testified, the defence opened its case.

*   *   *   *

As soon as Hugh Logan got on the stand, he accused his brother of shooting me, just as Sutcliffe Logan's lawyer suspected he might. At the time I was in England with my mother. I wish I had been there to see him deny it. Despite the overwhelming evidence, including several witnesses who testified that they saw Sutcliffe at the nightclub during the time of the robbery and the fact that Sutcliffe was at least five inches shorter, Hugh Logan calmly stood day after day, steadfastly denying his crime and pinning the blame on his brother. He claimed he wasn't even in the store but outside, standing by the car.

What was even more preposterous was his concoction of a bizarre, elaborate story in which he claimed that he had lived in mortal fear of his brother throughout that whole summer of 1983. He testified that "Cliff" had forced him, among other things, to admit to the shooting, and that he said he would "take care of everything." Hugh said he had agreed to take the fall almost to the minute he got into the witness box.

Hugh Logan's responses to the questions posed by Sutcliffe's lawyer, Ken Danson, revealed exactly how cold and calculating this nineteen-year-old was — and how easily he lied under oath.

"After the Becker's shooting you say that you went to another club after Heartbreaker's closed for the night, and you danced, right?" Danson asked.

"Yes I did. But that I did out of request from Cliff."

"You weren't forced to?"

"No, no. He did not, say `Get up there or I'll kill you.' No, he did not. He asked me to dance and I went and danced. To tell you the truth, a lot of my own feelings were involved in my dancing."

"Don't you think, upon reflection, that Clive Brown had the more appropriate response? He just didn't feel like going out to party that night because a young girl had been shot."

"I wasn't asked, I was told to come back up to Heartbreaker's. Cliff, at the time, wanted to talk to me in more detail about what happened."

"Did you think it a little bit unseemly to dance to Michael Jackson, at your brother's request, at a club in the early morning hours of September 24, after Barbara Turnbull was shot? That was therapy, right? That was good therapy?"

"It was, you see, my dancing is something they requested of me many times, to dance at Heartbreaker's."

"You didn't have to, did you?"

"No. I guess I could have, maybe I could have told him I didn't feel like dancing, maybe I could have. I had already told him that I would."

"Would you concede, I know you're not conceding very much, but would you concede that it was a bit of bad taste to dance to Michael Jackson that night?"

"Depends on how you look at it. Is it in bad taste to sing Gospel music when you're down? It depends on how you look at it, sir. You cannot call dancing bad taste. There are different types of dance."

"Well, Gospel music, as I understand it, is in the context of religious prayer. You're not suggesting that dancing to Michael Jackson that night was comparable to going to church?"

"No. I'm just asking you if that is what you're saying. How could it be in bad taste? That's what I'd like to know."

"When was the last time you shot a nineteen-year-old [*sic*] girl?"

"I didn't. I did not shoot anyone, Mr. Danson."

At one point, with Hugh Logan insisting he had not pulled the trigger and that his heart "ached" when he saw me in the courtroom, Warren Johnson suddenly sprang up in the prisoners' box and started screaming.

"Let your heart ache now because you know you shot her."

"All right," the judge said, trying to impose order.

"I can't take this farce any longer. I cannot, I cannot take this farce any longer. I cannot take it." Then Johnson sat down and started crying.

The outburst was unquestionably genuine and spontaneous. Unfortunately, I missed it all; I got home just in time to see Warren Johnson testify. That's when I heard the one piece of information that had a bigger impact on me than anything else. Johnson testified that as they were about to enter the store, Hugh cocked the gun.

He cocked the gun.

Any doubt I might have had about Hugh Logan's intent to shoot me vanished with those words.

At one point, while Warren Johnson was up on the stand during a pause in the proceedings, I caught his eye and gave him a half-smile. Looking confused, he turned and glanced at the judge, sure that I must have meant it for anyone but him. Why on Earth would I smile at a guy who walked out of the store while I lay bleeding on the floor, then went to a club, not even calling anonymously for help? But for some stupid reason, I felt some sympathy for him.

From the beginning I had the feeling that he truly felt remorse about what happened to me. It's a combination of things that made me feel that way: he was the only one who didn't have a stable family background; he was the only one to turn himself in; he told the truth on the stand; and, in particular, there was his reaction to Hugh Logan's testimony. It was mainly a gut feeling. Bill Whitlock, the detective in charge of the case, agrees with me, calling him "the best of the bunch."

*   *   *   *

There was more dramatic and emotional testimony to come. Ken Danson, Sutcliffe Logan's lawyer, called the Logans' mother, Jenny, to the stand. She had testified earlier, but he subpoenaed her a second time. This time she recounted what happened after Hugh's testimony, claiming that his brother had forced him to take the fall. Hugh's testimony was, as one would expect, extremely upsetting for her.

In her testimony, Mrs. Logan recounted a conversation she had had with Hugh after he testified that his brother was the shooter: "I said to Hugh, `I'm going through hell. I know that somebody could be listening in. I know that what we say could be taken out of context. I do not expect you to answer me straight yes or no, but I am begging you, please indicate to me if you're telling the truth `cause I have to know, I'm going to die. Cliff asks one thing of you, if you could please tell the people who he loves the truth. I think I'm one of those people, and I'm asking you, please, tell me the truth. I want you to indicate to me by nodding if it's a yes, or by shaking your head if it's a no.' I says to him, `Is what you're saying in court the truth?' and Hugh did that, indicating a no."

*   *   *   *

After the four defence attorneys finished, all that remained were the closing remarks and the judge's instructions to the jury. Of the closing remarks I vividly remember only those made by Leo McGuigan for the Crown. Leo's remarks were so eloquent and impassioned that I honestly felt like standing and applauding when he finished — and I say that not just as the victim, but also as an admiring spectator.

While the jury was deliberating, I was hanging out in front of the courthouse with Chella and my attendant. It was almost bizarre to be mingling with the media, waiting in the warm summer sun as though nothing particularly important was going on.

I was waiting for the verdicts in a case that had affected my life in every possible way, changing it irrevocably for the worst, but I felt very removed from it all, as though I were watching from the sidelines. Part of me realized that this trial really had nothing to do with my life, that it was going to change nothing for me. But a bigger part of me was expecting *something* at the end of it. A sense of closure, perhaps? Acceptance? Understanding?

That part was going to be disappointed.

When the jury was ready, we were called in. The air was electric with anticipation. This was the most dramatic moment for me; there had been a total of thirty-three charges and the jury foreman had to answer each one individually.

The court clerk read out the charges that applied to each accused, starting with Sutcliffe Logan. "How do you find him on count number one?"

"Guilty."

"Count number four?"

"Guilty."

"Count number five?"

"Guilty."

"Count number six?"

"Guilty"

And on it went. This was repeated for each of the accused, one after another.

"On Hugh Logan, count number one?"

"Guilty."

"Count number five?"

"Guilty."'

"Count number six?"

"Guilty."

"Count number seven?"

"Guilty."

"Count number eight?"

"Guilty."

When they got to Clive Brown, the dramatic momentum was broken. As the clerk asked, "On Clive Brown, count number one?" the jury foreman stumbled a moment.

"Pardon me. On the attempt murder, which number is that please?" It was obvious that they had found Clive Brown not guilty of attempted murder. Unfortunately, that stumble took some of the tension out of the moment, but I sure felt sorry for the foreman with all that pressure.

Of the thirty-three verdicts, for each of the four suspects, that was the only one that came in as "Not guilty."

While the verdicts were being read, some of the reporters leaned forward and looked at my face to see my reaction. I made damn sure that I had no expression on my face whatsoever. I didn't want my feelings being interpreted and reported.

What my reaction actually was is a good question. I was most happy for the Crown attorneys and the police. They had worked so hard and I felt that the verdicts were warranted and justified the effort they had put into it. I was glad that Hugh and Sutcliffe Logan's game of accusing each other hadn't worked. Instead of acquitting them both, the jury found both guilty of attempted murder. But truth be told, I felt nothing with the convictions. I didn't feel elated. I didn't feel victorious. I really didn't feel anything. Of course I would have been upset had they been found not guilty, but there was little chance of that happening.

*   *   *   *

Sentencing was held a month later. Obviously the Crown's job was to get the lengthiest sentences they could get, and going into the details of my shooting and the effects of my paralysis was a large part of that. Back then, victim impact statements were not a standard part of sentencing, as they are now. Now they are filled out in writing by the victim and usually read in part into the record by the Crown. Occasionally, victims will read excerpts themselves. Since the statements were virtually non-existent at that point, the Crown had to decide who they were going to put up on the stand to show how the crime had affected my life. Obviously, I was the first person they considered, so I was called in to meet with Brian Trafford.

At that point I was so hell bent on showing how well I was coping, and minimizing the impact as much as possible, that I probably would have been a better witness for the defence. Every question Brian asked me I answered as only a true Pollyanna would:

"Really, it's not so bad."

Brian must have been so frustrated with me. At one point during our conversation, he suddenly burst out with "Good God! What do you think about these guys?"

My answer?

"I don't know. I feel a bit sorry for Warren Johnson."

This must have driven Brian crazy. Here I was insisting "I'm just fine," instead of being honest and saying what was in my heart, talking about the difficulties and the loneliness and how badly I ached for my life back.

Why didn't I tell him how much I had loved to dance? I should have admitted how often I closed my eyes and went back to the big dining hall at my summer camp, with the tables and chairs pushed back, and danced with total abandon. Or how hard it was some days not to cry my eyes out when my attendant couldn't fix my hair properly and I had plans that night. Or how sick I was of drinking through a straw and how much I missed wrapping my hands around a hot mug of tea in the morning, blowing gently into it and feeling the steam on my face. Or how I couldn't get used to people wiping my face. And how it tore at my gut to watch my younger sister run out of the house and jump into her boyfriend's truck.

At the time I was just not capable of expressing any of that. I was still denying it to everyone but myself, so I certainly could not have spilled my guts to a man I hardly knew, and especially not to a courtroom full of reporters.

At the same time, part of me felt that I should have been put on the stand. I was just not thinking rationally. The whole meeting was uncomfortable. I kept stressing that I was upset that I would never have children. I made that a major point, when in reality it wasn't one of the major things affecting me then. But that was one thing that I felt I could express, even though it wasn't accurate — in fact probably *because* it wasn't accurate.

The one thing that bothered me about the Crown's handling of the sentencing was that they kept me guessing until the very end about whether they would put me on the stand. They kept saying they hadn't decided, which might well have been true, but I wish they had made me a part of their decision-making process. Finally, on the afternoon of sentencing, they came to me at ten minutes before the proceedings were to start, in the room that had been reserved for me for the duration of the trial.

"You're welcome to come and watch if you want to." Then they turned and walked out. I sat feeling deflated and very upset.

I had anticipated going on the stand again. I shouldn't have expected it, but I did. Instead, I went in and I watched others testify for me. I watched Janet, my occupational therapist, answering all the questions. One of the defence attorneys tried to demonstrate that there was a lot I could still do, including attending university.

To everything Janet answered, "Not without a great deal of difficulty." I thought she did an excellent job.

Unfortunately for my lawyer, Bruce Day, he was also called onto the stand to testify for me, mainly to talk about my finances. Bruce and I had never spoken about what was important to me and he was forced to make some assumptions, based on his observations about how my life had changed. I was very upset watching him because he wasn't hitting what was important to me — never mind that I'd never told him or anyone else what that was. He said that many quads succumb to depression, alcoholism, drug abuse and suicide, which made me feel ashamed, and angry, because I knew those would never be a factor in my life. He talked about how I couldn't get a bottle of milk out of the fridge if I was at home on my own, or scratch an itch. They weren't particularly significant details to me, but he had no way of knowing that. In hindsight, poor Bruce probably could not have given testimony that pleased me no matter what he said.

I was unhappy with the whole situation. I was completely closed off, not telling anybody what life was really like, not revealing the truth to anyone and expecting them all to just *get* it. Yet, had anybody really nailed it, I know I would have been very embarrassed. I couldn't have the truth aired at that point in my recovery. It was a no-win situation for everybody.

*   *   *   *

Clive Brown got nine years; Warren Johnson, eleven; Sutcliffe Logan, thirteen; and Hugh Logan, the shooter, twenty years. Hugh had a very carefully folded napkin that he dabbed his eyes with. I remember how fake it looked, dabbing under his eyes with this perfect square of tissue, as though he really cared. It didn't fool me for a moment. I resisted the urge to snicker or shake my head in disgust; I didn't want my reaction noted by any reporters.

*   *   *   *

Years later, I did have the opportunity to submit a victim impact statement, during the appeals. In 1988, Warren Johnson and Sutcliffe Logan had their convictions for attempted murder reduced to armed robbery; Hugh Logan made a similar appeal but was unsuccessful. Johnson and Logan also appealed their sentences, and at that point the Crown submitted my statement. I was pretty sure that the judge would not reduce the sentences, and I knew that the victim impact statement was not going to change things one way or the other, but by then I was able to be considerably more honest and thorough. First, this was written, so I didn't have to speak about it in a courtroom. And second, I knew there was going to be less media attention, which also helped.

I wrote two statements. I was hoping that the Crown attorneys would be able to have my statement closed to the media, so it would be read by the judge only. I wrote one that was remarkably frank, and then I watered it down, in case it was going to be on the public record. The watered-down version became my official statement.

The reason I wrote such an honest statement was really for the Crown attorneys themselves. I felt I had been unfair to them over the years after the trial. In subsequent interviews on the subject of victims of crime, I had stated several times that I considered it unfair that I had been unable to testify at sentencing or submit a victim impact statement. I held the Crown attorneys accountable for that. As I thought about it years later, I realized that I had made it virtually impossible for them to put me on the stand — it would have hurt their case more than helped it. So my statement was, in my own way, an apology or explanation to them. I don't think the statement made everything right, and I have no idea what they thought of it, but it helped my conscience a bit.

The sentences remained unchanged. The Crown appealed to the Supreme Court of Canada, which upheld the Ontario Court of Appeal decision.

The case had powerful constitutional implications with respect to individuals who are a party to a crime of murder or attempted murder. It is now studied in criminal law classes and frequently cited in courtrooms across the country.

*   *   *   *

I made no comment to the media at any point during the trial. I was glad to keep silent, because the question they first asked would inevitably be the question I didn't want to answer:

"How do you *feel* about the verdicts?"

My comments were reserved for after sentencing.

I kept it quite brief. I thanked the Crown attorneys and the police for their efforts. I thanked the jury and said I was satisfied with their verdicts. I thanked the defence attorneys for their courtesy.

I made one comment at the end of the statement for the media.

"For the most part it was nice to pass the time with you. It's just unfortunate that some of you were always looking for a story."

That was a comment I regretted somewhat, because, for the most part, they were really a good group of people. The comment was in fact meant for one particular reporter, who bothered me throughout the trial. She always seemed to ask stupid questions.

"So, do you hope to put all this behind you when it's over?" she asked one day.

Of course I answered "Yes," but I joked with my family later that I should have answered, "No, I'm going to let it haunt me for the rest of my life."

Funny thing was, for about a year I felt as though the trial really was haunting me. It was on my mind all the time.

It mostly came to me at night as I lay alone in the dark. I'd replay scenes over and over in my head, sometimes as they happened, other times as I wished they had happened. Often I was more assertive in my mind, unless the other players followed a script as I would have written it.

I wished I had stood up for myself and said, "Excuse me, that isn't right," a couple of times. I felt I should have complained right at the beginning when I had to find out through the media that the trial date had been set. I wished I had told them how upsetting it was to see that crime scene picture without warning, how the image was burned into my brain and how often it flashed before me. I wanted to tell them that they should have been frank with me about their decisions regarding sentencing; perhaps I could have chosen the people to put on the stand in my place.

I was angry at the system, angry at the Crown, angry at the police. But I still wasn't angry at the four individuals who caused it all.

What's wrong with me?

I was able to let it go a little bit after I started writing a university paper on victims and the justice system. I never finished the essay — I switched the subject to capital punishment — but it helped me get my thoughts down on paper and out of my head. Mostly, it enabled me to articulate my feelings in subsequent media interviews on the subject.

I realize now that a lot of the frustration was a factor of having gone through the system for the first time, and looking back on it with the clarity of hindsight. Victims are so out of their element, we don't know where we can stand up and scream for our rights. We don't even know what rights we have, few as they are. And I have to keep reminding myself that I was treated far better than most victims are.

That's why it's even more important for there to be someone telling victims about their rights, telling them what's going on when nobody else has time. When the police and Crown have so many other duties, it's not all that surprising that keeping the victim informed is not the highest priority. It's not an intention, it's just what happens. There is nobody whose sole responsibility it is to keep the victims informed of proceedings as they happen, and as a result I just got lost in the shuffle a few times. I don't blame any specific people, I blame the system for not having some sort of a liaison set up among the Crown, the police and the victim at that time.

Happily, that is changing. There are victim coordinators now in a few jurisdictions in Ontario, with plans to create more throughout the province. They work closely with the police and the Crown; in fact, they share offices with the Crown in some places.

Perhaps my biggest complaint about the justice system is the fact that victims are treated primarily as witnesses and are therefore unable to attend any part of a trial until they have testified. What bothers me is that the accused sits through all the witnesses and there's no question about whether that might taint his testimony. I understand that it is *his* trial, but I also see it as the victim's trial, in a sense.

It was my trial too. Why did I have to see so much of it through the eyes of the media?

Chapter Six:

PALM TREES AND PARADISE

I remember giving my younger sister Christine some advice when she was trying to decide which university to go to.

"You've got to go away to school," I told her. "Everyone should go away for university. It's important."

Yeah right. That applies to everyone but you.

I'd started classes at a local campus of the University of Toronto a year after leaving the hospital, right after the trial ended, but mine was nothing even remotely close to a "normal" or average university experience. I went to one class a day, with an attendant in tow to take notes, then went straight home. I didn't meet more than a couple of people in most of my classes. There were no school clubs or activities, no pub nights for me. It's not that I was barred from such activities, I just made no attempt to participate. I saw only difficulties and used them as excuses not to do anything. I was far too shy and uncomfortable around my disability. I didn't look for the similarities between myself and other students — I only saw what was different, and I let the differences overwhelm me.

I was taking general courses, plus ones that interested me, mostly English, which had always been my best subject. Taking only two courses during the winter and one during a summer session, it would have taken me a decade to get a basic degree — not that I knew what I wanted to do with one. But at least I had some schoolwork to occupy some of my mind and time. I still had no idea what I was going to do with the rest of my life, but I had papers to write, so I didn't have to think about that.

Then, on a cold, rainy night in March 1987, my life took a U-turn.

"I think you should go to Arizona State University in Tempe," said my good friend Bob, out of nowhere.

"And why should I do that?" I replied, laughing at the suggestion.

"It's warm all year round, you can get away from Toronto and living at home, and the Sun Devils just won the Rose Bowl," he replied. A big college football fan, Bob is.

I was incredibly unhappy. I hadn't told anyone, but I was just going through the motions of living my life. So, as extreme as the suggestion of going to Arizona sounded, part of me immediately embraced it.

"What would I do about attendants?" I asked.

"Get some down there. I don't know, you work it out."

Foreign student fees are heavy, but I knew the Workers' Compensation Board would cover tuition and books, as well as my attendant needs.

I hardly slept that night, I was so excited. I envisioned myself at parties, going from one class to another with friends, sitting in glorious, warm sunshine. The Arizona climate made sense for me on many levels. I had been rear-ended while in my van one day the previous year and had been living with near-constant neck pain since. The pain was always worse in cold, damp weather. And without snow and winter wear to contend with, I could take a much fuller course load and do it independently.

The next day I called a friend whose parents wintered in Arizona. Not only did she think it was a great idea, but, coincidentally, she was taking her kids down the next week for March Break. And her parents' place was close to the campus. She said she'd stop in and check things out.

I thought of little else while she was gone. In my mind, I was there already. The fact that it was over two thousand miles away, I had never been before, didn't know a soul there and was totally, physically dependent on people didn't even enter into my equation.

When she returned, she was armed with an application, a course catalogue and a whole lot of enthusiasm. She had spent an hour at the school's Disabled Student Resources centre, talking to the coordinator for mobility-impaired students. The whole campus was very accessible — there were even dorms with wheel-in showers. That was it, I was sold.

Though nearly everyone I told thought it was a good idea, one friend kept urging me to research other schools. She thought there might be one that was even better for disabled students. She'd heard about a university in Ohio that had attendant services already set up for students who needed it. But I wasn't going to consider any other place. This felt right.

One day I brought the course catalogue to school and showed it to my friend Alexandra, hoping that she might be tempted to join me. I was still sitting on the application, and I hadn't chosen a degree or department to focus on. I just knew I was going.

In starting university, I had discussed my plans with my case worker at the Workers' Compensation Board. His words to me, spoken one sunny afternoon while we were meeting outside on my patio, were very memorable:

"You really only have two choices. You can plan on a career in counselling, or working for the government — probably working for the government."

Neither area interested me in the slightest. After he left that day I sat and fumed. "There must be something else I can do," I kept repeating to myself. Then it came to me: radio! All you need is a voice, I figured. And hell, I had lots of media contacts, surely I could get a job doing that. But I didn't really know how to go about it, so I had been aimlessly letting time pass.

"Hey look at this," Alexandra said. "This is what you should do." She showed me the department she was looking at in the book: The Walter Cronkite School of Journalism and Telecommunications.

"Right," I said, without the slightest hesitation. "That's what I'll do."

It was all serendipity.

Everything moved quickly after I got accepted a few weeks later. Classes started in the third week of August. I planned to leave Toronto at the end of July, spend a week in Vancouver, then have two weeks in Arizona before school started. I advertised for someone who had four to six weeks free to train as my attendant, then come down and train people I would hire down there. There were only two applicants, and my choice was easy. Liz had finished an undergrad degree in something she wasn't using, had sold real estate for a year, hating it, and there was nothing tying her to Toronto. She was perfect.

The next few weeks flew by. I had a couple of going-away parties, and there was a blast of media coverage about what I was doing. Friends were going to drive my van with my computer down for me, then fly back. Everything was falling into place perfectly, except for one tiny detail: I had absolutely no idea what I was about to do. I was living on automatic pilot.

My sisters were excited for me, but my mother was starting to feel separation anxiety long before I left. I'd become a social crutch for her. She didn't have to have a life outside of work because there was always a reason for her to be at home: me. One day she expressed her feelings to me.

"What am I going to do when you're gone?" she said. "You're always here when I come home. I don't want to come home to an empty house."

"So get a dog," I replied. I had no sympathy for her. Desperate is the only word for my state of mind at that time. Today, the thought of moving to another city is completely unfathomable to me, but my unhappiness then made it easy to make a split-second decision to do it. Someone had thrown me a life ring and there was no way I was going to let go of it. Even in the worst-case scenario, I knew I couldn't be more miserable than I already was.

One curious thing happened about a week before I left. I developed a couple of large, painful canker sores in my mouth. It struck me that I often got those when I travelled. "Must be stress," I thought to myself, though I didn't think I was stressed. The whole move seemed a bit of a lark for me.

The day I left was chaotic. I was taking three wheelchairs: my electric chair, a manual one and a shower chair. I had a ton packed, since I wouldn't be home again until Christmas. It seemed as though there were a hundred extra things to find room for in my luggage. Friends had given me lots of going-away presents. My favourite was one my local MPP, Margaret Marland, left between our doors, with a note wishing me luck — a Canadian flag.

As we arrived at the airport, my mother, walking behind me, leaned down and croaked, "Bye," then turned around and ran out of the terminal before I could say anything or turn to face her. I was hit with guilt.

How could you leave her? She needs you.

I felt worse about the glib and casual way I'd been talking about leaving, and I felt terrible the entire flight to Vancouver. As soon as we checked into our hotel, I called her, ready to apologize.

"Don't be silly," she assured me. "I'm fine." She was lying, but I did feel better.

The next day, a Saturday, Liz and I were shown the city's sights by my mother's sister and her husband, who live there. It was a busy day that passed swiftly. It was only the following afternoon that the enormity of what I had done hit me. Liz and I were driving around in a van I'd rented and some sappy song I can't even recall came on the radio. Suddenly it all sank in. I wasn't sure if I'd faint or throw up — or both. I felt positively ill.

I met someone just before I left who had done a similar thing. "The first day I woke up there I thought, `What have I done?'" she'd said.

"Oh, I'm sure it'll happen the same way for me," I blithely replied.

But I was not prepared at all for such a panic attack.

My god, I've got to go back home. How can I make that happen?

I frantically tried to figure out a way to go back to Toronto.

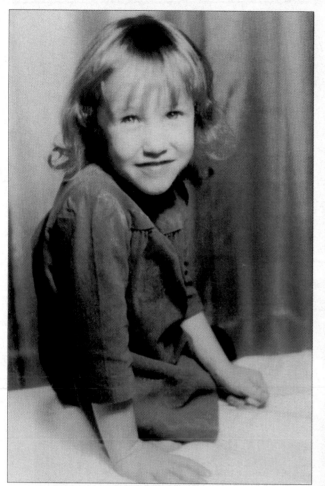

From top left, clockwise: What kid isn't cute? Me at 4. At 7, with Alison, my youngest sister. My parents did what good, Catholic couples were supposed to do and produced five kids. Starting at back left, Lynn, me, Chella, Alison, Christine.

Right: The proud parents with the brood, at my father's company Christmas party, me, Lynn, Christine, Alison, Chella. Below left: Us five in front of the tiny house in Montreal we quickly outgrew.

Above right: My grade two school picture – my teeth were almost too big for my head. Right: Me at 7, shortly after we moved from Montreal to Mississauga, Ontario.

Left: With my parents at my grade eight graduation, where I was valedictorian – a hint of things to come!

Above: At a family reunion in 1980. Chella, my mom, Alison, me, Lynn, Christine.
Left: Me at 16, at camp during the summer of 1981, the best summer of my life

Is this the face of pure happiness, or what? My first full summer at camp in 1981.

Yes, that's me, caught with a beer in one hand and a cigarette in the other at a party. I was your average teenager in most respects.

Above left: My photo, released to the media after the shooting. Above right: September 23, 1983. Where one life ends, and another, far more difficult one begins. Right: Christmas, 1983, in traction in the hospital with my mom.

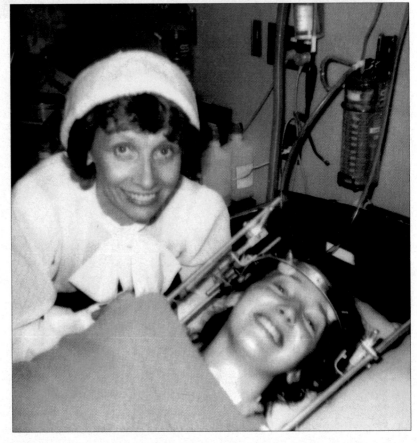

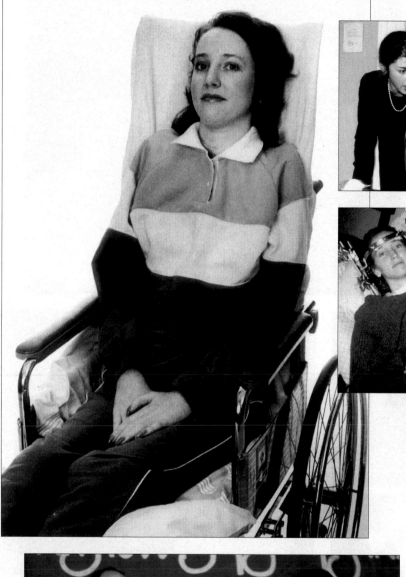

Left: At Sunnybrook, just before going back to rehab after needing extra surgery.
Above right: With my friend Annette, at a fundraiser for Sunnybrook Hospital.
Below: My first time home for one day, Christmas Eve, 1983.

Left: My high school principal, Jack Zarn, presenting my mother and sister Christine with a cheque for $25,000, raised by the students.
Wish I could have been there!

Right: Receiving my first "Good Crip" award, from Toronto Mayor Art Eggleton and Father Sean O'Sullivan. Below left: Another award, presented by former Governor General Roland Michener.

Above: With Betty Fox, mother of runner Terry Fox. Right: Me with Dr. Charles Tator – the man who put me back together after the shooting and one of my heroes.

Left: In London at Canada House during NHL annual meetings in 1985. From left, The Honourable Roy McMurtry, Alan Eagleson, Rod Langway, my mom, me, Darryl Sittler, Lanny McDonald.

Below: At a gala fundraiser with my good friend, Dini Petty.

Top right: With my friend, comedian Kelly McDonald at Yuk Yuks comedy club, soon after my discharge home. You can see how much weight I needed to put on! Below: With Dini and another friend, Lise, at another gala event.

Right: With Liz, my friend who helped me change my life, on our first spring break at Arizona State University. Far right: Us with a school friend.

Left: Home on summer break in 1990. Liz and I on her wedding day. Liz had graduated, but I still had another semester of school left to finish.

Below: At the Grand Canyon. Anyone in need of a humbling experience should go and look out at this sight for awhile.

On the set of the TV docudrama "Scales of Justice." Top: With director David Cronenberg. You can see the camera on the dolly attached to my chair. Middle: Me, the "serious actress" listening intently to Cronenberg – a great director and a prince of a man. Bottom: Clowning around on the set. David Cronenberg and the four "attackers" (actors) wearing wigs. Weren't hairstyles awful in the eighties?

Top: Graduation day, finally! Me, with Arizona Governor Rose Mofford (after my speech, when I could relax).

Left: The first family wedding, in 1992. From back left: My dad, Lynn, Christine, Alison, my mom, Chella and me.

Right: In Sedona, Arizona, at the Boynton Canyon vortex.

Top: The busy
reporter. At my
desk at
The Toronto Star,
Canada's largest
daily newspaper.

Below: On the job,
interviewing Rick
Hansen, Canada's
Man in Motion.

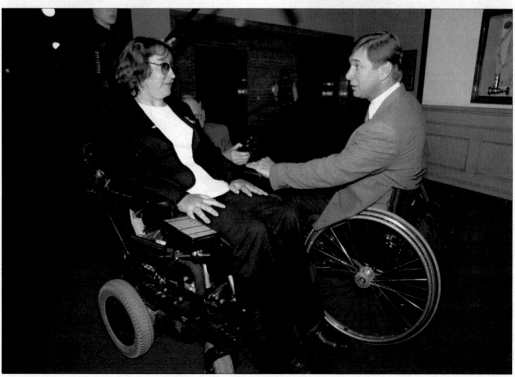

*With Rocky, my
trusty sidekick, who
sat on my shoulder
and "talked" me
through the writing
of this book.*

I'll have to go into hiding. All that media, those going-away parties. They'd all know I failed.

The fear that people would think me a failure is the only reason I didn't come immediately back home with my tail between my legs.

We flew into Phoenix the first week of August. "This is my kind of place," I thought, as the plane descended at midnight and the pilot announced it was 100 degrees Fahrenheit.

We were staying in a motel near campus until the dorms opened up a week later. Our first morning we got up and, after breakfast, decided to drive over to the campus and look around. As we got outside, we were hit with a heat unlike any we'd ever known. It was like bending over an extremely hot oven, or near the engine of a car that's been running for hours. It's the kind of heat you need to turn your face away from to breathe, except down there in summer there's nowhere to turn for cooler air.

The campus was deserted. Thankfully no one saw us as we gleefully took a picture of the first cactus we saw. We laughed at ourselves as soon as we turned the corner and saw that there were dozens more! Palm trees waved lazily in the hot breeze and I felt my first jolt of excitement. I could hardly believe I was there!

We quickly learned the first rule of summer desert living: don't leave home without water. Within minutes we were completely parched and dashing from shady patch to shady patch looking for any open store or kiosk. We stupidly had no American money, so we high-tailed it back to the motel.

Over the next week a pattern developed. I'd feel really hungry, order something from a menu, then start talking out loud. "What am I doing here? I must have lost my mind. I can't stay here by myself. Oh my god, what have I done?" By the time the food arrived, I'd have talked myself right out of any kind of appetite. Weight was quickly dropping off. Liz, who at that point hardly knew me, thought I was certifiably nuts.

Not that there was much I could eat anyway. By this time I had canker sores all over my mouth and all along my gums. Anyone who's had these knows how unbelievably painful they are. As soon as one disappeared, another replaced it. They continued, in fact, for my entire first year in Arizona. As well, my menstrual cycle stopped for the first semester, another sure sign of stress. It was incredible how much went wrong, mainly with things I'd forgotten to bring or do before leaving. I spoke to my mother almost daily for one reason or another for three weeks.

When the dorms opened, the first major glitch occurred. The room I'd been assigned was not accessible. Silly me, I'd thought filling out the form saying that I used an electric wheelchair and had a high spinal cord injury was enough information! It wasn't. So for the first few days I had to share a room with another disabled student, while Liz slept in an adjoining room. No one was thrilled with the arrangement. When a room did come up, it was in Mariposa, the graduate dorm, slightly off campus. But the fiasco turned out to be a blessing, because the graduate dorm was much more suitable for me. At twenty-two, I was the same age as the grad students anyway.

Mariposa was a motel that the university had purchased and converted. It was like a square doughnut: two sides had two levels, where the rooms were located; the office and front desk, a common TV lounge and a sitting area were in a squat building at the front; and a cafeteria ran along the back. In the middle was a pool. Our room was small, with its own washroom, shower and separate sink area.

The next hurdle was school itself. Right away, I made an appointment with an academic adviser in the Broadcast/ Journalism department.

"I'm here for broadcasting," I told her. There was a long pause.

"You don't have real good use of your hands, do ya honey?" she asked, with a southern drawl.

"Uh, no."

"I'm sorry, but I don't think you'd be able to keep up with the deadlines," she said.

"Fine, I'll do journalism," I said quickly.

"Mmm, same thing, honey. There are so many deadlines in these programs. I really don't think this is the department for someone like you," she said. "Let me just go see if the dean is here."

She got up and walked out, leaving me in her little office. I sat looking at the posters on her walls, the plant on her desk, the filing cabinet in the corner.

This can't be happening. Good lord, it cost me a thousand dollars just to get my van down here. Okay, I've just got to talk my way in. Journalism. That makes so much more sense than broadcasting, anyway. I've always liked writing. I love English. Okay, just wait for her to come back ...

When she returned she was with a tall, serious-looking man. It was Douglas Anderson, dean of the school. After speaking with him her attitude had completely changed. It seems she had forgotten that another disabled student had graduated from the program some time before. I wondered how easy it had been for *that* guy to get in and who his adviser was! Dr. Anderson was very pleasant and had come along to welcome me to the school. The relief was enormous, although it took me several minutes to mentally put my fists down. I had been prepared for a fight. After a few minutes of chit-chat, he left us to figure out the courses I'd take that semester.

With that organized, I next tackled the attendant issue. I didn't have a clue where to begin. As things stood, once Liz left I'd be on my own. Did I want a roommate? If so, was I prepared for all the potential problems that could pose? But if not, what would I do if I needed something at night? How many people should I hire and train? I'd contacted a domestic agency but hadn't had any luck at that point, nearly three weeks after my arrival there.

As things turned out, the best possible solution came about. And it was something that had never occurred to me. I still remember exactly, *precisely*, where Liz and I were on campus when the following conversation took place:

"It's really nice here," Liz said as we turned onto Palm Walk, one of the campus's nicest walkways, with sixty-foot palm trees lining both sides of the path.

"Sure is."

"It's such a beautiful campus," she said.

"Yeah."

"I really like Arizona," she said.

"Yeah, me too."

"Well, I'm thinking it might be nice to stay," she said. "I've been looking through the course catalogue and there's a teacher's certificate I could get."

My heart jumped into my throat. We'd been getting along really well. She was a lot of fun, had a great sense of humour and was very attractive and outgoing. She attracted people to her and, by extension, to me. It seemed as though she met someone every time she went out to the pool or down the hall to do a load of laundry. I was meeting people in the dorm because of her, and we'd been invited to parties, parties I was sure that by myself I would not have been invited to. If I could have fallen to my knees at that moment I might have done it. I wanted to beg and plead with her. For me it was the perfect answer, but I told myself not to be selfish.

We talked about the practicalities of it. She clearly couldn't start classes that semester, it was too late. But we easily figured out a way to organize the situation. She would do the bulk of my attendant needs that semester, except for a few nights she'd have off each week. The next semester she'd get me up and ready three mornings a week and I'd hire students for the rest. She would be free while I was in classes each day, and each night we'd have dinner in the dorm cafeteria. With those details worked out, everything fell nicely into place.

She ended up staying two years and became my best friend. I still wonder whether I would have made it if she hadn't stayed. She thinks it would have been fine, but I credit her decision to stay as a large part of why it worked as well as it did for me.

That first semester Liz was Mariposa's den mother. Because she had no school-work, she was often hemming some guy's pants or typing someone's term paper. It was a small dorm where everyone knew everyone, and our door was open more than it was shut. We went to tailgate parties, football games, pubs. I felt like I was finally having the university experience everyone else had. Most nights before din-ner we'd sit out by the pool for a few minutes, and there was always someone to talk to. Oh, and the sun shone *every day*.

For some reason Liz and I were known around the dorm as "the quiet girls." We didn't realize this until the night we tied one on and forever shattered the illusion. The scene of the crime was the pub right next door to our dorm, The Dash Inn. It was a small place, and always very crowded. One Friday night Liz and I went over for a margarita with some friends. The "one" margarita turned into three pitchers, with a beer chugged down for good measure. I have no idea how I drove my chair out of the packed place, but I do remember hitting a parked car and Liz driving home on my lap. My glasses were on sideways. When we got back to the dorm we tore up and down the hallway. Word spread throughout that "the quiet ones" were hammered. People came from the TV lounge to witness it. I still have the pictures of Liz passed out cold, crumpled in a little ball around a toilet bowl.

The semester moved along quickly enough, though I was terribly homesick. I was taking some basic courses that had very little work outside the class, so I spent much of my spare time writing letters to friends in Toronto. Going home that first Christmas, I received a huge dose of reality: life had continued without me! I had been convinced that everyone had my arrival date circled in red on the calendar and was waiting with bated breath — just like me. Though I talked to all my friends and saw most of them during the month-long break, I realized that I wasn't really miss-ing all that much by being away. Within two weeks I was itching to get back.

Back at school, I was loving the change of scenery more and more. As callous as it sounds, I was really enjoying the distance from my family. I felt free there, in a way I've never felt in Toronto since the shooting. I still do when I visit Arizona. There were no expectations placed on me. No one ever knew who I was or what was in my past. Those who did find out did so after meeting and getting to know me, the person, first. Plus, the fact that I'd been the victim of a shooting wasn't such a shock because guns and violence are so much more common in the States.

In fact, someone at Disabled Student Resources once asked me to speak to a guy who had been shot walking home from a party several years earlier and was para-lyzed from the shoulders down as well. He had just started classes at ASU. Our con-versation was very unsettling for me.

This guy had only just started getting out of his house after years of living with his elderly parents. His father had been his only attendant, but a heart attack forced them to hire outside help. It turned out to be a great thing for this guy, who had literally not been in a restaurant or shopping mall until his attendant started getting him out. I don't think he had even been in rehab, because he had been under the impression that he was setting a medical precedent.

"I thought I was the only person alive like this," he told me, referring to the extent of his paralysis. He was almost tripping over his words, he spoke so quickly. He talked about being cooped up in the house and how he had just assumed his whole life would be spent that way. He also had just hired a nurse for some of his needs and a romantic relationship had sprung up, something else he had assumed would never happen. This guy poured out years of pent-up thoughts and feelings to me. This tremendous tragedy had been multiplied by years of isolation. The whole scenario was so appalling I had trouble coming to grips with the fact that it was true. If this had been a movie I would have scoffed at the far-fetched notion of someone living like that in modern North America.

All this makes my reaction all the more shameful. Far from becoming a friend, confidante or role model, I never spoke to him again. I avoided giving him my number and I never called back. I couldn't. It was too overwhelming. His need scared me. And, truth be told, I felt a bit jealous that a guy like that had fallen into a romantic relationship so easily, something that had eluded me at that point. I had it so much more together than this guy — it wasn't fair! I also figured he was doing okay, with his attendant and new girlfriend changing his life so dramatically. "He's in school, his isolation is over," I reasoned. But he still desperately needed a friend, a *paralyzed* friend. I am not proud of my attitude or my behaviour. Even a year or two later my reaction would have been very different (and more compassionate), but at that point I just couldn't cope with it.

What I could cope with were all those deadlines that the adviser had warned me about. I was excelling at school, taking four courses each semester and doing well in everything (except biology — my only C at ASU). Degrees at ASU are more general than at some universities. They require courses in pretty much every area, even math (ugh). Actual journalism courses comprised only 25 percent of the total curriculum. I took an introductory media course my second semester and my first newswriting class the following fall. The transition from writing English essays to news stories was not automatic for me, by any means.

I still didn't have a future career plan. Journalism seemed like a good degree because of its versatility. By then I knew writing was in my future, I just didn't know what kind of writing. My skills had been flourishing in the English classes I'd been taking, but starting newswriting threw me right off. I went to see one of my English professors.

"Newswriting is plain bad writing," I lamented. "It's improper sentence structure. I don't know if I can bring myself to do it."

She tried hard to convince me to change my major. "Your skills would be wasted," she told me. "You belong in the English department."

But that night I gave myself a mental shake. If I really was a good writer, I should be able to learn any style and adapt accordingly. I forced myself to give it another try. It started coming more easily pretty quickly. Now I don't think I could write an essay to save my life!

It was right after that first newswriting course ended and I was home for Christmas that newspapers entered my life. I received a call from Mary Deanne Shears, then an assistant managing editor at *The Toronto Star*. She wondered what I thought about a summer job at the paper. Not wanting to burn a bridge, I agreed to meet with her, but to me that job wasn't even a remote possibility. I was not about to make a fool of myself on the pages of Canada's largest daily newspaper.

Mary Deanne came to visit me at my home. She told me about the summer program, a bit about how reporters worked in the newsroom and a bit of her own background. We talked about how I would do it physically — telephones, recording interviews, etc. In truth, though, newspapers were not my personal interest. The only reason I was even discussing it was because in my program a newspaper internship was heavily stressed. And it made sense to do one in Toronto, where my "celebrity status" might open a few doors or at least make a company more willing to make the kind of adjustments necessary for someone with my disability.

I had strong reservations, and I voiced them to her. With only one newswriting course and no direct experience, I knew I wasn't capable right then. The course had even provided all the details for each story; all we did was write them into a news piece. I certainly didn't know how to put a story together from scratch. In the semester coming up, however, I was taking a course we'd all been warned about. It was called Reporting, and it was supposed to be really tough. I told her my decision about the job would be based on the outcome of the course.

The Reporting class *was* demanding. We only met once a week, but a lot of leg work was involved. We had to sniff out and come prepared with three story proposals. For each idea that was complete and well researched we got a point, extra credit, that would be added to our final grade. We wouldn't know which story we'd be writing until the class started, and we'd have to hand in our work at the end of each class, finished or not. The computers in the classrooms were on tables I couldn't reach, so I hired someone to type for me. The school was willing to work out an accessible table, but I couldn't use a mouse and didn't know anything about the Macintosh computers used. Anyway, since I do type with a stick in my mouth, one key at a time, I wanted a fast typist to make sure I made the deadlines (Lord knows I didn't want to miss one of those!). I was determined that my disability would never interfere in any way with requirements, and it never did — in fact, I never missed one deadline the entire time I was there.

That class taught me how to be a reporter. I remember at the end of the semester we all counted up our points from our story ideas. I had seventeen, I think about nine or ten more than the next highest in the class. I can still hear the professor's reaction, heard by everyone standing in the hall, when she screamed: "Oh my god, she just blew the curve right out of the water." When the marks for the three Reporting classes were posted, I had received the only A.

Now I felt confident enough to say yes to the offer from *The Star*. I went back to Toronto for the summer and spent five exciting weeks getting my feet wet as a reporter.

*　　*　　*　　*

ASU is the fifth-largest university in the United States, and its size attracted some heavy-hitters to lecture and perform. Musical giants like U2, Tina Turner and Sting performed at various campus venues while I was there. The most notable speaker to visit during my years was undoubtedly former president Ronald Reagan. Reagan came just a few months after finishing his second term as president, when much of America still looked at him and his tenure through rose-coloured glasses. He had given a couple of lectures in California, but ours was his first visit outside his home state. Whether or not I agreed with his politics, I was not going to pass up the opportunity to see a man who had had such an impact on the world.

Like a scene out of the movies, security agents were crawling all over the huge complex, wearing earpieces with wires disappearing under their collars and many sporting what must be standard issue sunglasses (even indoors). I sat wondering how many guns were on the premises. Try as I might, it was impossible *not* to feel incredibly excited when "Hail to the Chief" played, the curtains parted and Reagan walked out to the stage. That audience was *pumped* — it was unlike anything I've ever seen anywhere. All these years later I can't recall his message, all I remember was that infectious hype that surrounded his visit — a reaction that no politician could create in Canada. Call Americans whatever you want, but they can never be accused of *not* wearing their patriotism on their sleeves.

And Walter Cronkite, America's best-loved broadcaster, was not an in-name-only affiliation with the Journalism school. He made annual visits to the school each fall, always taking time to meet with students and have an informal chat session. I was invited to participate in one of these one year. We sat in a circle and were first asked to introduce ourselves and tell him a bit about our background. He asked the first couple of students to speak up a few times, then sat and appeared to listen intently as we each gave our spiel. As each student finished he smiled graciously and said, "Very nice to meet you." Later, when I asked him a question, I had to repeat it "a bit louder" so many times that I was screaming by the time he finally heard it. I realized that he must have been pretending to hear our introductions. Cronkite was kind, generous with his time, experience and opinions — and deaf as a post!

*   *   *   *

As much as I loved being at ASU and as well as I continued to do academically, everything wasn't peaches and cream. I was alone on campus each day for my classes, which meant I didn't eat or drink anything, but I was used to that limitation, so that didn't bother me much. One thing that did bug me, though, was watching other students before lectures. I was always early, so I had loads of time for this activity. They'd look through their backpacks, be writing something, reading a book or, frequently, the school's daily paper, *The State Press*. I'd sit for those ten or fifteen minutes, filled with such envy because I couldn't do any of those things.

Getting around on my own wasn't difficult, but it did lead to trouble once in awhile. Trouble almost always involved a muscle spasm. I can usually tell when one is coming, and, if I'm driving my chair, I stop and wait it out. But now and then a spasm erupts out of nowhere, and if it's big enough *and* I'm still driving, anything around is a potential target. I had the old-style wheelchair for my first two years there, the one with the leaf switches above my shoulders, and big spasms would sometimes jerk me back in the chair so hard that it would knock the switches out of my reach. So I'd have to sit there until someone walked by I could flag over to help. Once it happened on a deserted street, and it was quite a wait. If my chair was moving, a spasm might jolt my body sideways, sometimes spinning the chair in circles, sometimes sending me into the nearest obstacle. One lovely afternoon a spasm took me through about twenty feet of bushes. By the time I got everything back under control, I was covered in leaves, which of course I couldn't brush off and wore for the rest of the day, supressing giggles throughout my remaining classes.

For me, each semester always began with a worry about how I would get notes from each class. I wanted to do it all as independently as possible, so I didn't want to bring a helper to any class I didn't absolutely have to. For the huge lectures, there was a professional note-taking business on campus. Graduate students were paid to sit in the classes and take notes, which were available for purchase for individual days for missed lectures or for the entire semester. That was the best solution, because they were guaranteed to be thorough. In smaller classes I always managed to meet someone, or I'd get the professor to ask the class for a volunteer to photocopy their notes. In the end, that worked out too.

Exams were easy to organize. Disabled Student Resources had a test-taking service available free for students. On the day of an exam, a DSR employee would pick up a copy from the department and bring it to the centre. At the designated class time, I'd go to DSR, where an employee would literally be my hands. Most of the tests in every subject were multiple choice, so I'd give the answers verbally, the scribe would take them down and the test would be returned to the department for grading with all the others. This worked for all disabled students, whether they were visually impaired or had learning disabilities and just needed extra time or a quiet room with no distractions. And it was all very aboveboard, no cheating possible.

Though getting around the campus was easy, getting into classrooms wasn't always straightforward. I hated classes that were on any floor other than ground. For most people, pushing elevator buttons is not an issue. For most disabled people, they aren't an issue either now that buttons are installed low enough to be reached from a wheelchair. However, for someone like me, with no arm movement, it was (and is) a neverending problem. Some of the taller buildings had busy elevators, so it was easy to catch a ride with someone else. But some smaller structures, ones that were only two or three storeys, were always a drag for me, because most students took the stairs.

For some reason, people often seemed spooked or uncomfortable when I asked them to press the button for me. If the elevator wasn't right there, more often than not the person would press the button and start to walk away. I'd fight my instinct to snap "If I can't press the up button, how the hell do you think I'm going to press the floor I need?" and nicely ask them to wait until it arrived so they could press the button inside. An awkward silence would always follow while we waited, which I usually tried to fill by saying something like, "It doesn't usually take too long," or "These darn elevators are so old and slow" or "I hope you don't mind waiting." I always arrived extra early, so I could carefully choose my "victim." The best targets were women, the older the better to cash in on the sympathy factor. I hated asking young guys, who sometimes looked like they were going to jump out of their skins. I always chose someone who didn't look like they were in a hurry.

The worst lecture hall, and I had three goddamn classes in it in my time there, was one in a very quiet building. There were four or five steps down from ground level, which put students at the back end of the huge hall. Once inside there were steps all the way down along the rows of seats — like a big theatre with steps instead of a ramped aisle. The elevator was tucked around a corner, totally off the beaten path. It opened into a small room behind the front of the lecture hall, the opposite side of the "safe" doors used by each TAB (meaning Temporarily Able-Bodied, a tongue-in-cheek way we crips refer to able-bodied folks). So to get in or out I had to drag someone out of their way.

Now it may sound like I'm making a big deal of nothing, but you would be amazed how much it bothered people. First off, I could never ask the same person twice, since it was such a big hall that no one ever sat in the same seat. And people really are like sheep — I was asking them to go against the tide of all the people who were *like them*. When I asked them to push the button for ground, they never said, "Oh, if it's going up I'll just hop in too." Nope, nope, nope. They'd push ground, then go back into the lecture hall, walk up the dozens of stairs, out of the building, then up the short flight to street level — to end up exactly where I did. It made me feel contagious or contaminated, and always very, very alone. I guess it's fear of disability, fear of the unknown, that caused this phenomenon.

I'm convinced this same attitude was the reason behind what I called "the two-seat rule." It went like this: the last two seats in every class to fill were always the two seats beside and the two seats behind someone in a wheelchair. It happened in every class, no matter the size. Actually, it stopped after the first couple of weeks in my smaller classes. In small classes where students were able to get to know one another a bit, it didn't take the others long to realize that sitting beside me wouldn't turn them into crippled newts. But in big lecture halls, forget about it.

It wouldn't be fair to say that all those students had an attitude problem and I didn't. I wasn't exactly comfortable with a lot of them, either. I was a fair bit older than most, and I had such different life experiences. I didn't get involved in clubs or try to fit in with the students outside of my dorm. I retreated because of my disability. I'd be willing to bet that ASU has more than its fair share of sorority chicks and fraternity brats. Though a serious university, it consistently makes *Playboy*'s list of top-ten party schools. You figure out the results of that. So, as my three and a half years there passed, I spent more and more time hanging out at Disabled Student Resources. I wasn't spending my time with disabled students per se, but with the permanent staff and student employees as well. They were all really nice people. There I knew I was accepted and I could relax and be myself. With a guaranteed cheery atmosphere, it was always a nice place to be. There were computers there for use and many other resources. I was asked to take over production of the centre's newsletter for my last two years, so there was a useful reason to be there as well.

The dorm was another comfortable place where I didn't feel like an outcast. Dinners were usually a fun affair, with Liz and I always sitting with friends. Because it was a dorm for graduate students, the age difference was much less, or non-existent, and there were lots of opportunities to get to know other students. People often left their doors open, and friends dropped in on the way by just to say hello. Emergency cookie runs were common.

*   *   *   *

Though I felt I could live forever with the way things were, Liz's program ended after our second year. I still had a year and a half left and I didn't know what I was going to do. I knew it would be difficult, if not impossible, to replace Liz. We spent an enormous amount of time together, getting along well, probably 99.9 percent of it. I was losing my roommate, main attendant and best friend. I had gone through some major growing pains during those two years and Liz had always been there supporting and encouraging me, yet pushing me at the same time. I hated to see her go and knew the friendship was impossible to replace.

I would have happily stayed put with Liz for the rest of my university life, but, since she was leaving, I had to admit it was time to move out of the dorm. At the beginning of our second year the residence association had opened our wing of the dorm to undergraduates. Suddenly it was a lot louder at night, with obnoxious, all-night weekend parties becoming the norm instead of the exception. It made me feel old, and I realized I had outgrown the place.

Things have a way of working out, and another workable situation came my way. Some friends had come down to visit Liz, and one of them made a proposition to me, knowing Liz was finishing her studies. This was an older woman, who had three children, two of them dependent on her. She was looking for a change of pace and wanted a break from her job. We ended up renting a house off campus and she became my full-time attendant. The situation was a nice change for me, too, in some ways. I quickly grew to love her kids — one of whom was an older teenager who did some night attendant work for me for pocket money. We rented a beautiful bungalow with a cowboy-boot-shaped pool, in the tradition of the true West. It was nice to host occasional dinners and parties for my friends. My sister Alison also came down and spent a semester with us, attending a local college while she was there.

Living in the house provided another excuse for not participating in extracurricular school life. I had briefly joined a couple of journalism/media clubs my first year but was too intimidated to go to more than one or two meetings. I'd see posters for formals, dances and other social events, but I never once considered attending one. Even when I was having fun with residents in the dorm, I was acutely aware of how my disability separated me from other students. I felt at home on campus, yet so very different from the others. I felt I was having the best university experience I could, given my circumstances, but that didn't stop me from longing for what I was missing. I knew I would never have been down there had I not been shot, but I still pictured what my life would be like there if I were able-bodied. I could clearly see me running from one activity to another, being on campus all hours of the day and night. I'd see students catching a nap in the library or one of the common areas, lying in the grass, putting up posters; or couples walking, talking, fooling around together, and it all reminded me of how different I was. I was social, but not in the way I used to be, the way that it was now impossible for me to be. My loss was always playing in my mind, just farther at the back on good days.

*　　　　*　　　　*　　　　*

During my third year at school I got a phone call from someone I hadn't spoken to in a couple of years. It was Gordon Wiseman, a Toronto writer and lawyer, who had written the script for a CBC Radio show I'd worked on just before leaving for Arizona in 1987. The show was "Scales of Justice," a series of docudramas on high-profile Canadian trials, narrated by well-known defence lawyer Edward Greenspan. I'd provided my own voice for the program based on my case. It was a bit of fun. This time they were preparing to do three pilot TV versions of "Scales" shows, to see how they would be received. They were to be directed by Canadian director extraordinaire David Cronenberg, known for such films as *Scanners, The Fly* and *Dead Ringers*. Gord wondered whether I was interested in being a script consultant, and also if I wanted to play myself again. He was just making the preliminary call, to let me think about it awhile; the producer, George Jonas, would call soon.

It was a lot to consider. Did I want to get dragged back through that again? Play the victim all over again? Would I always be known for something that was done to me, rather than for something I did myself? Being a script consultant was an easy decision; it was playing myself I wasn't sure about. I decided to do it for a number of reasons. Obviously, I'd never had an opportunity to do anything like that before, and I knew I wouldn't want to do it once I'd finished school and was more concerned with my career. I thought back to my drama club days in high school and how much fun I'd had in one play, where I'd played Winnifred, "a wisecracking cynic of unmistakably easy virtue" (friends joked that I was typecast). I also knew how much it would bother me seeing someone else play me if they got it wrong. But above all the chance to be directed by someone with the talent, imagination and stature of David Cronenberg, a once-in-a-lifetime opportunity for sure, was too irresistible to pass up.

George Jonas, a creator, producer and writer of the "Scales" shows, is an extremely talented man, and he was remarkably generous. He allowed me to change or eliminate absolutely anything in the script that I disagreed with or was uncomfortable with — not just my dialogue but that of all the other characters as well. It wasn't that he gave me great licence to rewrite, and I never took advantage of the privilege he gave me, but I was very impressed that he never questioned one of my changes. Every word I say on the show I either actually said at some point or wrote myself.

The summer before my last semester of school we shot the one-hour show. Almost all of it was a novelty and fun. Working with David Cronenberg was really cool. I learned one difference a great director can make when I continually stumbled over one word take after take. After four attempts David came over to me, leaned down close to my ear and quietly said, "Take a short pause and a breath before you say that word." I nailed it perfectly the next take.

There were a couple of really neat shots that stick out in my memory. One was a shot of me reading from the statement I made to the media after sentencing, that called for me to drive my chair down the ramp beside the courthouse as I address the reporters. David wanted to see the camera *actually* move with me, so they built a dolly extending from my chair and mounted the camera right on it. The other strange shot was the very first one, after Greenspan's introduction. It was me on the phone with my sister Lynn before the shooting. Since the event took place prior to the shooting, I did the close-up and a double played me for the long shot. But even the close-up required a hand to hold the phone. The person providing the hand had to hold it in a way that looked like I was really holding it, an awkward angle to be sure. After debating whose hand to use, they asked my younger sister Alison, who had been driving me to the set most days. This suited her just fine — it gave her the chance to participate, take her hand to make-up *and* she made about eighty dollars to boot. As it was set up David said, "This is the weirdest shot I've ever done." Considering the source, that really said something!

The last shot I had to do was one I had originally asked to be excused from. It was a reenactment of the statement the police took from me two days after the shooting, when they had asked me to identify the ski masks the guys had been wearing at the store. George suggested using a double and having the camera aimed at the police only, but David felt it was important I be in the shot, so I agreed to do it from my chair (the shot initially called for me to be lying in bed). I was supposed to be in traction, so a halo vest was borrowed from a hospital.

The shot came at the end of a long shooting schedule, made tiring for me by the fact that I was working full time at *The Star* on a summer internship. My days began at 6:00 a.m. I'd work all day, then I'd go directly to the set, shoot for the evening, drive an hour home and get to bed, if I was lucky, by midnight. We shot over my weekend off, too. Though this lasted less than two weeks, I was pretty exhausted by the end. We'd gone over schedule, so it was around 10:00 p.m. just as we were setting up. I wasn't exactly in strong shape for what was about to hit me.

As soon as I saw the vest in the make-up room I knew it wouldn't work. There was no room at the back of my chair for the hard plastic to fit, and I could see that wearing it would leave me leaning forward toward my knees. I realized I'd look unreasonable without making an attempt, so, against my better judgment, I allowed them to try putting it on me. As soon as they pushed my trunk forward, slipped in the back piece, then sat me up, I knew for sure I couldn't do it, not physically or emotionally. Before the front piece was even on I started to panic, but couldn't speak.

They fit on the front panel and clicked the vest together. I felt my throat close as they quickly put a blue hospital gown over top. I glanced in the mirror but couldn't look for more than a split second. The image staring back was me in September of 1983.

Over the years, as I questioned my seeming lack of strong emotion about my victimization, I always wondered if something would one day trigger an avalanche. I'd heard of people who had lived through horrific traumas seemingly unscathed until one day something simple sent them to a psych ward. I was afraid that all the emotion was down "there," waiting to erupt, and that something would one day bring it all up crashing over me. I was as afraid of it happening as I was of it *not* happening and remaining buried, holding me back from achieving some kind of closure. Well, that vest got the ball rolling.

As I sat there, the woman doing make-up, Shonagh, said immediately, "Let me go tell David you can't do it." Shonagh and I had really clicked, and though we hadn't known each other long, she could tell just by looking at me that I was a basket case. I was not capable of speaking, so I couldn't answer her, but the others set about trying to rig it all up to make it work. They called for some rope to try and tie me back, so I'd be sitting somewhat upright. I knew I just had to go out and deliver two lines, but it was taking every ounce of effort just to keep myself from bursting into tears. Finally I looked at Shonagh, shook my head, and she went and talked to David. I had to get that thing off me quickly, but I agreed to do the scene in a neck collar. I immediately reburied the memories that had been rearing their ugly head, did the scene and kissed my acting days goodbye.

*   *   *   *

After my bit of television stardom ended, I boarded a plane for my last semester of university. One drawback to attending school in Arizona was all the flying we had to do. Flying wouldn't be a bad thing at all if I could stay in my own chair, where I am actually much safer, as well as more comfortable, than I ever could be in an airline seat. But aviation rules state that all passengers must sit in airline seats, so that's what I must do. Alas, I could never find a direct, non-stop flight to Arizona, and we always had to change planes in Chicago, requiring an extra seat-wheelchair-seat transfer.

I find flying very stressful, and I always have giant fields of butterflies in my stomach en route to airports. After checking in, I stay in my chair until boarding time, when I go to the door of the plane. There I get transferred to a chair small enough to fit down the aisle, and finally I'm transferred again onto the airline seat. Because of the curve of my spine, I cannot sit comfortably with any stability in any chair other than my own, so simply getting down the aisle in the tiny chair is a challenge. I travel with an attendant, who can only do some of the lifting required. I do need help from an airline employee, who, whether or not he or she has received training, doesn't usually do a great job of moving me from seat to seat. It's not an easy transfer.

One nice thing many airlines do is bump up disabled passengers to business class when possible. The difference in seat comfort is enormous. My first choice of airline is always Air Canada, which seems to provide above-average staff training. However, that airline didn't fly to Arizona during my years there, and I was forced to fly on an American carrier. During my last year, I discovered that Canadian Airlines did have a direct flight during winter months, which was great for my last couple of flights. The difference between American and Canadian carriers, with respect to travel for people with disabilities, is wider than the Grand Canyon.

It seemed that something went wrong every time we travelled, lost luggage being the easiest to deal with. On one trip they realized, after I was on board, that they couldn't fit my wheelchair into the hold and they took it apart. When we flew into Toronto that night, absolutely exhausted at close to midnight, it took an hour to locate a screwdriver to put it back together. Once, while getting from one plane in Chicago to another, I was being carried on an aisle chair by four people. As we rushed on to the crowded, fully boarded plane, one of the people helping me loudly chirped, "This is just like moving furniture." On another trip, we were upgraded to business class but stuck there with exercise-guru Richard Simmons. That man does not shut up, ever. It was the only time a complimentary upgrade felt like a punishment.

It got so that by my last year I didn't want to see the inside of an airplane ever again. Fortunately, my love for travel returned after a couple of years of sticking close to Toronto.

*　　　*　　　*　　　*

I could hardly believe my university career was almost over. By the time I was finishing up my program, in 1990, I was pretty sure newspapers were in my future. For the first time I could imagine myself living on my own, somehow, in downtown Toronto. And I knew that going to Arizona was one of the best things that could have happened to me. I was graduating *magna cum laude*, with high academic honours.

I had one surprise headed my way that I never, in my wildest imagination, could have seen coming. I received a letter that said my name had been put forward as a candidate for valedictorian. Each department nominated one of its students, and a selection committee interviewed each one. As honoured as I was, I wasn't sure if I wanted to go for it. I had to think carefully, because if I was going to compete, I'd be upset if I didn't get it. I'm not the "Oh well, at least I tried" kind of person. I'd have to succeed, or it would bug me forever. But I knew I was qualified, and I knew I could do a great job.

The interview went well, and I wasn't really surprised when I got the phone call telling me I'd been selected. I was excited, though nervous about speaking to the twenty thousand people expected to fill the stadium for the graduation ceremonies. By then I knew that both my parents would be there. I thought about not telling them the news and letting them just see me on stage, but I was advised against it. That would have been quite a shock for them.

I agonized over the speech. I had a good opening joke about parking on campus, a huge issue (and headache) at ASU — it seemed to be on the front page of the school's daily paper at least once every couple of weeks. I wrote it all slowly, taking a couple of weeks and refining it every time I read it, which was several times a day. (My speech is reprinted in an appendix at the end of the book).

Sometimes I wanted to tell everybody I ran into that I, *moi*, me, was the valedictorian! I've never been one to brag so I usually held my tongue. There was only one time I couldn't resist. One of my journalism professors had been a broadcaster for many years and was a regular MC at commencements. One day, as class ended, he and I were the last at the door.

"Well, I guess I'll be sharing the stage with you at graduation," I said, assuming that by then he knew I was valedictorian.

"Yes, they sometimes invite students who have overcome difficulties to sit on stage during the proceedings," he said without hesitation.

I was stunned by the comment. Though his words were incredibly patronizing, that was not the worst of it. It had never occurred to me that my "difficulties" had anything to do with my selection as valedictorian. I was tremendously disappointed at his immediate assumption that I was to be a token figure on stage. He didn't ask why I'd be there, he leapt to my disability as the reason. I couldn't think of anybody who would want to sit on stage in front of twenty thousand people just because they were a crip. It made me rethink the whole thing. I wasn't sure I wanted to deliver the speech anymore. I called the woman in the commencement office that I'd been dealing with. She was as appalled by the comment as I was and convinced me my qualifications all came from me, not my disability.

As graduation day drew nearer my life got more and more complicated. My exams took a back seat to everything else. Aside from having to prepare the speech, I was packing up three and a half years of belongings. I had accumulated an incredible amount of stuff — a waterbed, television and VCR, microwave and ghetto-blaster — and on top of that I had my computer, books I wanted to keep and all my assignments and notes. My father, who had planned to come down for graduation anyway, offered to drive everything home in my van. Because the graduation date was so close to Christmas, I'd be flying home with Alison, my mother and my friend Holly the day after the ceremony.

To further complicate life, media in Toronto had found out I was valedictorian and they were calling the house. And ASU must have issued a press release about graduation, because I was getting lots of calls from the Phoenix press. *The Toronto Star* wanted to print my speech the day I was giving it, an idea I hated; the speech was written for Arizona graduates of ASU, not readers in Toronto. I felt as though I was being pulled in a dozen directions. All this was happening during the last few days I would spend in the place I had grown to deeply love, and it just wasn't fair! For the first time ever, I completely ignored all of the media calls. I didn't even return them to turn down interviews. As a journalism graduate, I felt a bit guilty, but I simply couldn't do everything.

I woke on graduation day to snow flurries. Snow in Phoenix. That's so unusual it was making news throughout the state. I'd been so nervous about the speech that I'd burned it word-for-word into my brain. I'd spent the previous evening doing nothing but practising it, saying it at several different speeds and in several different ways. I knew it cold.

Everyone in the proceedings was to meet on campus, then go from there to the stadium. I actually had a personal police escort leading my van. My notes were on my lap, with my graduation cap sitting on top. At the stadium I lined up in place with all the administrators, faculty and podium guests; the butterflies in my stomach increasing with every minute. A television crew had hooked me up with a wireless microphone. I had an escort with me, to help me up and down the steep ramp to the stage. I had told him clearly that I only needed help up and down the ramp, but I discovered after that he followed me all the way in and out, with his hands on the handles on the back of my chair, making it look as though he was pushing me and I couldn't control my own chair.

Faculty and other dignitaries were lined up in a tunnel leading to the stadium, and I started forward when I was given the cue. As I came into view a roar went up. I could hear the crowd chanting, but I couldn't quite make out what they were saying.

Wow! They like me. They REALLY like me!

Halfway up the aisle I suddenly realized that Rose Mofford, the popular governor of the state, was walking beside me. The crowd was chanting "Rose, Rose, Rose," and cheering for her, not me! That was a good dose of humility to bring me back to earth!

By the time I got on to the stage and had my first look at the multitudes, I was *really* nervous. My mouth was so dry, it felt as though I'd had cotton stuffed in it for hours. It was a little hard to talk that way.

The ceremony was fun, though. One thing about Americans, they sure have great grad ceremonies. Canadian ones are so solemn in comparison. There was tons of cheering and laughter. The speaker who went before me had the line of the day: "For all you graduates whose critics said it would be a snowy day in Phoenix before you got your degree …"

Then it was my turn. I moved my chair to the front of the stage, still with the worst case of dry mouth I'd ever had. On someone's advice I paused before starting, trying to savour the moment and enjoy the fact that twenty thousand people were sitting waiting to hear me speak. Then I began with a confidence I suddenly realized I possessed. My opening joke was *very* well received, and about halfway through my speech, when I paused while the crowd cheered at another appropriate moment, I realized that it was going extremely well. I was even salivating again!

What a rush it was, hearing that many people applaud at the end and knowing I'd done a great job. The governor, who presides over every one of the three state universities' graduations, told me it was the best speech she'd ever heard. She asked for a copy of it. It's possible she told every valedictorian the same thing, but it was flattering, nonetheless.

The next twenty-four hours — my last in Arizona — flew by. Making my rounds to say goodbye on campus was difficult. I managed to stay dry-eyed until I left DSR and the people I would miss the most. There were no wild graduation parties for me, just a quiet family dinner and more packing.

The most disappointing aspect of graduation was the media coverage. On one hand it was my fault for ignoring their calls, but it was appalling how the only thing they focused on was my disability. I made the mistake of allowing a TV station to put that wireless microphone on me, and for their broadcast they included my voice asking the man next to me on stage to move my cap so I could see my notes. Though every news piece talked only about my disability, the worst article appeared in the local Tempe paper. The lead said: "For fifteen minutes, blood pumped from a hole in her neck as she lay, not moving, sprawled behind a cash register. For the following nine weeks, she couldn't either utter a word, nor move her head. But for seven minutes yesterday, as the twenty-five-year-old gave the commencement address to the Arizona State University's fall class, Barbara Turnbull forgot that 1983 nightmare." One line in my speech was: "I know there were times when I thought this day would never happen, a feeling I'm sure all graduates share." The paper had a cutline under my picture quoting me as saying: "I never thought this day would come." A bigger insult and tremendous disappointment was that my own, dear *Toronto Star* paid that guy a freelance fee and ran his piece of garbage in my hometown. Even if I'd cooperated with them, the media had their mandate to paint me as a crippled inspiration for the masses. Nothing I could have done would have changed that.

The day after the ceremony I flew back to Toronto, acutely aware that my life was entering a new phase. Although I knew my time in Arizona would remain close to my heart, I was excited about the future. No matter what lay in my immediate future, I was confident it would be better than what I'd had before I left, three and a half years earlier.

Chapter Seven:

SETTING UP HOUSE

I was anticipating four lovely, free months when I got back from Arizona that Christmas. They stretched before me like a delicious treat I'd earned and felt I totally deserved. At first I moved back home with my family, but in those months, I planned to find an apartment, move downtown and enjoy myself before starting work at *The Star* in May for another summer. I was eager for life without homework. Time is never really free when you're in university, there is always something that could be read or worked on or started. In those years, any time I was doing anything other than schoolwork I always heard a nagging voice that made me feel a twinge of guilt.

I wanted to act like a tourist and get to know Toronto again, and I thought I might take some overnight trips around Ontario and Quebec. An attendant from Arizona, who had become a friend, came up to work for me for those months so she could get to know this area too. We were eagerly looking forward to it all.

But fate intervened before we could do anything on our "fun list." In early January I was ordered to go to bed and stay there. I had a major pressure sore on my hip. It had started two or three months earlier in Arizona as a slight red mark. It took me a few days to discover that a piece of plastic was pushing up from my chair, putting pressure on that one area morning until night. Even though we fixed the chair as soon as we found the problem, the spot got worse. The responsible thing to do at that point would have been to spend a few days in bed, but I was in my final semester of school and figured I just couldn't take the time. Plus, I'd never had a major pressure sore, and I didn't know the consequences of letting something like that go. Without the ability to feel pain, a paralyzed person can sit on a sore until it gets as deep as the bone. Even if it's not that severe, a bad pressure sore takes a long time to heal — much longer than it takes to create. My skin had given me no unmanageable problems for many years. My attendants were telling me it was getting worse, but I wasn't listening. After getting home, I continued to tune out warnings, while getting through the Christmas and New Year festivities. Then in early January I had to promote the "Scales of Justice" TV docudrama we'd shot the previous summer. There was always an excuse to pretend the sore wasn't there. By the time I saw a doctor, I had a serious problem.

"Go home. Stay in bed. Come back in three weeks," he told me. I felt the blood drain from my face.

"I can't spend three weeks in bed," I told him, a note of desperation clear in my voice. I was seized with panic at the mere thought of it.

"You have no choice on this one," he said. "There isn't anything else that will help."

Three weeks later he repeated his "prescription." Another three weeks later there was so little improvement that I didn't even bother getting out of bed to go see him. After eight weeks down I saw another doctor, but got the same advice: "Bed rest until it's completely healed."

The term used in rehab is "grounded," and from start to finish, I was grounded for four and a half months. Aside from three showers a week and the odd doctor's appointment, I was in bed at my mother's house from early January until mid May.

For me, being grounded is psychological warfare. That's partly why I put off the whole thing for so long. I just wasn't mentally ready for what my subconscious knew was headed my way. There is a whole state of mind to living in bed, even if it's only for a few days, and it takes a lot of work not to lose the mental battle. It starts with day and night switching places. It's very easy to doze all day, then lie awake at night in front of the television. It's also easy to lose every day to sleeping and the tube. I was careful to work out a schedule and, for the most part, I stuck to it.

I never slept past 8:00 a.m. I'd listen to CBC Radio until noon. Then I'd either have my shower or wash and brush my teeth in bed. Lunch was next, followed by the newspaper and any mail that came in. I never switched on the TV until 4:00 p.m., then I'd watch talk shows, the news and whatever was on that evening. I almost always turned everything off by 11:00 p.m. and tried to sleep. I never watched a single soap opera, a fact of which I am quite proud! But I probably could have kept the local video store in business by myself. On bad days I'd rent three or four movies and tune out of life, watching one right after the other. The whole ordeal would have been easier if I could have read in bed, but that wasn't an option. I didn't get a reading stand that worked for me in bed until very recently.

Part of what makes being grounded so difficult is how taxing it is to start getting up again. After a short while, even a shower would wipe me out and I'd actually look forward to lying back down — an urge that alarmed me.

I didn't know it at the time, but my whole family was affected by that grounding. Everyone was suffering from depression. As they later told me, they don't dwell on my disability when I'm up and around, but having to face me day after day, lying in bed and more dependent than usual, they lost the luxury of denial. At least when I was up and about I could spend time on my own, read, access my computer and, most importantly, have a life outside the walls of my home. During this time my family were pretty much my only social contact. I didn't tell most of my friends what was going on until I was ending my third month down and the end still wasn't in sight. In general I don't like visitors when I'm in bed; it reminds me too much of the hospital. But I eventually stopped putting people off. Some of them were upset that I'd kept it from them; they told me they would have liked to visit and be supportive.

I'm sure anyone with a spinal cord injury reading this can relate. Most of us get at least *one* of these suckers. For me, I'm pretty sure it will never happen again. Prevention is possible. It's a hell of a lot easier to spend even a week in bed than to let something get out of hand. It's really hard to put life on hold suddenly, particularly if you work, but it just can't be helped. With paralysis, taking care of your body is a serious responsibility.

That's what they try to teach in rehab. Checking your skin every night and every morning is critical. Sitting on a wrinkle for a day can lead to big problems. There are other things that rank high in managing a disability like this. Because most quads have indwelling catheters, it's important to drink lots of fluid (beer doesn't count). A catheter means that a foreign body is always present in the bladder, making the person very susceptible to bladder infections. In addition, with spinal cord injury the ability to regulate temperature is gone, so it's important to be careful in extreme weather, both hot and cold. Since we can't feel what is paralyzed, frostbite and sunburn are serious concerns.

Colds and flus can wreak havoc on a paralyzed person. Without the use of stomach and chest muscles to add punch to a cough, a cold can land someone in the hospital. If a chest is congested, we often need help to cough. For me, when I need help, a person pushes in hard and fast on my stomach just as I start to cough. But all this does not mean we are "sickly." In fact, for me it's the opposite. I'm lucky to have an incredibly tough immune system — in all these years I've only had one cold that made me need assistance coughing.

*   *   *   *

As bad as the paralysis is, it's the side effects that make it so much worse — everything from bladder infections and skin problems to societal issues and attendant problems, and, for far too many, constant financial pressures to take care of what's needed — medications, equipment, modifications to homes and vehicles.

For an individual with a high level physical disability to be a fully integrated and contributing member of society, there are several elements that must be present: attendant services that are sufficient, flexible and affordable; accessible and afford-able housing; technologies, like wheelchairs, environmental control equipment and computers; external accessibility, like curb cuts, snow removal and accessible build-ings; affordable, reliable, sufficient transportation; society's support and acceptance of some of these as a right, as demonstrated through legislation like the Human Rights Code; and, ultimately, the individual's desire to use these resources, benefit from them and give back. If any one piece of the puzzle is missing, it all falls apart. These things merely compensate for the physical limitations the disability imposes. Members of our society have these limitations, and require these things — it's as simple as that. They do cost, though there are ways of making the costs reasonable and feasible. For example, universally accessible design — including that for new houses, offices, public buildings — benefits society as a whole, particularly our aging population.

There are limited living options for people with disabilities. One is simply living in the community like anyone else, requiring what is detailed above. In the past it was more typical for disabled people to live in chronic care institutions, but, as you can imagine, this kind of housing is neither helpful nor necessary for most of us. There are now some very good transitional centres that act as halfway houses for people who have lived years in chronic care and have an opportunity to move into the community.

After living in Arizona and taking care of my own needs for so long, it was easy to decide that I wanted to live in my own home in the community, managing my own life. I think it's the best way someone with a disability like mine can live. It's not problem-free by any means, but, of the options available, it gives the individ-ual the most control. For example, there are government-funded outreach services through which a person in the community can get attendants to come right to the home. This helps allow for the flexibility of independent living.

Independence sometimes comes with a price, though. I have a friend who fell over in his chair one evening and spent four hours with his head in a box before being rescued. Many of my friends have hilarious stories about times they've fallen out of their chairs, and I have a couple of my own. I have an impish parrot that learned how to turn my chair off. One morning, not two minutes after my attendant left, he killed the power. For three hours I was stuck at a table with no phone, nothing to drink and nothing to do but read the section of the newspaper that lay in front of me. Fortunately for me the radio was on! Though these situations can be awful at the time, it's usually easy to laugh afterwards.

The twenty-four-hour attendant facility is the second best option. This kind of housing is basically a regular apartment building, with one accessible apartment on each floor that is government-subsidized and one apartment in the building turned into an office/lounge for the attendants. Residents then share a pool of attendants who are available around the clock, booking them ahead of time. The waiting lists for these buildings are typically several years long. Another problem is that choices for services can be limited. Take mornings, for example. The attendants are *so* busy then that people sometimes have to start getting ready as early as 5:00 a.m. in order to be ready for an average workday.

Some twenty-four-hour projects are excellent and some are dreadful. Some have terrific attendants and some have staff that abuse the residents and steal everything they can carry out unseen. It's usually one extreme or the other. They generally work best when they are run by the residents themselves. I have friends who live quite happily in a couple of these projects. In the bad projects, however, attendants are chronically late or fail to show. The residents are totally at the mercy of the attendants — even though the attendant is the employee, the roles get reversed and the attendant chooses what he or she will cook, clean or do. The residents in the bad projects are more likely to be undereducated, on fixed incomes, have little outside family interest or intervention and either be unaware of their rights or unable to fight for them. As in other areas of society, the weak and marginalized members are taken advantage of and victimized.

A great solution — for those who have the ability and motivation — is self-managed funding. In this scenario, the funds that come from the provincial health ministry go directly to the disabled person, instead of to a housing facility or attendants. The recipient can then have control over how the money is expended. It is a more cost-efficient arrangement and it gives control to the individual, but not every person can handle such responsibility. There are currently pilot projects in provinces across Canada testing to see how many people are capable of living more independently this way. That number is certainly way higher than the number of people receiving the funding now. This is how I live, but I'm in a different situation because my funding comes from Workers' Compensation and Criminal Injuries Compensation instead of the health ministry.

*   *   *   *

As soon as I was able to get out of bed, I started preparations to move into an apartment in downtown Toronto. During my last semester at school, a friend who lived in a co-operative apartment building had informed me about an accessible apartment there, and I'd been on the waiting list for a few months. The apartment had become available in March, right in the middle of my nightmare with the pressure sore, so I had already been paying rent for three months before I moved into it. After living on my own in Arizona for years, I was looking forward to continuing my independence, and I was excited about buying my first furnishings for my first real place.

The apartment was great for my needs — which was lucky, because it was the only one I looked at! It was a two-bedroom unit with lots of windows and a large solarium. Some friends had decorated it for me while I was stuck in bed, so it was beautiful, too. And it was very close to *The Toronto Star* building, where I would be working.

Twice I had a live-in attendant, who worked all week long for me, morning and evening, with the day free while I was at work. It was what I had done while in Arizona, and though it worked there, back in Toronto it was an experiment that failed miserably. I was putting far too much on one person's shoulders, and the apartment was too small to offer much privacy. So for the next eighteen months or so my sisters Christine and Chella took turns living with me, knowing it was to be a temporary situation until I found a bigger place, and I hired a few attendants who came at specific times of the day to do what I needed.

Though I was in my own apartment, I was still fairly dependent on my family. Even when my sisters were living with me, there were numerous times when I was stuck and needed a hand. On weekends I frequently needed help with dinner — my dance card wasn't exactly full. I was used to drinking a lot of water and I needed help in the washroom quite a bit. The situation had some unwelcome similarities to the way my life had been before I went away. My family always came through for me, but often at the expense of their own plans. They weren't always happy about the situation, which was clear to me, but, as before, I didn't have a solution. At times we were all more resentful than understanding. My sisters might stop by on their way out to clubs or parties and help me with what I needed and I wouldn't try to hide my unhappiness, though I knew my attitude would make them feel guilty. I *couldn't* pretend I enjoyed sitting at home by myself while they skipped off and had a blast. I wasn't interested in going to loud, smoky bars where everyone danced and tried to meet that special someone. I couldn't get attendants to come late anyway, and my sisters usually stayed out with their friends past closing time.

*   *   *   *

The expression "good help is hard to find" may be a cliché, but it is an understatement when it comes to personal attendants. Some consider it mindless work, but in actuality, being a good attendant involves skills not easily found. What I'm looking for is a person who does not judge or question what is asked of them (unless it's radically illegal and they have a problem with it). I need someone who is extremely responsible, reliable, trustworthy and punctual. I need someone who understands that I am an adult and I make my own decisions about my life. I mainly need a pair of hands and nothing more — not a parent, not a manager. However, an attendant is a partner in one sense. Good attendants make the difficult task of living with a disability a little easier.

Look at spontaneity. That's something that's an uncommon luxury to most disabled people with high levels of dependence. It's important that attendants get trained and learn routines, yet it's also important that they remain flexible. I may do things a certain way every day, then one day decide to switch it. It's important for me to be able to do that without having to explain myself, and it's important that my attendant not get irritated by it. This may sound like nit-picking, but believe me, it can be a huge issue.

That goes for scheduling, too. Let's say I have an attendant booked to arrive at 11:00 p.m. to help me get ready for bed and I get a sudden invitation to go to a party, or I've rented movies with friends and we're running behind. I end up on the losing end because I can't adjust the start time with my attendant. Each side has a point — I'm an adult, life is not always predictable, and I should be able to go to bed whenever I want. Yet from the other perspective, it's not fair that my attendant's evening gets thrown off by my sudden schedule change. I have had some friends and roommates who have known my routine and been willing to help me instead of my attendant, but then cancelling has its implications, too. That means the attendant loses the payment, which she often depends on. In addition, she has set her evening around my schedule, and a sudden cancellation is unfair. The solution is for me to pay her at least part of the wage she would have earned, if I cancel at the last minute.

I've gotten so used to going to bed and getting up when my attendant arrives that I've completely forgotten what it's like to crash or rise whenever the mood strikes. There are many nights when I'd prefer to stay up later and days when I'd like to sleep in, but without knowing that ahead of time that's not a choice I have. It's definitely difficult to get attendants to come late at night, especially on weekends. It's not surprising really — who wants to leave their nice, cosy home late at night (particularly in winter) and work for one hour?

My life must be planned, extraordinarily planned. That it's impossible to always know in advance exactly what my schedule will be is a never-ending source of frustration for me. My choices are very limited. Even with an understanding about flexibility, it can be tough for both employer and employee.

Privacy is one of the biggest issues to deal with. Attendants learn a great deal about the life of the person they work for, and it's critical they keep that information to themselves. Whether it's the way I manage my bowel and bladder, or who calls me on the phone, it's all personal. My phone is a hands-free unit, which means the person I'm speaking to is on a loudspeaker. This has always been a sensitive issue for me. I've had people regularly participate in my phone calls, not even pretending they aren't following my conversation. It's not easy for me to ask someone to leave the room. I always feel as though I'm offending people, or that they'll think I'm discussing them.

This issue applies also to banking business. Someone must use a bank machine for me. The responsible thing to do is to check that the correct amount of the transaction appears on the slip, but the courteous thing to do is to either ignore the balance or forget about it quickly, and the information should certainly be regarded as confidential. I'm sorry to say that I once heard one of my attendants dishing out my personal financial information to a friend over the phone. And mail — I need someone to open my mail and be my hands to organize my paperwork. When I need private mail opened I feel as though I am being insulting if I say something like, "By the way, this is personal." Then it sounds as though I've assumed the person intended to read it.

I have found that attendants close to my age are best, at least for the bulk of my needs. It's a physically demanding job, so they must be in relatively good shape. And it must be a person I can relate to if it's going to be more than a temporary situation. It must be a trustworthy person, though I discovered that's not so easy to judge (I've had money taken from my wallet, as have other disabled friends of mine).

The turnover rate for this kind of work is pretty high. Occasionally I find an attendant who sticks around a long time, but the average person lasts about a year, if they work more than a day or two a week. I've had the good fortune a few times to have an attendant last two or more years, but that's not common. I typically have as many as eight or nine people in my working pool at any given time.

Training attendants causes the most stress I ever feel. My regular routine goes out the window. It can take almost double the time to get ready in the morning while training and for a while after, until the person is used to the job. Part of what makes it so stressful is that I have to hide the effect it has on me. I must appear to have infinite patience, even when I'm screaming on the inside. It's also stressful for the person being trained, particularly if he or she has no experience.

Unfortunately, it's a job with few benefits. Someone like me, living on my own in the community, can't afford to provide medical or dental benefits or vacation pay for my attendants. I get a monthly allowance for what I need, but it doesn't stretch beyond that. There are no tax breaks. To get the kind of people I need I pay an hourly salary that's considerably higher than minimum wage. The hours are all over the place, and it's not always steady income.

People usually assume that an attendant has nursing or medical training, which is not necessarily correct. Sometimes it's actually better to train a person without any relevant background; then it's easier to mould them into the kind of employee I want.

It's partly because disabled people are so devalued that attendants are, too. They are facilitators, enabling someone like me to live as independently as I possibly can. But none of them can get far with just that on their resumé. People don't realize that a good attendant has many valuable skills — organization, efficiency, flexibility, people skills. One common assumption is that the person is doing charity work. "Oh, how wonderful of you," they say. "You must find it richly rewarding." "Uh, it pays the bills," they usually reply, or, "I'm just getting myself through school." Unfortunately, they're usually considered either unskilled or a saint.

I have people help me up in the morning, others to help me get ready for bed, one who comes to cook dinner during the week, a roommate who spends some time doing odd jobs for me and others who work backup when I need it. I need a pair of hands for grocery shopping, doing paperwork, having a bite to eat. It's a constant juggle to fit my needs around everyone's schedule, and there are times when it seems like everyone is quitting at once and I have to replace the whole bunch.

Trust me, managing it all alone is not idyllic and problem-free; those words can never be associated with disability. But I still have no doubt that self-directed funding is the best solution. I'm occasionally asked the question "Who takes care of you?" The answer is simple: I take care of myself. I don't hire "caregivers," I hire attendants. I receive my attendant allowance each month, and with it I hire people to follow my directions.

I'm certainly more independent now than ever before, but it's taken me many years to get here. I'd have to say relative independence, or at least the knowledge that it was possible, really started in Arizona. Before I went there, I had no clue what kind of life I would lead or *could* lead. It took years of trial and error.

*   *   *   *

In 1993, after a couple of years in my apartment, I started looking at condominiums. I needed a large place, with two good-sized bedrooms and two complete bathrooms. That way I could have a roommate, privacy wouldn't be as difficult, and it could be a more permanent solution. Other than that, my only criterion was to be very close to a wheelchair-accessible movie theatre (not an easy feat in this city). Amazingly, I found the building for me right away. It's in my favourite neighbourhood in the city, with loads of shopping and entertainment an easy distance for me to reach in my wheelchair, and work is a five-minute drive away. Soon after moving in, I set about modifying it with environmental controls.

I've always been acutely aware that I'm better off financially than most people with spinal cord injuries. Dealing with the Workers' Compensation Board has been frustrating at times, but for me it's been a comprehensive kind of insurance coverage. I now have a state-of-the-art wheelchair that I can operate with my head. The head control that I have is one that can also work environmental control equipment that is wired in, all with infrared light. I can open my front door, and a door that leads to an outdoor deck adjoining my condominium. I can operate the TV and VCR, the lights, raise and lower my blinds, trigger a device that pours water into a teapot on my desk, empty the bag that my bladder empties into, even open the door of my parrot's cage. I have three telephones in my home I can operate.

Extravagant? Some might think so. What does having this equipment mean to me? I don't know if I can adequately convey the importance. It all comes down to control and quality of life. The more control a person has over their environment, the better. Sure, many times when I open or close my blinds someone is home. I can ask someone to open them each morning and close them at dusk, *or I can do it myself, whenever I choose*. Until you are in a position of having to ask someone to do every little thing for you all day, every day, you might not appreciate just how satisfying a motorized blind can be.

Most of the equipment I have is fairly new. I lived without the ability to use the washroom independently for about eleven years, and now I don't know how I did it. My bladder empties into a bag that's strapped to my leg, and attached to the tubing at the bottom is an electric clamp, with a wire leading to the battery on my chair. By triggering the clamp through the head control of my chair, I can empty the bag whenever I need to, without having to ask someone to help me. It's a fairly simple device but an indispensable one. When it needed some work recently and I faced the prospect of living without it for a couple of weeks, I purchased a backup to use instead. I knew I couldn't justify a request to WCB to pay for a second one, but I am not willing to be without it if it can at all be helped. I feel fortunate that my salary enabled me to afford the $300 for the backup — not everyone is so lucky.

Every disabled person should have financial access to every gadget available and all attendant needs. Unfortunately this is not reality. There are multitudes of people who must somehow come up with the cash for just about everything they require. There are government programs to assist with some coverage for basic equipment, such as wheelchairs and some environmental controls, but they are not exactly liberal with funds, nor do they make quick and easy decisions.

Now I'm more independent in my home than ever, and I don't rely on my family in any regular way. We're a healthier and happier group for it.

*   *   *   *

A whole other set of problems comes into play when I'm out with friends. Food and eating have been, for me, big issues to deal with. My arms don't move, making it necessary for someone else to bring food to my mouth. Many call it "feeding," but I always refer to it as someone "helping me" with a meal or eating "with me." It took me years to realize that in my desire to make my needs as inconspicuous as possible, I was actually giving up control. Instead of giving somebody (a novice, say) directions on how I like to eat, I too often expected them to just "get it" and slide right into a routine I like. Therefore, I sometimes ended up eating much faster or slower than I like, but instead of giving a direction or stating my preference, I'd sit and fume inside.

As in many areas in life, communication is the answer. I have to take the chance that when I communicate what I want, people won't take offence or chastise themselves, thinking they *should* have figured it out on their own. It amazes me how many questions about me are asked to people I'm with once I'm out of earshot. Strangers mainly ask how I operate my chair or get into my van. Most frequently the person waits for me to pass, then asks whoever is walking behind me. This is unbelievably frustrating, because I can't turn my chair around in time to answer. Sometimes the people they ask don't know the answers, or at least don't know how I would personally answer those questions. I think I'm very approachable, and I wish the questions would come directly to me, so I could answer them the best way. When people do approach me directly it can lead to some terrific, informative conversations that I really enjoy. I believe able-bodied people, at least the uneducated ones, are afraid of disability and afraid of offending someone "less fortunate." There is an air of mystery around disability that needs to be broken for us to be accepted in the mainstream.

The mystery is handed down from one generation to the next when parents say to their children, "Don't stare," or shush them when they ask, "Why is that lady in a wheelchair?" I'd love it if the parent said, "Let's go say hello and maybe we can ask her," but perhaps that's not realistic. In general, children can ask me anything they like. I love talking to kids, and no child has ever asked me an offensive or inappropriate question. As for adults, you should treat a disabled person with the same respect you would show to an able-bodied person. If you get too personal, be aware that your question might not get answered. I think all my friends who use wheelchairs feel the same way I do about this.

But even personal friends have contributed to this problem of building walls. I was once meeting a couple for lunch who had children I did not know. While confirming plans on the telephone the night before, my friend said, "We're bringing the kids, but we've prepared them." Taken aback, I didn't respond to the comment, but my mind wondered, "Prepared them for *what*?" Perhaps it was my imagination, but I could have sworn those kids looked frightened of me when we met the next day. If children need *preparation* to meet a person who happens to have a disability, they can only grow up considering our differences, not our similarities.

It's usually obvious to me when I meet someone who is uncomfortable around my disability. It almost always stems from inexperience or a lack of exposure to people who use wheelchairs. People don't know what to do or say, how to act. They are often afraid of doing or saying the "wrong" thing. People have patterns in how they interact with others, but someone like me comes along and interrupts the pattern. So whose responsibility is it to ease the discomfort? I usually end up taking it on.

The language people use in reference to people with disabilities is one indication of how we are viewed. I'm not one to get too hung up on semantics, but I have gotten pretty tired of being reduced to the status of a "wheelchair." Take wheelchair seating in concert halls and theatres, for example. These are areas where a disabled person can remain in his or her wheelchair to see a show. Because of limited space in such venues a person who requires such seating can only ever sit with one other person. While I don't take issue with that, I am fed up with the language the ticket-sellers use. When I call to order, I'm asked to confirm, "One wheelchair, one attendant?" I always reply, "Actually, they're for one *person* in a wheelchair and one friend." The inference, aside from turning me into an inanimate object, is that I can only go out with attendants or trained members of my staff. The reality is that I go out with any friend who has a driver's licence — unless we're headed somewhere that's within walking distance, in which case there are no limits at all.

I was on board an airplane once, patiently waiting for my wheelchair to be brought up from the hold, when I overheard an airline employee report over a walkie-talkie, "No, the plane's not empty yet. There's still a wheelchair on board." Call me confused, but wasn't that what I was waiting for? But of course the person on the receiving end of the intercom message understood perfectly.

This kind of terminology has sometimes led to rather hilarious encounters. Cineplex Odeon, a Canadian film distribution company, has a policy of charging half price for a disabled person and one person they are with. For starters, I'm not all that comfortable with the policy. I felt patronized every time I saw "One Child/One Senior" appear on the ticket screen. I now politely refuse the discount. At times I want to retort indignantly that I can afford to pay fully for myself, but I keep reminding myself that the majority of people with disabilities are on a fixed income and are much more limited than someone like me, who is fortunate enough to be working. One day, some time ago, I went to a matinée at my regular theatre with a friend. The teller, who looked very young and somewhat unsure of herself, asked for half of what I was usually charged. When I inquired why, she looked at me and stated, "Because you are a wheelchair." Fortunately I was in a good mood, so my reaction was only to laugh myself silly.

I've gone to the Toronto zoo once since the shooting, and I have to say it was one of the worst experiences I've had going out in public. It was very soon after I came home from rehab, so this is going back to the mid-1980s. We were a group of five people, three adults and two children. When we stepped up and told this to the ticket-seller, she responded, after noting my wheelchair, "One adult, two children and one handicap with a supervisor." Then, after listening to two visitors discuss — totally within my earshot — whether I was actually "the" Barbara Turnbull, then conclude "She must be, because everyone else is staring at her, too," I decided I'd encountered enough animals for the day, though I'd barely made it through the front gates.

I'm the first to admit that political correctness is taken too far; consider the nauseating terms "physically *challenged*" and, even worse, "handicapable," but I do resent the implication that I am what I drive. And guess what, folks? We "wheelchairs" have friends, partners, spouses and family members to go out with, not just attendants. And no matter how hard I try, I never seem able to be wild enough to need a supervisor.

The media, in their efforts to provide concise newswriting, have made terms like "wheelchair-bound" and "confined to wheelchair" common ways of referring to people with disabilities. Taken literally, those expressions would be amusingly inaccurate if they weren't so offensive. Everyone I know who uses a wheelchair sleeps in a bed and often sits on couches or armchairs. The only time I've ever seen a person "bound" to a chair was in a gangster flick.

While I'm on the subject of language and communication between able and disabled folks, I'd like to take this opportunity to assure readers that I've heard every cheesy joke about wheelchair usage there is. Whether it's about doing wheelies, speeding, drinking and driving, racing or getting a driver's licence, it ain't original, okay?

Nowhere is my disability thrown in my face more than at music concerts. The moment the audience gets to their feet my spirits plummet. At some concerts it only happens in encores, and I reached a point where I just accepted, and anticipated, that I would miss those highly charged concert closures, but at other shows I sometimes miss much more. One of the first concerts I attended after the shooting featured a group I really loved. In particular, they had one ballad that had meant a lot to me when I still lived a carefree existence. The audience jumped up as the band stepped on the stage, before the lights were even up. At one point the lead singer told the screaming fans, "I don't care how much you paid for your seat, I want you up out of it and dancing." At a cost of about $15,000, I was sure I had the most expensive seat in the house, but I didn't even get a glimpse of the band the entire concert. Already totally depressed, when they performed the ballad I'd been so looking forward to, I sat surrounded by the standing crowd, choking back tears.

*   *   *   *

Being accepted is a goal most disabled people have. Except in certain circles, I don't think it's one that is realized, even in today's supposedly more enlightened society. We live in a society that often "heroizes" people when it doesn't know how to respond to them. I have no doubt that some people enjoy being heroes, but I'm someone who has been put in that position, and I don't find it particularly comfortable. In a way, I feel it's kept me at arm's length from being a regular, accepted member of society. In its attempt to boost me up, it is ultimately devaluing.

I've never been comfortable with the label "inspirational." The most difficult times for me in this regard have been when I've been recognized with "courage" awards. The first one I received was the short-lived Steve Fonyo Medal of Courage, given by the City of Toronto (established right after the one-legged runner raised millions for cancer research with his cross-country marathon, but before his fall from grace amidst charges of fraud and assault). Privately I've always referred to these as "Good Crip" awards. They were undoubtedly heartfelt gestures, but they felt a bit patronizing. It took me years to figure out my feelings on this subject. I am not thumbing my nose at the awards I've been given, nor am I trashing the idea of them. I think they are important because they do recognize people who have made tremendous contributions to a population that has a harder time than most. I don't yet belong in that category. However, if I'm ever able to make a significant, concrete contribution, I will be proud to be recognized for it.

To me, a courageous act is one in which a person chooses to make himself vulnerable or take a risk and carries through for the good of another person or people. An example: someone is in a burning building, screaming for help. A good deed is to call for help, then get a hose and try to douse the flames. An act of courage is to run into the house to try and get the person out.

Getting out of bed every day does not take courage. Going to school — no matter how much more difficult it is for one person than another — does not take courage. Getting and keeping a job does not take courage; it takes skill, but not courage. I was shot and I am paralyzed. I have spent too many years living as a quadriplegic, years I'd give anything and everything to have lived in a fully functioning body. I've done well, and I've made the best of a horrible situation, but I haven't done it with courage. I've simply done it with strength and sheer will, the same way thousands of people live their lives every day, disabled or not.

I have not devoted my time to helping the disabled community. I've lent my name to fundraising activities, but I've lived for myself first and foremost. I've done what interests me. That's why those awards have made me so uncomfortable. What I feel they've done is recognize me for being a good cripple, and that's not something that deserves special mention, because thousands of people do it every day. Why is it that we are either ignored or exalted? Living like this is not my choice, it's just the way it is.

Having said that, I do realize that many people have been affected by my story and, perhaps more so, by the way in which I have forged ahead with my life. I do appreciate their admiration. Sometimes I'm recognized by someone and I sense that they feel actual *affection* for me, even though we've never met before. That does make me feel good. Part of the reason I struggle with the image people have of me is that I have a hard time accepting that people think so highly of *me*.

Once in a while, I can see the positive impact my actions can have and I feel I can give myself some credit. My sister Christine teaches high school at a minimum-security jail in northern Ontario, and in the fall of 1996 I visited and spoke to three of her classes about journalism and what it's like to be a victim of crime. A few of the inmates approached me afterward and thanked me, saying that my comments had given them a new perspective. On my way out, I was handed a letter written by an inmate who had just seen me in the hall and recognized me. He said he was too ashamed to reveal his name, but that he wanted to convey how much my "mere presence" at a jail meant to him. In his three-page letter he wrote: "It must take a person with your history a great amount of strength, faith in God and humanity, and understanding to be able to come here. Very few of us in these places ever see the result of our actions up close. As much as I dislike what I am confronted with in you, I do thank you for it. It, for me, affirms the decision I made some time ago, that I needed to make changes, both in my choice of lifestyles and within myself."

That letter in itself made the trip worthwhile, but, in addition, it helped me to understand a little bit of how others feel about me and what I have accomplished with this life I've been handed.

That people in Canada care as much as they do is one of the things I love so much about this country. And that I will never take for granted.

Chapter Eight:

SEX AND THE SINGLE CRIPPLE

Self-esteem has never been a strong part of my character. In fact, it's more accurate to say I've suffered from low self-esteem my whole life. Before my injury, my low self-image sent me fleeing from potential romantic relationships. It was easier and safer to set my sights on someone unattainable. If a guy was nice, sincere and looking for more than a casual fling, I'd either squash it directly or delay dealing with it until it played itself out and he moved on to saner pastures. After all, there had to be something wrong with a guy who wanted me.

I was only eighteen when I was hurt, so it's not as though the pattern was too well established, but whenever a guy showed real interest, all I remember feeling was panic. I never questioned it or tried to figure it out or get past it, I just reacted instantly. Sure, I had some dates and some flings, but I never had a "regular" boyfriend-girlfriend, long-term relationship.

So if you add a severe disability on top of that, you get one hurting individual.

Since the shooting, I generally don't look in the mirror more than I have to. I usually rely on my attendants to tell me if my clothes are sitting right, and I use a small, hand-held mirror to check my hair. Sometimes days go by in which I don't look at my full image. Then there are times when I actually forget about my disability — at a party, in a clothing store, going down a street — and suddenly I catch my reflection. The shock of seeing *me*, in a *wheelchair*, plunges me into a depression, and I quickly avert my eyes.

The first time I was privy to any discussion on romantic or sexual relationships after the shooting was close to three months later. I was still in intensive care, though in one of the isolation rooms, so I had a bit of privacy. My nurse was flipping through the channels on my tiny television when I saw someone in a wheelchair. I had her stop on that channel and saw I was tuned into "The Shulman File," a talk show hosted by Dr. Morton Shulman.

133

It wasn't a show I had ever been interested in, but I certainly knew who he was and that he was controversial. He usually managed to offend his guests one way or another, and it was not uncommon to see someone getting angry or upset. This night the guest was a high-level quadriplegic, and he sat in a head-operated wheelchair. I only remember one comment that Shulman made; it is one that has never left me.

"You say you people can have sex. Who wants you?"

Those words were like a derisive laugh aimed just at me. At that point, the indefinite aspect of my disability had not yet sunk in, nor had any of its implications. My fantasies all consisted of me hopping into a sports car and driving for days. The only thing I varied was the type of car.

Though the topic had been lurking in the back of my thoughts, I had not yet dealt with it in my own mind. That comment devastated me and shook me up for years.

I asked myself then, as I have many times since, if I were able-bodied, would I ever be attracted to someone with my disability? And if so, would I ever act on it?

The next time the issue came up was in rehab, at Lyndhurst Hospital. There was a sex education seminar for patients. Run by Paul Stirling, the hospital's psychologist, it consisted of four or five sessions that each lasted about an hour or more. It involved mostly dialogue and conversation about relationships, and there was a film shown during the last session in which couples with one disabled partner discussed and demonstrated their sex lives. In one of the sessions we broke into two groups and met with a psychologist of our own sex to discuss our own specific issues. These days at Lyndhurst the classes are always broken up into three groups, one for each sex and one for couples.

As Paul Stirling recently told me, not many of the patients attend the groups. Except for couples, it's too soon to be dealing with that aspect of life for most. Patients haven't worked out their own body image with their new status as a disabled person. It definitely wasn't good for me at that point.

Each session was agonizing, and my body reacted to the stress I was feeling. As soon as a session started, I would start to sweat profusely, but I dried up the moment I left the room. I couldn't bring myself to ask a single question, a problem that was compounded by the fact that nothing that we learned addressed a disability as severe as mine. At the course's end, I borrowed a book that included a chapter focusing on a woman with a C4 level injury — my level. But I was disappointed to discover that the woman's injury was not a complete one like mine. She had partial movement and feeling in different parts of her body. There just didn't seem to be anything that dealt specifically with my concerns and my disability, and I was in no state to be able to ask.

While I was still in rehab I attended a wedding with a friend from camp. I was spending weekends at home by this time. As we drove, I told him some stories about the hospital. In one, I mentioned my roommate's husband.

"She's married?" he asked.

"Yes," I replied, prepared to go on with my story.

"Is he in a chair?"

"No."

"She was married before her accident, then." It was a statement, not a question.

"Yes," I said, wishing I could say otherwise.

This was the attitude I was facing from my own friends, even before I was out of the hospital. The message to me was clear: if you're a single crip, stay in your own backyard.

My friends didn't talk about it, my family didn't talk about it. So neither did I, for years. Meanwhile, I ached with loneliness and silently prayed for my Prince Charming.

I had decided that if I ever had a relationship, the lucky guy would have to fit certain criteria. He had to be able-bodied, for starters. A relationship in which one person is disabled would be hard enough, the logistics if *both* were disabled would be too difficult. Sense of humour was high on my list, coupled with someone I found attractive, obviously.

But I figured my only chance was with someone who was involved in some way with the disabled community. That way, he would already realize that we're people, just like everybody else; he would see past the wheelchair. That sure narrowed the field.

Once in awhile someone, usually my younger sister Christine, would say something about the possibility of a relationship, or tell me that some day I'd meet someone. I would always say I had no intention of marrying or I knew it wasn't going to happen. I always felt compelled to say a flat "No." But inside my heart screamed "Yes!"

More typically, the subject was simply never broached. Friends would never ask me, "So, are you seeing anyone?" the way friends often ask each other. Nor would anyone ever say, "Hey, I've got a friend who would be *perfect* for you." The topic just seemed easier to avoid than confront. Of course, on the odd occasion when a friend did ask about it, I scoffed at the notion, then changed the subject. My dating personality remained stuck at eighteen — and a dysfunctional eighteen, at that.

Life in the romance department didn't get any easier for me after I left home for university in Arizona. It got worse, in fact. I fled from opportunities. One afternoon, shortly after arriving, I was in a stereo shop in a local mall. Liz was shopping elsewhere and we had agreed to meet there so we could buy a tape-player for our dorm room.

I struck up a conversation with a salesman and we really hit it off. In the span of a short conversation, we discovered several things we had in common. Suddenly, he looked at me differently. He looked at me as a *woman*, and he looked as though he was interested in asking this woman out for a date. I panicked, mumbling some excuse about meeting someone, and fled the store.

The next time I did it was months later, on campus. Disabled Student Resources had a transportation service for those temporarily or permanently disabled. The battery-powered carts were driven by student employees, and anyone with a mobility problem could sign up for rides around campus (Arizona State University is one *huge* campus). My dorm was slightly off campus, and I used to get rides to one early class and home again one late afternoon a week.

My schedule fell during the shifts of a student named Seth. The ten- or fifteen-minute rides always flew by with us chatting a mile a minute, and it wasn't unusual for us to spend another few minutes finishing up a conversation. We discovered, among many similarities, that we had been born on the same day, the same year.

This time he even fit all my criteria — cute, funny, and he clearly saw past the wheelchair. One day he casually suggested that we get together after school hours. I stammered an agreement, then beat a hasty retreat. We continued our rides and great chats, but things never progressed beyond that. Then, using every ounce of nerve I didn't actually have, I took another step one day a couple of weeks later. I had tickets to a Sting concert and my friend had backed out at the last minute, so I called Seth and asked him.

"Wow, I'd like to, but I can't. I've got plans already," he said.

I hung up and tortured myself for having asked. I figured that I must have misread everything, that he was just being pleasant to the crip he had to drive around to make money. The fact that I asked him the day before the concert didn't matter to me, I was sure he'd lied about having plans.

A day or two later he phoned me. Not for business, just to chat and to see how the concert had gone. Not only did I make up a lame excuse and get off the phone as quickly as I could, I cancelled all my bookings on the transit service and never talked to him again.

Now I can see that it was my old pattern surfacing, "saving" me from ... what, I don't know. Being hurt, perhaps; taking a chance, definitely. Back then, I just reacted and tried to forget about it. Inside I was no different from anyone else, or so I thought, but I kept sabotaging the very opportunities I was so desperately wanting.

It wasn't just me. I was also getting discouraging messages from the rest of society. I remember listening to a live, national phone-in show right after the "Scales of Justice" radio docudrama. A woman from Winnipeg phoned in to criticize the sentences the four accused received and said, "What about that girl? She'll never marry, she'll never have children." I cringed as people from one end of Canada to another heard those words.

Was that true, I wondered? Based solely on the issue of disability, the answer would be no. Even in my own small circle, several of my friends had met a partner and married after their spinal cord injuries. As well, many disabled people have children. There are tremendous technologies that make reproduction a reality even for men and women with severe disabilities. I know of a disabled woman in Toronto who has two children — she was artificially inseminated with both. She is currently single and has been since before she began her family. And nobody can put a negative spin on it, because she's a great mom. I personally would not try to bear a child, but I'd consider adoption or surrogacy if the circumstances were right for me. I *know* I'd make a good mother, too.

While none of my friends would ever make such a callous comment, their attitudes have hurt me at times. A couple of close friends, people completely comfortable with me, admitted they would never even consider dating a person with a disability. Another friend, visiting me in Arizona, met a friend of Liz's and mine on campus. He was very good looking, and my friend repeatedly asked Liz why she wasn't dating him. She even asked me, "Why doesn't Liz go for him?" It never occurred to her to ask *me* if I was interested. Someone else once suggested I hire a male attendant because, like therapists or nurses, "they often fall in love with their employer or patient."

I was sitting with some friends at a coffee shop once when the subject of marriage and children came up. Everyone at the table was asked if they wanted to marry, then if they wanted kids. Everyone but me, that is. I'd suddenly become invisible.

But again, I wasn't willing to take any risks. One night in my dorm the phone rang, with its distinctive on-campus ring. It was a wrong number. I'd just hung up when it rang again. It was the same guy, looking for someone else. The lines must have been crossed, because he said he'd been dialling a different number. We started joking and chatting, and, after several minutes, he said I sounded "cute" and asked if I would give him my number so he could call me again. I made an excuse and hung up, suddenly depressed. I pictured the look of shock I'd receive if I ever met him on a blind date. It became a vicious cycle that kept perpetuating stereotypes and resulted in my continued loneliness.

A person with a disability has so much to fight against to have a healthy self-image. One thing I've observed is that disabled people don't get the messages from society that, I believe, go a long way to shaping how we feel about ourselves. These can be as subtle as an appraising look from a stranger or as obvious as a wolf whistle from some guy driving by in a souped-up sports car. These messages simply say "You are attractive." The recipient of these messages is an accepted, "dateable" member of society. Crips like me don't get these messages.

When I'm in public, walking with another female approximately my age, I watch the eyes of men, approximately our age, as they pass us. They almost always check out the person I'm with. It's an obvious look of appraisal. These men never cast their eyes on me — in fact they usually don't see me at all. I find myself often issuing a silent challenge, mentally *daring* them to look my way. If they do, their eyes pass with mild interest over my chair. "How does that move?" is clearly written on their faces.

It's enormously hard to fight against all that. How does a person feel attractive without ever receiving messages that they are? And how does a person draw someone toward them if they think there isn't anything attractive about them?

Much of society views us disabled folk as asexual, and my attitude has never helped to educate even those close to me. But why on Earth *wouldn't* I be interested in a relationship? Low self-esteem aside, I had been in every way a normal teenager. I had not been chaste. My hopes, dreams and desires mirrored those of all teenagers. In a split second my body became paralyzed, but why would my mind and heart change? Why would desire vanish?

Good sex comes mostly from the head, experts will tell you. Being strictly logical, it all comes down to two things: desire and imagination. These things are not diminished by disability. If anything, they are enhanced.

I doubt that I need to remind any reader that sex is one of our basic human needs. I also don't need to say that sex is pleasurable. But suddenly I was kicked out of the club. I certainly don't blame all of society for my long drought. It took me a good ten years to figure out my own hang-ups, the ones that kept setting off my flight instinct.

Over the years some close friends told me they thought I was closed off to the idea of a relationship. The first time a friend said it, I dismissed it as being way off base. Then a second friend said the very same thing. I tossed that off as well. When a third friend repeated the same thoughts, I realized I had to do something to break the pattern. I had to get a bit of control over the situation. Then came a completely new idea, one that had certainly never entered my mind before.

"Why don't you hire someone?"

The suggestion, coming from a long-time friend, shocked but intrigued me. We were discussing the whole dating issue, and I was telling her that the longer it went, the harder it got for me.

"Hire someone?" I asked. "I could never do that."

"Why not? Think about it," she urged. "You certainly wouldn't want to be alone in your place with him, but I'd wait in your living room and make sure everything was okay."

My mind raced. Could I do that? Where on Earth would I ever find a male hooker? Like so much else in life, even prostitution is easier for men. Female hookers are found on many street corners all over the downtown core. But I wouldn't want that. There were several considerations: cleanliness, safety, privacy and definitely discretion. With the kind of image "Barbara Turnbull" had in Toronto, that's all I'd need is some guy spouting off that I'd hired him to ... what did I even want?

I'd thought about taking out a personal ad before, but had already ruled it out. Firstly, I'd obviously have to mention my disability, and what if I heard from sickos who targeted me *because* of my disability? What if some pervert was only curious about what sex would be like with a crip? Then there was the problem of my name being so recognizable. And it was bad enough that I'd need help with a drink, I certainly wouldn't do *that* on a blind date. No, a personal ad was out of the question.

The next day, I got a *NOW* magazine, a Toronto weekly, and as soon as I was alone I flipped to the ads at the back. Just reading them left butterflies in my stomach.

Aaron! Boyish, 20, 6 ft, 165 lbs, swimmer's build

Arabian Stud!

! Hot Hard Hunk !

Gymnast — Tanned, muscular and smooth

College boys, the ultimate fantasy!

I thought about dialling one of the numbers.

Just to get some basic information.

I wished I had the nerve but I knew I would never actually do it. I put the idea out of my head.

A few months later the subject surfaced again, this time with a couple of my attendants. I had started talking about the issues of men, women, disability, romance and sex more often. It was freeing, after so many years of keeping all my thoughts bottled up. These attendants were so open and comfortable talking about it all, even providing examples of people they'd known who had sought out such services. Some were disabled, but certainly not all.

"I know a lawyer who doesn't want the hassle of a relationship or the pressure of having to phone the next morning, he just wants sex. Twice a month he calls an escort service," one told me.

"All that is far easier for men than women," I'd argue.

"If you're interested I could make inquiries," one said one day.

"Really?" I laughed. "How would you do that?"

She explained that a friend of a friend of a friend worked as a Dominatrix — a woman who is paid to sexually dominate and humiliate men. It had started out as a way to pay for university, but she'd stayed with it. She apparently had the right contacts.

"Sure, what the hell, make inquiries," I said, trying to sound casual.

A possible perfect solution.

Meanwhile, I continued my education about this issue I had allowed to elude me for so many years. I went to the Lovecraft store in Toronto's Yorkville area, feeling completely self-conscious. "Why is *she* here?" I was sure the other customers were thinking.

I bought two books, one the autobiography of a famous New York Dominatrix, and a book of erotica, "By Women, For Women." I consumed the autobiography in a matter of days, but the erotica stayed unread on a shelf. I wasn't comfortable enough to read it, even in my own home, though at the time I passed it off as disinterest.

It took a few weeks before the information came back to me, but yes, the Dominatrix knew a male hooker. Questions and answers went between my attendant and her "source." Basic questions, like cost, age, background, sexual orientation. I learned that he worked as a stripper, too, not just a prostitute. The whole thing didn't seem real, it was like a very weird game. Finally my attendant couldn't play the go-between anymore.

"Here's her number, you really should talk to her yourself."

After staring at the number for another week or two, I called one afternoon, my heart pounding. Not quite believing what I was doing, I left a message with a time when I knew I'd be alone. I didn't even want my roommate in on this.

She called, and we had an easy, comfortable, twenty-minute chat, about everything from travel to education. I told her about a friend of mine who was thinking about becoming a Dominatrix. She offered to talk to her and pass on some tips. She told me about herself, how she got started and why she'd stayed with it after finishing school.

"There's a demand for this," she stated simply. "And it can be extremely satisfying work," she added, laughing.

"Steven" was twenty-eight, dark-featured, muscular and easygoing, she explained. Heterosexual in his own life, he serviced couples fairly often. I asked her what he charged and how long he stayed. Since I had never seen male strippers, I had decided to have him do a "show" one night for me and a couple of friends. There are no male strip clubs in Toronto that are wheelchair accessible (believe me, we checked).

It made sense to have him come strip first, anyway. Once we'd met, a second night with just him and me would be easier.

"I think he charges $200 for about an hour or so, but he's not a clock-watcher," she said.

I gave her a time and day when I knew I'd be alone and she promised to pass on the information to "Steven" (obviously not his real name), who would call me himself.

"Are you sure you're comfortable with this?" she asked me twice.

Is it that obvious?

"I don't know about now, but I intend to be," I vowed.

"By the way, I think it's really great you're doing this," she said as we signed off.

I sat there digesting our conversation and, particularly, her parting comment. My attendants thought it was great, the two friends I'd told thought it was great, the Dominatrix thought it was great.

Damn it all, it *was* great. Wasn't it?

Without a doubt, my first phone call with Steven will always be the most bizarre conversation I'll ever have with someone I've never met. It consisted of him asking a ton of questions and me stammering out mostly noncommittal answers.

"Is there an occasion? A birthday?"

"No. Well yes, actually, it's mine. Birthday, that is." (Dini had already said that the first night would be a birthday present from her to me).

"What music do you want playing?"

"Gee, I never thought about that. It doesn't really matter. Do you have any, uh, favourites you like to...? No? Well, let me give it some thought."

"Do you want me to strip right down, or to a G-string?"

"Well, I guess, uh, whatever you prefer, I guess right down. Or whatever."

"Do you want me to have an erection?"

"Oh. Well. Uh, whatever. Just, uh, go with the flow, I guess, or, whatever. I don't know. I'm not making this easy for you, I know."

"What do you want me to wear?"

"Oh, god, I don't know. I don't care. Whatever you want, it doesn't matter."

Then it started getting easier.

"Do you want me to bend over?"

"No, that's okay."

"Do you want me to physically interact with you or your guests?"

"Uh, no."

"Will anyone want to touch me?"

"No."

"Any fetishes?"

"NO!!"

He wanted to know everything: the lighting in the room, where everyone would be sitting, the names of the guests, if alcohol or drugs would be consumed. I suppose he deserved credit for preparation. I explained that this first night was for me to get comfortable, then I'd probably hire him for a second night, as a hooker. I told him I had a disability and hadn't been with anyone for a long time.

"So are you just looking for something visual?" he asked.

"Well no, I'm looking for intimacy," I replied, hit with irritation and my first flash of disappointment. Didn't he understand? Where was his imagination? Was it so hard to figure out? Don't able-bodied people know what *they'd* miss if they were disabled?

Start with basic touching. For the most part that vanishes when you're a crip. Sure I was touched every day, but by attendants, as they helped me get dressed, as they washed my hair, as they spread moisturizer on my face. That's not exactly the same as being touched with affection. And I'm not talking about a chaste kiss on the cheek by a family member or a friend.

And what about kissing, necking, *making out*, for hours, or what seems like hours. I'd be willing to guess that most people who go through long periods of celibacy — and here I'm talking about longer than a year or two, or five — don't miss the basic act of intercourse or penetration but the intimacy that goes with it.

When all that goes in a flash, and stays gone for years, it's hard not to obsess about it. I had reached a point where I thought it wouldn't matter what qualities a body possessed, as long as that body was with me in bed.

Anyhow, he wanted to get together the night before our little Friday night party, to meet and to see where everything would take place. I was nervous that whole Thursday. I'd planned everything around a weekend when I'd be alone, so no one else would be home. He called to confirm just before coming over and asked if I wanted him to bring a joint.

"Sure," I replied. I was not a seasoned pot smoker, but not being a drinker I thought it might calm my nerves.

I was hit with my next flash of disappointment when he walked in. He was an attractive person, from a objective point of view, but he was not my type at all. He was very muscular. I've never been particularly attracted to well-built men.

So what? Get over it. You need the practice, this opportunity is sitting right before your eyes, you will not back down.

He might not have been my type, but he was extremely cool and laid back. Friendly, too. I don't think much would have fazed him. Of course I'm sure he'd done things and seen things that I couldn't even begin to imagine, certainly much stranger than sitting in a room with a person in a wheelchair. He got himself a beer and we started chatting while he rolled a joint.

"Don't make it too big," I said, knowing I couldn't pretend to be cool if I was really stoned.

He told me about his "regular" job (computers), regular customers of his "moonlighting" job (married couples looking for extra spice, unsatisfied married women, women who hired him to serve food or drinks nude at a party), his dating life (girlfriends usually knew about his extracurricular activities), his family (sisters and mother knew nothing).

I cannot believe I'm sitting here with a hooker. A HOOKER, for chrissakes. Me!! This is so weird.

We chatted more about plans for the following evening.

"Do you want a little demo?" he asked me two or three times.

"No thanks, I'll wait," I repeated.

"Not so many lights tomorrow," he said at least ten or twelve times. I assured him it would all be done by candlelight.

"Do you want me to have an erection?" he asked again.

"No preference, just see how the evening goes," I said, again. "But how can you do that on demand and in front of strangers?"

"Well, it doesn't happen instantly. I just think about it and play a little. I'm a bit of an exhibitionist, I guess. I can have an erection right now while we sit here, if you'd like."

"No thanks," I said in a rush.

"Really, it's easy. I can do that if you'd like."

"NO! It's quite all right, I'll wait," I said. "But thanks, though."

This is so weird.

As it turned out, he had figured out who I was during our initial telephone conversation, just from me giving him my first name, saying I was disabled and that I had grown up here. He had been fifteen when I was shot, but he remembered all the publicity.

The third strike against him was how excited he was that he'd be stripping in front of Dini Petty.

"Maybe she'll want to start hiring me," he said.

Don't hold your breath.

I had decided to be totally frank with what I was looking for in a second "date." He had obviously not automatically known what I'd want, but why should he? I thought of the Dominatrix's book and took strength — her first customer had plunked down $200 and asked her to pee on his face, for crying out loud. Practising the art of kissing was pretty tame in comparison. I didn't get too specific, since my enthusiasm for this whole scene was quickly waning, but I still thought there was a chance I might go through with it.

"Look, it's been so long I think I've forgotten how to kiss," I said. "I'm not looking for major sex."

"Well, it's good you know what you want," he said absentmindedly, licking the rolling paper and sealing the joint and his fate as my personal hooker at the same time.

After he left I sat trying to convince myself I wasn't completely disappointed. He could have said a number of things that would have made a difference:

"This is something to look forward to."

"That sounds like a nice evening."

"What a nice change of pace that would be."

They'd have been lies, but it would have made the whole charade a lot easier to take.

The following night was even stranger than the previous one had been. Dini was going to be late, she was actually skipping out of a party she was hosting to participate in my get-together. The other friend I'd invited, who happened to be about seven months pregnant at the time, arrived a bit late too, only twenty minutes before Steven was scheduled to arrive. Having come directly from work, she was still eating dinner when he showed up.

When Dini finally arrived, we all sat around the table making small talk. I had decided on a movie soundtrack, and he knew it was the next CD coming up. It seemed to take forever for it to start, and when it finally did he disappeared into the washroom.

He emerged after several minutes, wearing only a baseball cap on backwards and a pair of jeans. I was sitting on one side of the dining-room table, while the other two audience members sat beside each other on the other side. Steven stood in front of the table and started swaying back and forth, slowly circling and looking each of us in the eye in turn.

He undid his jeans and slipped out of them. He was wearing what looked like tight cotton boxers. I learned later that this was the underwear style made famous by poster boy/actor Markie Mark. They were Calvin Kleins, and apparently in every fashion magazine and on billboards everywhere. I hadn't noticed. What did I know? I didn't follow trends in men's underwear. Women were supposed to love them, but they did nothing for me. Those came off right away, as he continued to sway and circle. Underneath he was wearing a plain, white, cotton G-string.

Where's the tiger stripes or the fluorescent pink satin? That's pretty boring.

"Steven, you have got a *great* ass," Dini said.

He definitely took care of himself, was very muscular and toned. But the more I saw, the less I was interested.

"You really have a great body," Dini added.

I sent a silent "thank you" her way for breaking the ice. I felt so awkward and didn't have a clue what to say.

Steven slipped the G-string off, covered himself with it for a moment, then cast it aside with his other clothes.

That's his striptease act? No bumping? No grinding? Is this supposed to be fun?

It was not exactly what I'd been expecting. For the next few minutes he continued to sway and circle while he started to rub himself. My dear friends had started a conversation about pregnancy, delivery and babies. Me, I sat on my side of the table, feeling like a bigger and bigger idiot with each passing minute. I worried that they looked rude for having a conversation while this man bared himself half-erect before us. There was so much more than the table that separated us. I badly wished I was on their side, part of that conversation, part of that life.

Suddenly my two friends jumped up, went to the other side of the room and started dancing together. Steven came over and stood by my side, swaying, circling, rubbing.

This is THE most ridiculous thing I have ever participated in.

"Why don't you go dance with them?" I offered, hopefully.

"No, I'll stay with you."

"It's okay, go ahead. Go dance with them."

"No, I'll stay with you."

Sway, circle, rub.

Now would be a really good time for the floor to open up ...

"I'd *like* it if you danced with them," I said, catching on to the game.

That had to be one of the longest hours of my life. The CD finally ended, Steven took his clothes to the washroom, came out dressed and exited with $200 in his pocket.

There was no question about a second night anymore, not with him or any other guy in that field.

It was an important lesson for me. I learned that "just anyone" wouldn't do at all; there had to be, aside from physical attraction, an intellectual connection that I would never find in a "man-for-hire." Besides, what I was looking for was the most intimate and personal kind of interaction between two people — not exactly satisfying with a stranger. If that meant a lifetime of celibacy, so be it. A friend once made an observation that, despite being a generalization, I think summed it up fairly accurately: "Most men are content with 'the act,' but for most women it's the meaning behind the act that's important."

But hell, how many women can say they've spent two evenings with a hooker?

It's not shocking at all that men hire hookers — look at Charlie Sheen: $53,000 for Heidi Fleiss's gals and to the world he's just a party-happy playboy. At least it's no big deal when able-bodied men do it. If disabled men hire hookers, there is a subtly different perception — is it because he can't get it anywhere else?

When I was considering one for myself, there were a few people I confided in. One of my attendants had worked in a couple of twenty-four-hour attendant care buildings in Toronto and had several friends with disabilities. She thought it was a great idea but wondered why I was planning an evening before "the night."

"Why do you want to meet him first? When the guys hire someone they always just talk for a while first," she said.

"What do you mean, '*When* they hire someone,'" I asked, incredulous. "Some of the guys have done this?"

"Sure, they do it now and again."

That made me so angry.

"Why should they be forced to hire someone? It's just because they're *crips*," I fumed.

But I realized I had my own double standard. It was fine for able-bodied folks to hire hookers but not okay for crips.

Realization came very slowly to me, but it came in the form of a man. This was someone who fit all my criteria, except that he'd had no previous exposure to disabilities. In fact, I was the first person he'd ever met who used a wheelchair. We met because of a mutual interest in books and found a lot more in common. It was the first time I let my guard down and took the first steps toward a "normal" relationship. What I discovered was that it wasn't until I became comfortable and confident with myself in that respect that others saw that in me and responded.

Having said that, I still think it's harder for disabled women than disabled men to meet partners and date. I base that mainly upon my own observations and from seeing what happens in my own circle of friends. I see many more disabled men in relationships than heterosexual, disabled women. If you look at plain anatomy, sex is easier for disabled women than men. So why is it the way it is?

The reason, I think, is twofold. Firstly, I think women are more open-minded than men when it comes to this area. As well, I think women have a more nurturing side to them. This is not to say that disabled people need nurturing or that these relationships are maternal or unhealthy or anything like that. I just think women are more willing than men to consider dating a person who has a disability.

Another reason is that the disabled person is usually the one who has to initiate a date. Women just aren't socialized to be the initiators. I don't care how things are supposed to have changed with the sexual revolution, men are still expected to lead.

So what am I looking for? The answer is simple. I want the same thing most people do. I want a partner who will love everything about me; one who will find me beautiful, even on days when I'm bloated and feel like garbage. I want someone who will want to rent a good video on a cold winter's night — or even a bad video, for that matter. I want someone I can laugh with, get mad at, share my innermost thoughts with and try to juggle family dinners with at holidays. I want to fall in love and have a really fabulous wedding day. I want to have someone I can call from work and say, "Honey, I'm going to be late tonight. Start dinner without me."

In short, I want to meet my soulmate. And in case it takes a long time to find him, I want to really enjoy myself in the process. And you know something? I don't just want it, I deserve it. I *deserve* it. Sure there's a chance that it won't happen, but I have to believe it will.

Chapter Nine:

STAFF REPORTER

At first glance, the newsroom of Canada's largest newspaper is an incredibly intimidating place. The newsroom is actually an entire floor of a very large building overlooking Lake Ontario. The first time I went through the doors, a few days before starting my first summer internship back in 1989, I must admit I felt a little faint. That night I didn't sleep; I lay in bed and fretted till dawn.

What on Earth have you gotten yourself into, and how are you going to pull this one off?

My first couple of days put some of my fears to rest. I was trained on their computer software program, unique to the paper, and I wrote only brief items using the information from press releases. That part was just like school. And talk about a friendly office — they all went out of their way to be helpful and make me feel welcome. It seemed as though every single employee stopped by my desk to introduce him or herself and say hello. "If you need anything, I sit right over there," became familiar words. Each day I had more offers of coffee or tea than I could drink in a week. It helped put me at ease.

The company had put an accessible washroom stall in the ladies' room, leased a hands-free phone for me and set up a table large enough for everything I'd need. Their tech wiz had found a tape-recorder I could use for interviews, which was modified slightly so the record button was easy for me to push with my mouthstick. I was put in the "general assignment" pool, where you do whatever assignment is thrown to you each day.

At the end of my first week I was "promoted" to obituaries. I handled the story just fine, and the following day, there was my first byline. What a rush! Printed underneath the headline was: **"By Barbara Turnbull, Toronto Star."** I sat and pondered it a long time that morning. I was so used to seeing my name *in* the headline, it had never occurred to me how rewarding it would be to see it appear as proof of something I had done, rather than something that had been done to me.

The rest of that summer went equally well. I was given at least one assignment every day, and I handled them all. I always kept a copy of what I had filed, to compare to what appeared in the paper after it had gone through copy-editing. Having had no previous "real" experience, I tried to soak up everything I could, including eavesdropping on colleagues' telephone interviews whenever I could do it unnoticed.

I think everyone was surprised at how well the experiment worked, certainly none more than me. I did not feel like a "token crip," and though I sometimes wondered if they only wanted me there for publicity value, I was confident that I had done a good job. On my last day the managing editor offered me a job for the following summer "without hesitation." I went back to school with several clippings, a school credit and the sense that I had found my niche.

Unfortunately, the experience the following summer was almost completely opposite. For the first few weeks of my job there was a different assignment editor replacing the one from the year before, who was on vacation. I was greeted every day with, "Well Barbara, it's a slow news day."

Part of a reporter's job is to come up with your own stories — it's important to have something to work on when things are slow. It's also another way to gauge a reporter's skill. I was very aware of this, but I found it extremely difficult to come up with much of my own stuff at that point. I had been out of Toronto and Canada for three years, and I wasn't out on the street covering assignments that might lead to other stories. So every day was a struggle to get through; I was constantly trying to look busy. The assignment editor was clearly treating me differently from everyone else, either because I was the most junior reporter or because of my disability. As far as I was concerned, neither reason was excusable, but I didn't have the guts for a confrontation.

At the end of the second week, something happened that made the bad situation worse. *The Star* has an employee publication called *StarBeat*. The new issue had a little item about me.

"Barbara Turnbull is back for a second summer. Last year, she impressed everybody with her writing ability and dogged determination. Turnbull, who types with a mouthstick ..." *blah, blah, blah*.

I was mortified. First of all, no other summer student was ever mentioned like this, even those returning for a second year. Secondly, there was absolutely no relevant reason to describe how I typed, except perhaps to inspire people and show how "brave" I was supposed to be. There was no denying that this was different treatment — tokenism, even — and I was devastated. The attention felt worse because I had no bylines to back it up.

About halfway through my time there, Mary Deanne Shears, the woman who had initially hired me, called me into her office.

"I'm just wondering what's going on. I'm not seeing any of your bylines."

I said I hadn't been very assertive at the assignment desk, which was likely a factor. I wasn't going to blame someone else, whether or not that person was part of the problem.

The last two weeks picked up tremendously when Brian McAndrew, the assignment editor from the previous summer, returned from vacation, but the whole experience made me feel I hadn't proved myself. I wanted to feel 100 percent that I deserved a job at a newspaper like *The Star*. It was agreed that I could return for a third trial the following summer.

My third internship came with its own complications. I'd seen the pathetic job the media did covering my graduation, which was immediately followed by the intense publicity for the "Scales of Justice" show, which ran two weeks later. I didn't like being a reporter and the subject of stories at the same time. It made me feel uneasy to wear those two hats simultaneously. I was ready to turn my back forever on "Barbara Turnbull, the Victim" and Toronto's media darling. The timing made sense to me, since I was really starting my career, so I used the "Scales" air date as the cut-off point. After that, I turned down almost all interview requests for the next four or five years. I occasionally did one if it was regarding a specific issue about which I felt I had something valuable to add, but I nixed anything that was just an update about me. By that time I'd been moved to the "Where are they now?" files.

After that third summer, I was a contract employee for the next couple of years, until September 1993, with one contract always leading right into another. My employee status always had a question mark on it, but I didn't mind that, because I still wasn't sure if the job was for me.

Although I am able to handle news assignments and file them on my own (it is all done on computers, which don't discriminate), I've never been completely independent at *The Star*. Each morning I require an initial set-up, which includes plugging in my tape-recorder, putting on my telephone headset and setting up a drink. That's usually done by one of the newsroom "messengers," a title given to some guys who are many things to many people. Craig, Nello and Vince spend most of their shifts running all over the building, but they also help me out from time to time during the day, whether it is opening mail, moving around papers or photocopying or faxing something. They are truly great, easygoing guys, always willing to help.

And for the rest of what I need, there is always someone around. I still get offers of coffee or tea, though many years ago I kicked caffeine and started simply drinking water. So many reporters, editors and other staff are used to my habits, they often offer me water as they walk by. If I need my headphones put on or taken off, there is usually someone close to hail over. No, none of this is in their job descriptions, but I have never had any indication that anyone minds. Many of these people have become good friends, personal friends even, outside the office.

One need I used to have, which was a big hassle, was help using the washroom a couple of times a day. I had one good friend who helped me every day, making it a simple thing, but that wasn't independence. Years later, when I had the electric device that enabled me to use the washroom independently, *The Star* modified a little-used single washroom and put on a door-opener I can use with the control on my wheelchair. Being able to use the washroom unaided is a luxury I still don't take for granted! I hated having to ask someone for help — and take them away from their job — every time I needed to pee. Fortunately I work with a supportive management, willing to accommodate my needs.

Finally I did get to a point where I felt good about the job I was doing. I had so many of my own stories to do that I could have stayed busy without getting any assignments, which to me defined the good reporter. I was producing some good work, learning a lot and pulling my weight. But I still felt inferior whenever I compared myself to my colleagues. There were some, I was sure, who felt my disability and the publicity were the only reasons I was there, and I began to wonder if they were right. I rarely joined the other reporters when they went out for drinks, and when I did I was acutely uncomfortable the entire time. I was afraid to open my mouth, in case something came out that would reveal me to be the imposter I considered myself to be.

One thing that drove me crazy was that everyone seemed to know who everyone else was in the business. Whether it was papers, magazines, radio or television, they all seemed to know who covered what beat, where. It took me a long time to realize that a lot of that knowledge came from going out and covering stories. Reporters gossip in scrums, waiting for press conferences to start, working out of town on big stories. Because the vast majority of my stories were done in the newsroom — except for the occasional feature or profile — I didn't ever have the opportunity to meet anyone other than *Star* colleagues. At work I was tied to my desk by the headphones. I'd see reporters stopping to chat at other people's desks as they walked through the newsroom, and it bothered me that I couldn't do that. For the most part, the only reporters I spoke to were the ones who stopped by my desk.

In those first years there, those years when I feared I was considered a token, I was extremely sensitive about my status as a disabled person and as a victim as well. I avoided any story that had anything to do with disabilities or wheelchairs. Not only did I never propose a story having anything to do with disability, I actively avoided them. I occasionally got phone calls from people who had potential stories and knew my name, but I always referred them to the reporter who wrote the disability issues column for the Life section. In my fear of being stereotyped, I passed on some good, worthwhile news stories.

I also carried a permanent chip on my shoulder about being not just a victim, but the victim of a newsworthy case. Any questions about the prison status of my attackers irked me to no end. "I am not here as a victim," I'd fume to myself, and maybe a few friends, if an editor asked me anything about a parole hearing. Instead of being happy they were interested in keeping the story alive — and keeping the public informed about a case they had responded to tremendously — I didn't ever want to have anything to do with it.

*   *   *   *

While I was at school in Arizona I learned through the media (as usual) that Clive Brown and Warren Johnson had been paroled in the late 1980s.

It was only after Warren Johnson's parole that I discovered that the victim of a crime must officially request that the parole board notify them of hearings and decisions. Nobody had volunteered that information to me. That seems to be one of those tidbits that victims must discover for themselves. Once I did notify the parole board they were very good about keeping me informed, but it's incredible and unacceptable to me that victims are not automatically notified at every stage of the process.

In 1992 Hugh Logan, the shooter, became eligible for full parole. Something inside me snapped. When I had learned about Clive Brown's and Warren Johnson's release I didn't feel anything. I honestly didn't care. But hearing that Hugh Logan might walk away, a voice inside me said, "Uh uh, this is way too soon."

It had been only nine years. I had been asked the question "How long would satisfy you?" and I didn't have an answer, but at that point my gut told me to do whatever I could to keep him in jail.

It might be fitting at this point to say that there really is no such thing as justice for victims, particularly those who have been physically affected by a crime. It wouldn't matter if all four of these guys spent twenty or thirty years in jail — nothing would change for me. No punishment dealt to any criminal can eradicate such a crime, or even ease it. Victims of theft or fraud can have their money or stolen items returned or replaced, but they have still been victimized. Any victim looking to our system for personal justice is bound to be disappointed. At the same time, obviously, criminals have to be punished, and most are eventually released back into society. So victims need to have realistic expectations from the system. The justice system has always revolved around the accused and his rights. Victims have been gaining some ground in the last couple of decades, but I very much doubt it will ever be a balanced scale.

Until recently, the Parole Act was similarly centred solely on the criminal. I wanted to be at Hugh Logan's parole hearing, but at that time the convict had total control over who could attend. He could either allow or bar the victim, or members of the media or any other interested party who requested admission.

The parole board passed on my request. They later told me Logan was thinking about it; his lawyer would call me to discuss the issue, then advise her client.

I decided to present my request in such a way that it would make him look bad if he refused to grant me access. I wrote a letter saying that I was having a hard time getting over the crime, and that facing him at his parole hearing would be "therapeutic" for me.

That was bullshit, but believable, I hoped.

His lawyer called me and I spent forty minutes on the phone with her. During the conversation she subjected me to pointed questions about my reasons for wanting to attend the hearing, my feelings about him and his possible parole and all my past submissions to the board. She also rambled on about all the ways in which Hugh Logan had been a model prisoner. Though I was fighting back angry retorts during the entire conversation, I calmly kept stating that the hearing would be a catharsis for me. We kept going in circles: she was trying to convince me to meet with Hugh privately, while I kept emphasizing that it was the "official" process of the hearing I needed. After all that, she promptly recommended that Hugh not allow me access. He initially ignored her advice and gave his permission for me to attend, but as the date for the hearing got closer he changed his mind.

The way he informed me of his decision to bar me was with a letter that was obviously written and signed by his lawyer. In the letter he offered to meet with me one-on-one at the jail another time and give me a cassette copy of the taped hearing. "Unfortunately, your mere presence could be interpreted by the Board as a very strong, unspoken objection to my release," he wrote. That was the ammunition I needed. I photocopied that letter and made my own written submission to the board.

"Obviously he is still only thinking of himself," I wrote, concluding with: "While you listen to evidence about Hugh Logan, I ask you to remember that less than nine years ago he completely devastated my life. Mr. Logan's deliberate actions created an existence for me from which there is no escape or reprieve. As you make your decision please keep in mind that he shot me and left me lying on the floor. Then he went dancing and drank champagne."

He was denied parole that time, but I knew he would not have been paroled yet anyhow, given that his brother, who wasn't even at the store the night of the shooting, wasn't out yet.

The following year he came up for parole again. This time I was able to attend because the Parole Act had changed and he no longer had control over who attended. I clearly remember every detail of the day: it was a hot and sunny day, the end of July 1993. A friend of mine, Sally, came with me to the hearing. We left early for the three-hour drive up to Kingston.

I had never been to a jail before, though what I saw of this minimum security institution was not jail-like in any way. Upon arriving we were greeted by several people from the board and the jail. I was told they had a room set aside for me to use while waiting for the hearing to start. Sally excused herself to use the washroom, and as soon as she left, one of the men with the jail asked everybody else to leave and he closed the door, shutting me into the room with him. He introduced himself and said he was a psychologist.

"Today I'm here for you," he said. A long pause ensued, while I asked myself if I was hearing correctly.

"You must be feeling somewhat anxious about this hearing?"

I was furious. I couldn't believe how he had manoeuvred me into this situation. Nor could I believe that he actually thought I would speak about my emotions to him, a prison psychologist and somebody I had never set eyes on before.

"No, I'm not anxious at all," I said breezily. Then I immediately turned the interview around and asked him some questions about the jail. After a couple of minutes, I said my friend would be waiting. He opened the door to the others. When Sally came in she was just as furious as I was.

Moments later they announced it was time to go in. I suddenly got hit with an intense dizzy spell, a bit of an anxiety attack.

I can't do this.

I asked for a drink of water, and I took a few deep breaths, trying to calm myself. I didn't want to reveal to anybody how I was feeling. There was no way I was going to buckle at that point, so I steeled myself and entered a tiny, airless room. Ventilation was one small air-conditioning unit in the window; it was the only thing making the air breathable, so I sat right by the noisy machine. I was dismayed to hear that they were going to turn the air-conditioner off when the hearing got under way, because the proceedings were being recorded and the din was too loud. I didn't know what I was going to do. It was so hot I knew I'd pass out without air, so I asked them to bring a fan to direct on to me.

Before Hugh Logan and his lawyer were brought in I was reminded that I was not allowed to say a word or I would be ejected from the hearing. Hugh's sister was there, and a reporter from the local Kingston paper.

It was awkward at first when Hugh came in, because neither of us wanted to look right at the other. He sat down while we continued avoiding eye contact, which wasn't easy in such a small room. The hearing began right away.

I didn't know what to expect, but I was really impressed with the depth of the board members' questioning. They asked about his background, his childhood, his relationship with his family and his parents; they went through everything. They had him talk about how his criminal activities started and they went through each crime before finally getting to the shooting. During the trial Hugh had denied shooting me, but he was now admitting it. They wanted to know why he had lied on the stand. He said he had been looking after his own skin. A couple of times he looked over at me and said he was sorry. Each time he was rebuked.

"Don't look at her, look at me. She's not allowed to talk to you. You're not allowed to talk to her." He said he found that frustrating.

His frustration was nothing compared to mine, because there was one crucial question that had never been put to him. I wanted to know why he cocked the gun before he went into the store, as Warren Johnson had testified.

It was a .357 magnum. The gun could have been fired without being cocked, it just would have taken a bit more pressure on the trigger. It seemed obvious to me that he'd intended to use the gun if he'd cocked it before he went into the store. If it was only money they were after, why didn't he give me a chance to cooperate? Why did he shoot?

They asked him why he thought he needed to take a gun into the store. They asked him why he took a *loaded* gun into the store. But nobody ever asked him why he cocked the gun first.

I was screaming the question in my head. It was so hard for me to hold back, but I didn't want to be removed from the hearing (even though it would have made good press). I still don't have an answer, and, to my knowledge, the question has never been asked.

My first thought when I looked at him was how good looking he was. He had obviously been working out and was well built. Then it hit me right between the eyes:

What an incredible waste of two lives.

The thought had never struck me with such impact before. His life was wasted too. I realized that all my efforts to keep him in jail had accomplished nothing. It really sank in that it didn't matter when he got out because it wasn't going to change anything for me.

I also realized that I was a little bit afraid of him. The fear might have come from seeing how well built and strong he was. Part of me was afraid that he was going to seek revenge for the efforts I had made to keep him in jail. Logically that didn't make sense. Why on Earth would he come after me? He'd put himself in that jail with his own actions, I certainly hadn't. But logic had nothing to do with it.

At the end I felt a strong sense of defeat and tremendous, overwhelming sadness.

Once again, parole was denied.

* * * *

Going into work the next day was extremely difficult. It was a Friday, so I decided to tough it out till the weekend and I ignored my impulse to call in sick, though I was not exactly well balanced. I worked with a bunch of reporters — people who ask strangers intrusive questions everyday. I knew they were all going to want details about the hearing.

From the start of my job at *The Star* I made it clear that Barbara Turnbull, the victim, didn't work there; Barbara Turnbull, the reporter, did. I've never had a problem discussing the shooting, the trial or any aspect of my case, but it wasn't my job to keep the news desk up to date on the latest events. If *The Star* wanted to cover them, fine, but I wanted nothing to do with it.

That day *The Star* ran the article from the Kingston paper, with pictures prominently displayed, on page three. I dreaded being in the newsroom. Hearing it on the radio news as I got ready for work didn't help, either. As for the article itself, the reporter did an exceptional job of writing about it, but I was extremely self-conscious. And on my guard.

Sure enough, the first person I saw was an assignment editor, who brought it up immediately.

"What was the hearing like?" he asked.

"I'd rather not talk about it."

"Oh come on, tell me!"

"I don't want to talk about it."

That became my mantra, as more and more colleagues approached me.

"What was it like to see him?"

"How did you feel when he walked into the room?"

"Was it hard to get through the hearing?"

They asked me questions that my family didn't even ask me. In fact, my family barely mentioned the hearing because we were preparing for my sister Christine's wedding at that time. Colleagues who knew me best simply asked if I was okay and said nothing else. It was a huge relief when I finally left the building at the end of the day.

That night I was hit with a wave of depression. I realized that I had just been holding myself together to get through the day on the job, and now that the weekend had arrived, I felt the weight of it all square on my shoulders. I had made plans to go out for dinner with my sister and some of her friends, but I hardly spoke through dinner. I just sat there depressed, mulling over the incredible *stupidity* of it all. I didn't know what to do with my feelings. I wanted a shelf I could put them on, but none existed.

That Sunday, there was a large Jack and Jill wedding shower for my sister and her fiancé up north in Muskoka. She was going to be getting married there a week later. It was not a particularly nice day, fairly overcast. The party was on an island, which we reached on a motorized barge. We were sitting outside. Late in the afternoon somebody put on Neil Diamond's Greatest Hits CD. I grew up listening to Neil Diamond and I have always liked his music, so I was happy with the choice, and sat following the familiar songs in my head.

I was sitting beside my sister as she opened her gifts when the song "September Morn" came on. The song jumped out at me because when I was sixteen I used to make some extra cash organizing the pop table at a monthly dance for single parents. That was the only song I ever really remember being played at those dances, because I always liked it so much.

I hadn't heard that song since the shooting. When it started, I had the strangest episode. I was suddenly transported back to when I was sixteen. I felt as though I were at the dance again, except that I knew what was in my future. I was terrified. I heard this little girl's voice inside of me screaming, begging, "Don't make me live through all of that."

I could hardly breathe. I certainly could not talk. There was only a small part of my brain that was still rational and stayed in the present, and it kept telling me when to take a breath. I felt the way I had on the floor in Becker's the night of the shooting, having to coach myself to get through the moment. I was praying that nobody would talk to me and desperately hoping my face looked normal. I was hoping the attention would stay on Christine and Scott — that nobody would look at me. I felt almost catatonic as I sat there listening to that whole song, and it took several minutes to compose myself when it finished.

I started to think I should get professional help of some sort.

The following weekend was my sister's wedding. I had an anxiety attack at the rehearsal in the church the night before the big day, but managed to keep it from everyone. I blamed it on the fact that I needed to eat.

Each weekday I would steel myself as I went into work, use all my strength to get through the day as though nothing was wrong, then feel myself sag as I left the building. Exhausted and depressed, I spent each evening wrapped in my thoughts. The only thing I looked forward to was going to bed, but once there I lay awake for hours.

The following weekend I spiked temperatures of over 39 degrees Celsius each day, though I wasn't sick. On the Saturday I was out with my best friend Liz in Oakville. I was a basket case all day, fighting back tears the entire time, but again I kept it to myself. When I got home my temperature was 39.6 degrees. I knew it was psychosomatic because both days I took Tylenol and it did nothing to reduce my fever. The only thing that brought my temperature down was going to the movies. I went to a movie each day, just trying to take my mind off it all. Both times my temperature was normal as I left the theatre. I know it was stress-induced — it didn't escape me that it happened on a weekend, when I didn't have to perform in my job.

Eventually the depression faded and I felt my true self break through again, but it took a long time.

*　　　*　　　*　　　*

When Hugh Logan came up for parole a third time, two years later, in July 1994, I didn't bother to attend the hearing because I was sure he would be denied again. His brother Sutcliffe, whose total sentence had been several years less than Hugh's, had only been released from jail less than six months before, so I didn't think he had a chance. It was only eleven years after the shooting.

I got the phone call that afternoon informing me that Hugh Logan had been granted full parole in exchange for voluntary departure from Canada to Jamaica, where he was born. This was the same deal that his three partners in crime had applied for and received before him. I was shocked. Even though two days previously I had told myself that it didn't matter, it was a slap in the face that he was let out so soon. I thought that violent offenders had to serve two-thirds of their sentence before being eligible for parole in Canada. The fact that he'd served just a little more than half was something that offended me as a victim.

Voluntary departure is different from deportation. It means that a convict can serve the rest of his sentence completely at liberty in another country, provided that country will accept him. If he is a Canadian citizen, he can come back to Canada after his sentence is finished. In these cases, "parole" meant going to sunny Jamaica to vacation through the rest of their "prison" sentences. Clive Brown is a citizen and returned to Mississauga in 1994. Sutcliffe Logan can come back in 1997, should he choose, and Hugh Logan, the shooter, is eligible to return in 2003. Warren Johnson is not a citizen and is the only one who cannot legally return to Canada without the consent of the Immigration minister.

There has been a good deal of press given to the issue of deporting people with criminal histories, particularly when the person involved has been in Canada from a young age, as was the case with these four. "They are products of our society. We created them and we should deal with them," the critics say. *The Star's* editorial policy is that it is "morally wrong" to deport these people, no matter how unsavory they may be. A 1996 editorial concluded: "Just as we don't want foreign criminals sneaking into Canada, we cannot offload our criminals to their countries of origin after they have spent their lives in Canada." Advocates for the convicts say it's cruel to send them somewhere where they have no memory and no recent contact. Designated countries, like Jamaica, don't like it either. They're having a tough enough time of it without getting our rejects.

Tell me, then, why it's okay for these guys to embrace their birth country when it means they can get early parole? It seems to me they hold this "Get Out of Jail Early" card that they play as soon as they can, when it suits them. If they are lucky enough to have attained citizenship before they victimize someone, they retain the privilege to return here when their sentence is up.

This is wrong. It should be one way or the other. If they want to remain Canadian, they should go fully through the prison system. If they want to get out of jail early by going back to where they were born, then their Canadian citizenship, and all the privileges that go with it, should be revoked.

In spite of my opinion, by Christmas of 1994 they were all back in Jamaica — except for Clive Brown, who was back in Canada in time to celebrate the holidays with his family.

Once they were all out I spent a great deal of time trying to put it all into perspective and figure out how I felt about it. Where was my closure? I had first expected it when the trial was over, and then when the appeals were over. I definitely expected it once they were all out of jail, but I didn't feel it. I wasn't sure what I was expecting, or what closure might feel like. As much as I had tried to convince myself that it didn't matter whether Hugh Logan was in jail, I discovered it did matter. It mattered a lot. I had a recurring image of him playing volleyball on a beach in Jamaica and it really bothered me.

I might have felt differently had he shown true remorse. He said that he was sorry, but I strongly believe he's only sorry he got caught. I have no doubt he's sorry for the effect that the crime had on his life, but I don't think he's had any true remorse for how his crime affected me. I've seen nothing to show he's capable of it.

From the beginning, I have believed that Warren Johnson was the only person who felt true remorse. It's ironic that he is the only one who cannot return. When he was granted parole he sent me a two-page letter just before leaving Canada. He wrote: "At this point, an apology for all the pain and suffering that I have caused you is wholly inadequate. The agony of your paralysis far outweighs any apologies I can make, but I hope that you will at least accept this letter as an expression of my sorrow for not being able to completely make amends for the wrong done to you." After writing about his version of the night of the shooting and his explanation for why he did not call for help, he wrote, "This is my solemn resolve: to make what amends I can, and let this be a positive rather than negative lesson. At the same time, I will never be able to forget — neither do I want to — what happened to you." He ended it: "Please accept my sincere apologies, and my deepest regrets — inadequate as they are." This from a guy who didn't even pull the trigger. I felt it was an honest and sincere letter, even gutsy. I appreciated his intentions. I did write him a short note back, agreeing with him that there was nothing he could do to make amends, except perhaps stay away from crime.

I have never received any indication that Clive Brown is remorseful. In the process of writing this book I sent Clive two requests to meet with me. I wanted very much to talk to him, but he completely ignored my letters, which were sent by registered mail to his home. Instead of taking the opportunity to demonstrate remorse — or at least some respect — he proved to be nothing but a coward. Perhaps I should not have expected more, but I did. How nice for him that he has the ability to make so many choices in his life.

I hope that all of them stay clean, but I won't be surprised to hear that the Logans are back in trouble. Many people involved in the case believe Sutcliffe to be a psychopath. He clearly had enough charisma to influence others and he has obvious intelligence. Too bad it's all such a waste.

I remember when Pope John Paul was shot in 1981. I also vividly recall that he visited the shooter in jail and granted his forgiveness. I wondered whether the Pope would have made that visit had that bullet turned him into a quadriplegic.

The best I can do is say I have no room in my heart for hatred.

I have no room for forgiveness, either.

*   *   *   *

With cutbacks and a poor economy, I was one of five reporters laid off by *The Star* in September 1993. At the time I really thought it was the best thing, although I spent the next two and a half years in career limbo. I was unemployed for part, and had another job in public relations for part. During that time away I came to terms with my differences. When I returned to the paper in May 1996, this time as a permanent employee, I discovered a confidence I had never before possessed.

Today, I am a very different reporter — certainly less sensitive. I don't disregard stories about disability, because I realize I might be the best person to cover some of them properly. That doesn't mean I write about that subject regularly in any way, but I don't turn my back on it anymore. And now I would be happy to offer information about my assailants and their parole. I am finally ready to bring *all* of who I am to my job every day.

I believe my experiences have made me a better journalist. Having been on the receiving end of much inaccuracy, I dread mistakes and try to be meticulous about facts. I'm not always successful — no one is perfect — but I have a pretty good record. At the very least, I never forget what it's like to be the subject of news stories, seeing the words you speak appear in print and living with the results.

I love my job. I have tremendous respect, admiration and affection for the people I work with. I am grateful for the writing talent that enables me to have such a rewarding career, one that offers satisfaction, some excitement, and is an important public service.

And I am grateful that I can still recognize what is positive in my life.

Chapter Ten:

LOOKING BACK, LOOKING FORWARD

For too many years, when I looked in the mirror, looked back over the events that so utterly changed my life, I saw something that darkened my view. It wasn't the image of a gun or the hand that held it. It was my own feelings of guilt. I had a secret that I carried with me for years, one about which I felt such shame that I couldn't even bring myself to write about it in my journal. I thought if I ever died and someone read my journal, they'd be horrified by what I'd done.

Over the years I've been asked many times — by interviewers and other inquiring parties — if I had any philosophical notions about why this happened to me. The great "Why" question. I always talked about bad luck and "drawing the wild card," while inside I told myself the answer was plain.

Don't forget, I was raised Catholic. We stopped attending church a few years before the shooting, but the kind of guilt imposed by years of confessionals is nearly impossible to erase. During my three and a half years in Arizona there were several times I almost went to confession in one of the local Catholic churches. I figured I could get "official" absolution where I was guaranteed the priest wouldn't know who I was.

What wracked me with guilt is that I stole from the Becker's store where I worked. Regularly. Pretty much every shift, actually. It started when my first boss left and the area supervisor told us it was okay to take cigarettes without paying for them. Before that, I'd diligently paid for everything I consumed. But when he was so nonchalant about it, I figured it was no big deal. It soon went from cigarettes to whatever I drank or ate on my shift. A bag of chips here, a can of pop there, licorice from the box on the counter. What did it matter? It got so that if my boss or another employee was working and I had to pay for something, I'd feel a bit resentful.

Before too long, I was taking change from the drawer. Not all the time, just when I was going downtown to visit friends. Going downtown meant train fare to the city and subway rides once there, so I'd take exactly what I needed in quarters. I assured myself it wasn't *that* wrong, because it was only change, and I only took exactly what I needed for the one specific purpose. And I did have standards: I never took bills, and if my mother gave me money for milk or something, I always used the money to buy it legitimately. Every time my boss would do inventory, I'd feel a twinge of guilt and wonder if he was personally affected by what I pilfered, but it was never enough to curtail my thieving ways. I have no idea if my boss suspected or knew. It would have been a good thing if he'd fired me before that September night!

No punishment could have been greater than what I put myself through after the shooting. It was disaster as retribution, and it made such perfect sense to me. I'd been stealing, so "God" took away my physical ability to steal. "God" could see that I was not an evil person and that my soul could be saved, so "He" intervened. And now I had to atone for my sins.

One day, not so long ago, I was having a conversation with a friend. He was talking about the two bicycles that had been stolen from him recently.

"But it's okay, because I had that coming to me," he said about the loss.

"What do you mean?" I asked.

"When I was young I stole a lot of bikes," he said.

"How many?" I asked, riveted to the conversation.

"I could never count. Loads. Whenever I wanted to go somewhere, I took a bike," he said. "So it makes sense that someone would steal mine. That's not all I stole," he added.

"My god, give me the whole story," I said. He couldn't talk fast enough for me. He told me that at one of his jobs, he and all the other employees would take cash from the register, as much as $300 a week each. At another job, the same thing. He figured half of his first car was probably paid for with stolen cash.

"And did anything ever happen to you?" I was afraid to ask.

"Nothing," he replied. "I grew out of it. I just stopped one day and never stole again. It was partly my bosses' fault for making it so easy for us."

"And don't you think it'll ever catch up to you?"

"Nah, I was a stupid kid. Kids steal."

I was absolutely floored. I asked another close friend if she had ever stolen anything when she was a teenager. Not only had she stolen plenty, she told me, but her brother stole so much in his teen years that at one point not one single item in his wardrobe had been legitimately purchased. When I confessed what I'd been thinking since the shooting, she thought I was nuts.

For the next couple of weeks I felt like I was walking into walls. I could think of little else. As crazy as it sounds, I had spent much of the previous ten years believing, being totally convinced, that I was being punished. And along the way I'd managed to convince myself that somehow the punishment fit the crime.

In a way, my ludicrous notion fits the textbook pattern of phases victims supposedly go through. The initial stage is disbelief, followed by a period during which the victim wonders what she did to deserve it. Finally comes a resolution and recognition that it was unfortunate, but it's time to move on. I got stuck in the second stage.

It took me weeks to get used to the idea that I didn't deserve this. With it came the freeing but scary thought: "If I didn't deserve this, is it okay to be angry?" Though I know the answer is yes, that hurdle is still too big for me to jump. The great rage within me remains buried.

When I'm down all I feel is tremendous sadness. It doesn't happen often, and it rarely lasts more than a couple of days, but when it does hit me I see my life as a videotape, one I wish I could fast-forward to the end. I figure my next life *has* to be a whole lot easier than this one has been. On the other hand, I also believe wonderful things are headed my way in this life. I'm overdue for them. I know that most people look at me and are just thankful they aren't me. But that's okay. Over the years I have looked at many able-bodied people and thought the very same thing.

I know there is a ball of emotion buried deep that will one day rise up. One evening, as I was nearing the end of this book, I got genuinely, deeply angry. More accurately, I acknowledged that I have much to be angry about. The intensity of the emotion terrified me, though I felt tremendous relief afterward. Usually I get angry about something I have some control over. I tend to get angry only when I'm in a position to do or say something that will at least provide a release for the emotion. Perhaps that's why I haven't felt anger over the shooting before — there's nothing I can do about it, so it could be that I'm simply protecting myself from the force of such a powerfully negative emotion. I know anger can destroy a person, and so in some ways I'm not sorry that anger hasn't surfaced. I trust that my inner self will guide me through it bit by bit.

*   *   *   *

Something else has happened recently to change my outlook on life. I have something now that I have not had since the shooting: hope. That hope can be traced largely to a man known throughout the world as "Superman."

Simply put, Christopher Reeve's paralyzing accident is the best thing that has ever happened to the spinal-cord-injured community.

165

That sounds like an incredibly callous comment, but let me explain. I wouldn't have wished this on him, as I wouldn't wish this on *anybody, anywhere.* But having said that, the fact remains: *Superman* broke his neck. The significance of it cannot possibly be emphasized enough.

Ironically, for years I'd been willing such an accident to happen. "What we need is a major Hollywood star to break his neck, then watch what happens to the research movement" is something I've said more times than I can count. But of course I never thought that it would come about. From a public awareness perspective, it definitely couldn't have happened to a more appropriate person. There are bigger stars in Tinseltown, ones with much more money, but that's part of what makes him the perfect person: he isn't a Michael Jackson or Marlon Brando, someone who is more mystery than real. He also has the beautiful, supportive wife, the cute, supportive kids. People can relate to him.

And from the start, Reeve has had the perfect attitude. Appearing on CNN's "Larry King Live" and with Barbara Walters on "20/20," the clichés that fell from his tongue were inspiring — even to cynical old crips like me. "Life is like a game of cards," he told Walters's global audience. "If you think the game's worthwhile, you play the hand you're dealt."

I must admit, when I first saw him on TV after his accident it was a shock to me. "My god, it really happened," I thought. "He *looks* like a quad." Part of me had somehow not accepted that he was really "one of us."

What Christopher Reeve has done since his accident has changed my life.

When I was hurt, a cure was not spoken about as a definite possibility in my lifetime. I knew about Dr. Tator's research, even in 1983, but there was a giant question mark at the end of it. I knew it was important to keep it going, but always, in my mind, I saw it as benefiting others decades from now. Even three years later, when Rick Hansen finished his round-the-world tour, raising $24 million for research, rehabilitation and wheelchair sports, no one was saying "We can cure this within your lifetime." Well, someone might have been saying it, but my doubts drowned it out.

Truth is, I refused to believe that the research would ever affect me. I *couldn't* believe it. I couldn't afford to have that kind of hope. I knew that great strides had been made that helped acute injuries, and I assumed that before long they'd know how to fix those injuries as they happen. I suspect my paralysis would not have been so extensive if the shooting had happened today. But me *move* again? It was safer to assume it wouldn't happen.

But when Christopher Reeve got thrown from his horse, suddenly Barbara Walters was telling millions of people that researchers believe they could cure paralysis, if only more dollars found their way into the labs. Before long Reeve was testifying before Congress, and getting results. President Bill Clinton coughed up $10 million, with more promised by senators. Reeve was on the cover of *Time* magazine, and in *Newsweek*, and talking to the Democrats at their convention. Then he issued a challenge to doctors and researchers in 1996, when he was forty-three years old: to get him on his feet for his fiftieth birthday.

Things changed most dramatically for me when the Toronto Hospital brought Reeve in to help kick off a fundraising launch. I had an assignment at work to do a set-up feature on what was actually happening with the research out there. Was Reeve realistic? For the very first time I actually *listened* to what the researchers were saying. I had to, it was my job as a reporter. I had to read up on it and write about it. And for the very first time I got excited.

The brain and spinal cord are unlike other areas in the body, which will reconnect and heal. Although it was proven in 1980 that nerves in the spinal cord could be regenerated, researchers have been unable to make them grow enough, reattach and start functioning again. In the last five years phenomenal strides have been made in this area. Two years ago, researchers in Sweden made paralyzed rats walk again. They severed the spines and, trying something totally new, grafted on nerves from another part of the body. It was a new idea and it worked.

Now, scientists are working together globally like never before. Diseases and disorders of the central nervous system are being looked at together. Research that benefits those with Multiple Sclerosis can be applied to that for Alzheimer's. At the Toronto Hospital, they've put together researchers working on seventeen different central nervous system disorders. And with his challenge, Christopher Reeve has infused those scientists with a gale force gust of enthusiasm. They have never had the world's attention before, but now the world wants to see "Superman" fly again.

Two things struck me while I worked on that story. First, I discovered that I'm going to move again. I don't expect to walk out of my chair like I did before that bullet put me in it, but I know I'll at least have arm movement back. I *know* it. And at this point, I think that would be enough. I don't really *need* to walk again, but I do need, and desperately, desperately want, my independence back. I want to get myself out of bed without assistance whenever I want, and I want to go to bed, the same way, whenever I want. I want to read again before I go to sleep at night, and I want to reach over with my arm and snap off the light with my hand. I want to lounge on the couch on a rainy weekend with a good book. I want to get in a car and drive again, by myself. And I believe now, with all my heart and mind, that it will happen.

*   *   *   *

Now, when I look in the mirror the view is clear. I see the events of the past in their total context, and I have made some sense of many things. I still prefer to look forward, though. I'm a survivor, and I see bright days ahead.

AFTERWORD

What is happening today in spinal cord research is unprecedented. Never before has there been so much promise that a cure will be found. However, never before has the need for funding been so great. Because governments are cutting back, researchers are being forced to turn to you and me, the public, for more and more financial support.

Soon after the shooting I allowed the Canadian Paraplegic Association to use my name to raise money for their programs, which focus primarily on rehabilitation. I think I can say that CPA has made, conservatively, $1 million with my name. Only recently, though, has my focus changed to research.

In 1990, CPA approached me with an idea to start an annual golf tournament in my name. The proposal was for 70 percent of the proceeds to go to Dr. Charles Tator's lab, at The Toronto Hospital, with the rest going to CPA for their administrative efforts and other rehabilitation programs. And so The Barbara Turnbull Open was born. It has been quite successful; we've sold out most years and raised tens of thousands of dollars. Each year I've gone and said a few words about the need for research funds.

But Christopher Reeve's fundraising efforts brought something home to me: I haven't *really* done enough.

Since 1983 I have had a public profile. I should have used the publicity but chose not to. I could have been lobbying governments, working hard toward the goal. I was always glad that there were people out there devoting themselves to the cause, but I didn't want to do that myself.

So now I am pledging myself to the cause. I thought about this very carefully while I was tapping out each letter of each word in this book with my mouthstick, on my computer. Now I'm putting my own money where my mouth is, beginning by donating 60 percent of my royalties from this book to a charitable foundation that will help raise awareness and financial support for spinal cord research.

With the help of an amazing, dedicated friend, a charitable foundation has been created, called The Barbara Turnbull Foundation for Spinal Cord Research. The money donated to this foundation will be funnelled, in partnership with the Neuroscience Canada Foundation, to worthwhile projects every year. This latter foundation is affiliated with the federally sponsored Neuroscience Network of Canada, which is an internationally recognized Centre of Excellence, concerned with supporting and optimizing neurological research efforts across Canada. A more detailed description of the extent and stature of the research being done in this field in Canada is included in Appendix A. Several of Canada's most highly qualified scientists and physicians in the field of neurological, and specifically spinal cord injury research, have agreed to serve as members of a scientific advisory board to help the Foundation make the best possible funding decisions.

If you have been in any way touched by my history, this book, or by anyone in your life who is paralyzed, please consider supporting neurological research in Canada. I'd love to see schools run annual fundraisers for this. I've asked my family and friends to make an annual donation — I'd rather have a donation than a Christmas present.

You see, I don't want to be paralyzed for one single, solitary day longer than I absolutely have to be. No one should be restricted like this. Tens of thousands are.

In my way, I'm reaching out to you. I hope that you will reach back. Incredible achievements can be accomplished when people join hands and work together for a worthy goal.

THE BARBARA TURNBULL FOUNDATION
FOR SPINAL CORD RESEARCH

C/O The Toronto Star
One Yonge Street,
Toronto, Ontario
M5E 1E6

INDEX

APPENDIX A

PROSPECTS FOR REPAIR AND REGENERATION IN THE SPINAL CORD

Charles H. Tator, M.D., Ph.D., FRCS(C)

The prospects for repair and regeneration in the spinal cord have been enhanced by the development of several new experimental strategies and by continuing positive results in older strategies such as transplantation. Also, researchers now have more reliable and objective outcome measures for assessing the anatomical and functional results of regeneration experiments. From studies on patients who have had spinal cord injuries, there is evidence and encouragement that scientists will ultimately achieve success in promoting human spinal cord regeneration and restoration of function. For example, these studies show that many patients with major cord injuries will have some remaining spinal cord tissue at the injury site which may be available for repair or regeneration. The following is a brief review of the principal current strategies for enhancing spinal cord repair and regeneration.

1. Transplantation

There have been many successful studies of the transplantation of foetal or adult spinal cord tissue or other nervous tissue into the transected spinal cord of adult or neonatal experimental animals. There are also many positive examples of the transplantation of nerves or specific cells in nerves such as Schwann cells. One recent study implanted nerves to bridge specific transected pathways in the spinal cord. All of these studies have shown a most remarkable anatomical integration of the grafted tissue, and some have shown evidence of functional improvement.

2. Growth Factors

Many agents have been discovered which promote repair and regeneration of the injured nervous system. The administration of these growth-promoting agents, termed growth factors, to the traumatized or transected spinal cord has shown positive results. For example, there is strong evidence for enhanced regeneration of the corticospinal tract of adult rats treated with at least two kinds of growth factors administered locally at the site of spinal cord transection. One recent experiment combined growth factors and nerve transplants and produced some restoration of function.

3. Gene Therapy

One of the purposes of gene therapy is to cause adult cells to regain the growth-promoting ability of young growing nerve cells. There are a number of hopeful gene therapy approaches designed to improve regeneration or recovery after spinal cord injury. Changing the genetic complement of injured neurons toward foetal conditions when axonal sprouting is active may be possible either by alteration of existing genes or by the administration of new genes.

4. Electrical Stimulation

In animal studies, electrical stimulation has not been as effective as had been forecasted on the basis of the initial studies on nerve cells growing in glass dishes, which had shown remarkable growth bursts. Similar studies in animals indicate hurdles to overcome with respect to reduction in toxicity and the development of useful stimulation paradigms.

5. Overcoming the Spinal Cord's Inhibition

There have been important discoveries about how the spinal cord resists attempts at repair and regeneration, and one important mechanism is that the insulation on nerve fibres, known as myelin, inhibits the growth of damaged nerve fibres in the spinal cord. The identification of myelin-associated neurite growth inhibitory proteins was followed by experiments showing that long-distance regeneration of lesioned motor tract fibres in the rat spinal cord occurred in the presence of specific antibodies to these proteins. Recently, there was further evidence for regeneration by this strategy when these antibodies were combined with growth factors in experiments on adult rat spinal cords, in which half of the spinal cord was divided. Another strategy involves rerouting the regeneration away from the inhibitory myelin-containing zones of the spinal cord. For example, nerve transplants were used as bridges to transport the regenerating fibres into more permissive zones of the spinal cord.

6. Enhancing the Spinal Cord's Naturally Occurring Regenerating Cells

It has been found that the spinal cord and nerve roots contain cells that can regenerate, and that trauma can cause these cells, such as ependymal cells and Schwann cells, to proliferate. Their regenerative capability, however, is minimal, and strategies are thus being pursued such as the administration of growth factors to enhance this inherent ability. In animals such as salamanders, the ependymal cells can even regenerate a new spinal cord.

The prospects are therefore excellent for repair and regeneration of the human spinal cord after injury. There are many new strategies being pursued by many researchers around the world. Canadian neuroscientists are at the forefront of this research. Almost all of the above strategies are being pursued in a Canadian laboratory today.

Dr. Charles H. Tator is Professor and Chairman of Neurosurgery, University of Toronto, and Playfair Neurosciences Unit, The Toronto Hospital.

APPENDIX B

Valedictory Address, Arizona State University

December 21, 1990

I said to a friend of mine the other day, "Isn't this exciting? Just think -- Friday is going to be the first day of the rest of our lives." "Actually," he joked, "I'm looking more at it as the *last* day of the *best* of our lives." He was clearly frightened of what lies ahead. "Look on the bright side," I replied, "at least we won't have to try and park here anymore!"

President Coor, Governor Mofford, distinguished guests and fellow graduates. Today truly is an exciting beginning *and* a sad ending. We each have spent at least four years (and some much more than that) working toward this goal. There were times when I thought this day would never arrive, a feeling I'm sure all graduates share. We have been at ASU through some big changes, ones that have hopefully prepared us for the next step. Although our education should not end here, we have acquired many skills that will guide us for the rest of our lives.

How ASU has changed, and changed so quickly! Our population grows almost as fast as this campus expands. With over 42,000 students registered for classes this year, we are the fifth largest school in this country. In the last couple of years we've seen the addition of buildings above and below ground, from the Hayden Library expansion to the Fine Arts complex, plus a few more. One of the special things I have found about ASU is the sense of community our beautiful campus possesses, even with the large student body and constant construction.

We were fortunate last year to get a new president who recognized the potential problems the growth presents, and promised to cap enrolment. President Coor, may I warn you that everyone was reading your lips -- except perhaps the fees department. I think the only thing students would like to see more than a cap on enrolment would be a cap on tuition increases.

We've banded together through good times and bad, trying not to lose sight of our Sun Devil spirit (and I *know* the Devils will beat that team south of us one of these years).

There is no doubt ASU has personality, and that personality has helped make this school one of the most diverse. We have over 2,200 international students, countless minority students and more than 1,000 students with disabilities. There are 300 organizations registered on campus, many celebrating our differences and similarities. Hopefully this has helped round out our education, and made us more aware of some of the issues various groups face.

There have been racial tensions that cannot be denied, but I feel confident that ASU students will always demand equality, and that this administration will respond to that demand. All in all, I feel proud to be graduating from a university that promotes and maintains such diversity.

But campus life aside, are we prepared for what lies ahead? We would be fooling ourselves if we believe the next step is going to be an easy one. The job market is far from being wide open right now. With the threat of war in the Middle East, businesses everywhere are tightening up. There is a distinct possibility that within a short period of time, members of this graduating class could be serving in Saudi Arabia. That disturbs me more than the fact we'll have trouble finding employment.

But it will be a challenge to fight the discouraging employment figures. It is one we must accept and overcome to the best of our abilities. Now, more than ever, is a time to believe in ourselves and in our abilities to succeed.

Some of us are continuing formal education and will be attaining higher degrees, but many of us will be moving on. Regardless, let us keep in mind that our education should not stop at these doors. With every new experience there is a chance to gain knowledge. Each opportunity gives us a chance to add to our depth of understanding, if we choose to grasp it and make it what it can be.

It is not only our good fortune to have a university degree to which knowledge can be continually added, it is our responsibility to pass on the values that we have acquired through our hard work and perseverance.

Today marks one great achievement. We should enjoy it, then let the next one begin. Thank you.

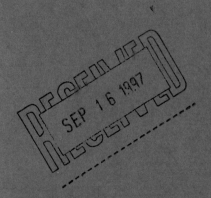